GLYPH 6

GLYPH

TEXTUAL STUDIES

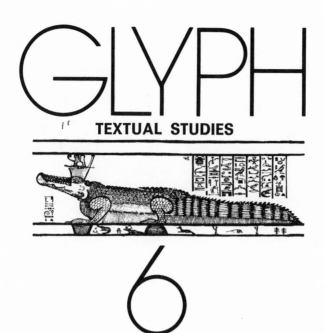

6

Publication of this volume was generously assisted
by the Melodie Jones Chair (currently held by Louis Marin)
at the State University of New York at Buffalo

THE JOHNS HOPKINS UNIVERSITY PRESS
Baltimore and London

STATEMENT TO CONTRIBUTORS

The Editors of *Glyph* welcome submissions concerned with the problems of representation and textuality, and contributing to the confrontation between American and Continental critical scenes. Contributors should send *two* copies of their manuscripts, accompanied by return postage, to Samuel Weber, Editor, *Glyph*, Humanities Center, The Johns Hopkins University, Baltimore, Maryland 21218. In preparing manuscripts, please refer to *A Manual of Style*, published by the University of Chicago Press, and *The Random House Dictionary*. The entire text, including extended citations and notes, should be double-spaced.
Copies of *Glyph*, both hardbound and paperback, may be ordered from
The Johns Hopkins University Press, Baltimore, Maryland 21218.

The illustration on the cover and title page, an Egyptian crocodile from the Ptolemaic period, is reproduced through the courtesy of the Walters Art Gallery, Baltimore.

CONTENTS

ONE

A "BUCHSTABLICHES" READING OF
THE ELECTIVE AFFINITIES
J. Hillis Miller

[*The Elective Affinities*] has possessed all along a disturbing power. In congenial temperaments this may rise to rapturous enthusiasm. In those who are alien to the novel the reaction becomes hostile consternation. Only an indefectible rationality is able to cope with it. Under the protection of such rationality the heart may dare to abandon itself to the prodigious, magical beauty of this work.

[Ein trüber Einfluss, der sich verwandten Gemütern bis zu schwärmerischem Anteil und in fremderen zu widerstrebender Verstörtheit steigern mag, war ihm von jeher eigen, und nur die unbestechliche Vernunft, in deren Schutz das Herz der ungeheuren, beschwornen Schönheit dieses Werks sich über-lassen darf, ist ihm gewachsen.][1]

    To interpret a work of such power and beauty as Goethe's *Die Wahlverwandtschaften* takes some courage. My excuse is that I too have been overwhelmed by its beauty, and that perhaps better than any other work of European fiction it dramatizes, within the form of the realistic novel, what is at stake in the use of line imagery to figure interpersonal relations.[2] Whether my calculating exploration of the latter, protected I hope by an indefectible rationality, will allow me to abandon myself safely to the novel's prodigious beauty remains to be seen.

    That *The Elective Affinities* is stitched together by figures of lines there can be no doubt. In one passage Goethe (or "the narrator") alerts the reader to look for the red thread of a recurrent theme running through Ottilie's diary, as the king's ropes are indicated as belonging to him by such a thread wound through each: "Just so is there drawn through Ottilie's diary, a thread of attachment and affection which connects it all together, and characterizes the whole" (139); ["Eben so zieht sich durch Ottiliens Tagebuch ein Faden der Neigung und Anhänglichkeit, der alles verbindet und das Ganze bezeichnet"] (115).[3]

What that red thread is, is by no means easy to identify. The narrator says it is there, however, and so it must be. The figure of the line appears once more for Ottilie at a crucial moment when, near death, she says, or rather writes, since she is past speaking: "I have stepped out of my course, and I cannot recover it again" (258); ["Ich bin aus meiner Bahn geschritten und ich soll nicht wieder hinein"] (209). A long catalogue could in fact be given of places in the novel where the relation between one person and another is spoken of as a line, bond, or tie. For example the narrator says of Ottilie, when her love for Edward has absorbed her whole life: "It seemed to her as if nothing in the world was disconnected [unzusammenhängend] so long as she thought of the one person whom she loved; and she could not conceive how, without him, anything could be connected at all" (190); ["Es schien ihr in der Welt nichts mehr unzusammenhängend, wenn sie an den geliebten Mann dachte, und sie begriff nicht, wie ohne ihn noch irgend etwas zusammenhängen könne"] (155). To Charlotte, on the other hand, her little son Otto seems "a new link [Bezug] to connect her with the world and with her property" (204); ["Sie erhält durch ihn einen neuen Bezug auf die Welt und auf den Besitz"] (166), while in the estate itself, which is an externalized image of the relations among the people living on it, newly planted trees and shrubs form a tie binding one part of the landscape to another: "and already the young plantations, which had been made to fill up a few openings, were beginning to look green, and to form an agreeable connecting link between parts which before stood separate" (205); ["und schon grünten die jungen Pflanzungen, die bestimmt waren, einige Lücken auszufüllen und die abgesonderten Teile angenehm zu verbinden"] (167). To give a final example, Edward, when he is determined to separate himself from his wife, marry her to his friend the Captain (now Major), and marry Ottilie himself, exhorts his friend: "Disentangle and untie the knots, and tie them up again" (229); ["diese Zustände zu entwirren, aufzulösen, zu verknüpfen"] (186).

Another form of lines is represented by all those paths, roads, and boundary lines which wind their way through Edward's estate or are made to do so by Edward, by Charlotte, or by the Captain. Those same lines are retraced in the carefully detailed scale drawing of the estate the Captain prepares. Much attention is given, an attention which may seem excessive or irrelevant, to topographical details of the estate. The changes made in it are described in oddly precise elaboration, as though it somehow matters whether a path goes this way or goes that way, or a new summerhouse is put in this place or in that, or whether the old gravestones in a country churchyard are moved or not to make way for a new path.

The most important use of line imagery in *Die Wahlverwandt-schaften*, however, is of course in the title and in the working out of the title's implications in a passage in Chapter Four, as well as in the book as a whole. The customary translation of the title, *The Elective Affinities*, is the correct equivalent English idiom, but it does not exactly match the play of metaphor in the German word. The German word says chosen (*Wahl*)—related (*verwandt*)—condition (*schaft*): a collective condition of being related which is chosen. The English suffix "ship" is not far from the German *schaft*, as in "relationship." The center of the word *Wahlverwandtschaften* is the image of relationship, and the word *Verwandten* is the ordinary German word for relations in the sense of those closely tied by blood or marriage. Goethe puts a strong emphasis, however, on the notion that related things and persons are drawn to one another by powerful forces of attraction. These lines of force pull things or persons which have an affinity strongly toward one another and make them want to meet, merge, combine, and make a new compound changing each thing from what it is into something else.

What it is in itself, in Goethe's notion of substance or selfhood, is made initially of its relation to itself. Its affinity for something else changes its self-relation, which is its self-identity. "In all natural objects with which we are acquainted," says the Captain, "we observe immediately that they have a certain relation to themselves" (32); ["An allen Naturwesen, die wir gewahr werden, bemerken wir zuerst, dass sie einen Bezug auf sich selbst haben"] (30). The Captain says this fact is "obvious" but it is an odd way to define an entity, since it appears to define a given single substance as drawing its unity and singularity from the fact that it is double. Each entity is divided into at least two parts, each of which has not merely a relation to the other but a strong attraction making the singleness and identity of the thing. Goethe uses here the word *Bezug*, which means "relation," but has a root indicating an act of drawing towards. A train engine or other means of transport is in German "ein Zug." Every entity which is in fact really a single entity has as a main feature of its identity a strong tendency to hang together, as a drop of quicksilver will recombine if it is broken into fragments. All the little parts run back together into a single globular whole, best symbol since Parmenides of oneness: "When we were children," says Charlotte, "it was our delight to play with quicksilver, and wonder at the little globules splitting and parting and running into one another" (33); ["Und schon als Kinder spielen wir erstaunt mit dem Quecksilber, indem wir es in Kügelchen trennen und es wieder zusammenlaufen lassen"] (30).

Nevertheless, this oneness in all natural objects, made of self-relatedness, has also, apparently as a feature of its intrinsic power to enter into relation with itself, also a tendency to enter into relations with other natural objects, as Charlotte, anticipating the direction of the Captain's explanation, perhaps already foreshadowing her elective affinity for him, says: "As everything has a reference to itself, so it must have some relation to others" (33); ["Wie jedes gegen sich selbst einen Bezug hat, so muss es auch gegen andere ein Verhältnis haben"] (31). The word translated here as "reference" is *Bezug* again, translated in the previous sentence as "relation." The word translated as "relation" in the second clause of the second sentence is "Verhältnis," perhaps a more neutral word, though it would be the word used to name an adulterous liaison.

Each thing, in any case, has a potential affinity for many different other things, as a person has many blood-relations and in-laws making up a whole network of connections, of *Verwandtschaften*. With only one at a time, nevertheless, can it be joined or compounded in a bond whose human correlative, for Goethe, is marriage and sexual union. This seems to be a matter of election or choice, so strong is the attraction drawing two elements, say sodium and chlorine, together and producing of their merging a new substance, table salt.

The interesting case is the one which manifests this power of election by showing an irresistible preference for this over that in a given substance, or as Edward puts it: "Affinities begin really to interest only when they bring about separations" (35); ["die Verwandtschaften werden erst interessant, wenn sie Scheidungen bewirken"] (32). The example Goethe gives, or has the Captain give, in this little lesson in nineteenth-century chemistry, is the power of sulfuric acid to displace carbonic acid combined with lime ($CaCo_3 + H_2So_4 = CaSo_4 + H_2O + CO_2$):

Thus, what we call limestone is a more or less pure calcareous earth in combination with a delicate acid, which is familiar to us in the form of a gas. Now, if we place a piece of this stone in diluted sulphuric acid, this will take possession of the lime, and appear with it in the form of gypsum, the gaseous acid at the same time going off in vapor. Here is a case of separation; a combination arises, and we believe ourselves justified in applying to it the words "Elective Affinity"; it really looks as if one relation had been deliberately chosen in preference to another. (35)

A "Buchstäbliches" Reading

[Zum Beispiel was wir Kalkstein nennen ist eine mehr oder weniger reine Kalkerde, innig mit einer zarten Säure verbunden, die uns in Luftform bekannt geworden ist. Bringt man ein Stück solchen Steines in verdünnte Schwefelsäure, so ergreift diese den Kalk und erscheint mit ihm als Gips; jene zarte luftige Säure hingegen entflieht. Hier ist eine Trennung, eine neue Zusammensetzung entstanden und man glaubt sich nunmehr berechtigt, sogar das Wort Wahlverwandtschaft anzuwenden, weil es wirklich aussieht als wenn ein Verhältnis dem andern vorgezogen, eins vor dem andern erwählt würde.] (32)

The most interesting cases of all, however, are those where four elements, combined at first in pairs, substitute partners in a crisscross exchange, each taking a new mate in a simultaneous quadruple manifestation of elective affinity. What was attraction becomes repulsion and is replaced by another irresistible attraction. This merging and flying away seems not only to indicate life and volition in "inanimate" matter, but also to indicate an occult transcendent power at work in, and behind, nature: chthonic, but hidden, below, profound; or higher up and hidden above. This universal power is an inner law which manifests itself differently in each particular all-compelling elective affinity, but which remains the same in its secrecy:

And those are the cases which are really most important and remarkable—, [says the Captain] cases where this attraction, this affinity, this separating and combining, can be exhibited, the two pairs severally crossing each other; where four creatures, connected previously, as two and two, are brought into contact, and at once forsake their first combination to form into a second. In this forsaking and embracing, this seeking and flying, we believe that we are indeed observing the effects of some higher determination; we attribute a sort of will and choice to such creatures, and feel really justified in using technical words, and speaking of "Elective Affinities." (37)

[(D)iese Fälle sind allerdings die bedeutendsten und merkwürdigsten, wo man das Anziehen, das Verwandtsein, dieses Verlassen, dieses Vereinigen gleichsam übers Kreuz, wirklich darstellen kann; wo vier, bisher je zwei zu zwei verbundene, Wesen in Berührung gebracht, ihre bisherige Vereinigung verlassen und sich aufs neue verbinden. In diesem Fahrenlassen und Ergreifen, in diesem Fliehen und Suchen glaubt man wirklich eine höhere Bestimmung zu sehen; man traut solchen Wesen eine Art von Wollen und Wählen zu, und hält das Kunstwort Wahlverwandtschaften für vollkommen gerechtfertigt.] (33-34)

The German word translated here as "technical words" is *Kunstwort*. Goethe wrote *das Kunstwort Wahlverwandtschaften*, "the technical word elective affinities." The word *Kunstwort* has a special valance in German missing in English. *Kunst* means of course "art." The word *Kunstwort* means the word peculiar to a certain "art" in the sense of a special mystery, such as the "art" of chemistry. It suggests also, however, "artistic word" or "aesthetic word," a word casting a beautiful veil of appearance over the substance it names, the veil of Maya, so to speak. An example might be the words Goethe himself uses to produce that magical beauty of *Die Wahlverwandtschaften* of which Benjamin speaks. Opposed to *Kunstwörter*, technical words, are what in the English translation are called "symbols," in the German *Buchstaben*, literally "letters," or more literally still, book-staves, from the staff- or stick-like lines used to make letters or runes. *Buchstäblich*, for example, means "literally."

The word *Buchstabe* has a complex resonance in the Germany of Goethe's time, since it is the word used by Martin Luther to translate the Biblical "letter" of the law as opposed to its spirit, *Geist*. The question of the interpretation of the Bible or of literature generally, for example the parables (*Gleichnisse*) of Jesus, is also at stake in the term. We should take the Bible as literally true, Luther enjoined, but what would be meant by a literal, *buchstäbliches*, reading of Christ's parables? Is *Die Wahlverwandtschaften* itself to be read literally or spiritually, parabolically, and what, exactly, would it mean to do either of these? In any case, one does not read far in *Die Wahlverwandtschaften* without feeling that, as in the Bible, every detail in this text, even apparently "irrelevant" details put in for mimetic truthfulness, are charged with significance, though whether these should properly be described as literal or as spiritual significances remains to be decided. The opposition between *Geist* and *Buchstabe*, with its Biblical and Protestant overtones, like the opposition between written and spoken language, is fundamental to romantic linguistic theory, for example in the speculations about language of Friedrich Schlegel.[4] A complex network of associations is present, then, in Goethe's use of the word *Buchstabe* to name the opposite of *Kunstwort*: "I quite agree," said Edward, "that the strange scientific nomenclature, to persons who have not been reconciled to it by a direct acquaintance with or understanding of its object, must seem unpleasant, even ridiculous; but we can easily, just for once, contrive with symbols to illustrate what we are speaking of" (37); ["Ich leugne nicht, sagte Eduard, dass die seltsamen Kunstwörter demjenigen, der nicht durch sinnliches Anschauen, durch Begriffe mit ihnen versöhnt ist, beschwerlich, ja lächerlich werden müssen. Doch könnten wir leicht mit Buchstaben einstweilen das Verhältnis ausdrucken, wovon hier die Rede war"] (34).

The opposition between *Kunstwörter* and *Buchstaben* is analogous to the opposition between figurative language and literal language. This opposition is crucial to *Die Wahlverwandtschaften*. The novel dramatizes interpersonal relations in terms of the exchanges of figure and the relation between literal and figurative language. Or rather, it might be better to say that it expresses the exchanges of figure and the relation

between literal and figurative language in the figurative terms of interpersonal relations. The peculiarity of the "laws of language" is that one
must use language to speak of them, so there is neither a literal language
about language, nor an appropriate technical language, *Kunstwörter*,
free of the metaphors of art in the other sense, in the sense of the
aesthetically beautiful. The story of marriage, passion, and adultery
which makes up the novel is in fact an allegory of the laws, powers, and
limitations of language. This is expressed literally, *buchstäblich*, in the
bare letter symbols in the passage which follows the one just cited. And
yet of course, in another sense, nothing could be more abstract and
figurative than the expression of chemical or human relations by bare
symbolic letters. There seems to be some difficulty, both in the words
of the novel and in the world those words describe, in manifesting the
literal literally. To that problem I shall return, since it is the fundamental issue in *Die Wahlverwandtschaften*, both in Goethe's own
language and in the story he tells. Meanwhile, here is his example of
the *buchstäbliches* reading, a literal way of speaking, or a way of
speaking with letters drawn out with straight or curved lines to make
the capitals of the alphabet:

Suppose an A connected so closely with a B, that all sorts of means, even
violence, have been made use of to separate them, without effect. Then
suppose a C in exactly the same position with respect to a D. Bring the two
pairs into contact; A will fling himself on D, C on B, without it being
possible to say which had first left its first connection, or made the first move
toward the second. (38)

[Denken Sie sich ein A, das mit einem B innig verbunden ist, durch viele
Mittel und durch manche Gewalt nicht von ihm zu trennen; denken Sie sich
ein C, das sich eben so zu einem D verhält; bringen Sie nun die beiden
Paare in Berührung: A wird sich zu D, C zu B werfen, ohne dass man sagen
kann, wer das andere zuerst verlassen, wer sich mit dem andern zuerst
wieder verbunden habe.] (34)

This is exactly the way the exchanges of metaphor have been
defined in the Western tradition since Aristotle. Every metaphor can be
reduced to a proportional relation: A is to B as C is to D, in which, as
in all ratios, the terms are potentially interchangeable, so that A is to C
as B is to D, and so A can replace C in relation to D. B and C then mate.
The lines can be redrawn to make a new ratio giving the same
equivalence: $A/B = C/D$ or $A/C = B/D$. The basic paradigm of *The
Elective Affinities* is the following: Human relations are like the
substitutions in metaphorical expressions, or, to put it the other way,
since these metaphorical analogies are reversible, the laws of language
may be dramatized in human relations. Edward makes this application
explicitly in a passage which just follows the one quoted above. The

passage virtually ends Chapter Four, the chapter which establishes the universal natural law the novel exemplifies. Edward, however, does not yet know that the irresistible new *Bezüge*, attractions, or elective affinities which he and the others will manifest, will not be the ones he imagines, but those destroying his marriage by replacing Charlotte with Ottilie in his own love and putting the Captain in Edward's place in Charlotte's affections. Nevertheless, what he says allows for that possibility and anticipates it, though not as necessity, since the formula itself does not tell which of the possible combinations will be stronger than all the others, breaking bonds and making them in defiance of any human or even divine law, such as the law of faithfulness in marriage:

"Now then," interposed Edward, "till we see all this with our eyes, we will look upon the formula as an analogy, out of which we can devise a lesson for immediate use. You stand for A, Charlotte, and I am your B; really and truly I cling to you, I depend on you, and follow you, just as B does with A. C is obviously the Captain, who at present is in some degree withdrawing me from you. So now it is only just that if you are not to be left to solitude, a D should be found for you, and that is unquestionably the amiable little lady, Ottilie. You will not hesitate any longer to send and fetch her." (38)

["Nun denn!" fiel Eduard ein: "bis wir alles dieses mit Augen sehen, wollen wir diese Formel als Gleichnisrede betrachten, woraus wir uns eine Lehre zum unmittelbaren Gebrauch ziehen. Du stellst das A vor, Charlotte, und ich dein B: denn eigentlich hänge ich doch nur von dir ab und folge dir, wie dem A das B. Das C ist ganz deutlich der Kapitän, der mich für diesmal dir einigermassen entzieht. Nun ist es billig, dass, wenn du nicht ins Unbestimmte entweichen sollst, dir für ein D gesorgt werde, und das ist ganz ohne Frage das liebenswürdige Dämchen Ottilie, gegen deren Annäherung du dich nicht länger verteidigen darfst."] (34–35)

Edward has understood the law but he is unable yet to make the right application of it, though the reader in retrospect can do so as the story unfolds of Edward's irresistible adulterous passion for Ottilie, hers for him, and of the scarcely less powerful attraction of the Captain and Charlotte for one another.

The model of exchange and relationship worked out in this early chapter is exemplified on three related levels in the novel: on the level of interpersonal relations, on the level of the language of the text itself, and on the level of the building of roads, paths, gardens, lakes, and houses on Edward's estate which makes up the topographical theme of such great importance in the novel. On all three of these levels the concept seems to be of a literal, self-related substance which is related to other such substances by lines or channels of force making possible transformations of that substance in which it nevertheless retains its identity. It fulfills itself or becomes truly itself in those relations to another.

On the linguistic level, the concept of figurative language depends on the notion of referential meaning, a substantial virtue in words which they borrow from the things they literally name. The power manifested by the exchanges of metaphor depends on the carrying over of this literal energy of words into the new context where the words in combination with other words are used in a translated or transported sense.

In the "same way," in the changes of the landscape effected by Edward and his household, the four lovers project a model of their changing relations on the estate, drawing it out as on a map, but giving those relations substance in the rocks, trees, water, paths, and houses they have reshaped, as a building is man-made but rests solidly on the earth below, in "the wedlock of the stone with the earth" (64); ["die Verbindung des Steins mit dem Grunde"] (55). The latter phrase describes the ritual of the laying of the cornerstone for the new house Edward has built on the hilltop, placing it there because Ottilie has chosen the spot as best. Goethe, or his narrator, gives the poem the young mason speaks at the laying of the cornerstone in prose. This is in deference, one may suppose, to the necessarily prosaic language of the novel as a genre. The oddness is that this is a prose translation of a poem which does not exist, as perhaps the novel as a whole may be said to be. The novel is, it seems, the literal which can give the spiritual only in "an imperfect rendering" (63); ["unvollkommen wiedergeben"] (55), but surely no words could be more artful than Goethe's in this text.

Interpersonal relations, finally, for which the other two levels may be seen as analogies or parables, obey the same laws. Each person, it would seem, has in Goethe's view a substantial selfhood which enters into relations with others and so becomes more truly itself, changing but only to become what it already is. This level, like the others, is securely grounded on a hidden energy which manifests itself especially in the intrinsic tendency of substances at all three of these levels to combine preferentially with certain other substances. These tendencies are stronger than any conventional human laws, such as laws of marriage, even though the latter may seem to have the divine spirit as their sanction. Such tendencies appear to be the *Buchstabe* which is stronger than any *Geist*.

The ontologically grounded system I have sketched would seem to be the key to a total reading of *Die Wahlverwandtschaften*. Such a reading would move back and forth among the various analogies, from the theme of landscape design and estate building to the crisscross relations among the lovers, to the functioning of the language of the text itself, in which everything is meaningful, *geistlich* or *künstlich*

J. Hillis Miller

and *buchstäblich* at once. As in the case of the beauty of Ottilie herself, the novel's surface of dangerous beauty is grounded on metaphysical laws which this surface manifests. Seen from this point of view, the novel is an admirable demonstration of the relation between European aestheticism and Occidental metaphysics. Far from being incompatible, these are mutually sustaining, as they are, for example, in Kant's third *Critique*. Metaphysics generates aestheticism, that mode of art in which the highest value is a surface of beauty open to the senses and feelings, a surface made of the transformations and substitutions of figure. Even the seeming glorification of adulterous passion over the obligations of the marriage bond in *Die Wahlverwandtschaften*, which has so troubled some readers of the novel from its first appearance, is only apparent. The divine ground of marriage in God's law and the occult chthonic ground of the elective affinities which draw Edward and Ottilie, Charlotte and the Captain, toward one another are in the end of the novel reconciled. God's law is stronger than the law of the elective affinities, or the former makes use of the latter, or perhaps the one is in fact no more than another manifestation of the other, mysteriously altered, a figurative version of it as literal. It is not just Ottilie's power to resist her love for Edward which makes her saintly. The passion itself touches her with spirituality. It manifests her attunement with powers more than human. The body of Ottilie, dazzlingly beautiful still in death, visible yet through the lid of her glass-covered coffin, has a miraculous healing power. The bodies of the two lovers, Edward and Ottilie, destined to die of their unfulfilled passion, lie at the very end of the novel side by side in the village church, their fate accomplished:

[F]alling asleep, as [Edward] did, with his thoughts on one so saintly, he might well be called blessed. Charlotte gave him his place at Ottilie's side, and arranged that thenceforth no other person should be placed with them in the same vault. . . .

So lie the lovers, sleeping side by side. Peace hovers above their resting-place. Fair angel faces gaze down upon them from the vaulted ceiling, and what a happy moment that will be when one day they wake again together! (274)

[(W)ie er in Gedanken an die Heilige eingeschlafen war, so konnte man wohl ihn selig nennen. Charlotte gab ihm seinen Platz neben Ottilien und verordnete, dass niemand weiter in diesem Gewölbe beigesetzt werde. . . .

So ruhen die Liebenden nebeneinander. Friede schwebt über ihrer Stätte, heitere verwandte Engelsbilder schauen vom Gewölbe auf sie herab, und welch ein freundlicher Augenblick wird es sein, wenn sie dereinst wieder zusammen erwachen.] (222)

Goethe himself seems to have given full support to this religio-aesthetic-metaphysical interpretation of the novel in a statement he wrote in explanation of its title:

A "Buchstäbliches" Reading

It seems that this strange title was suggested to the author by the studies he carries on in the realm of the physical sciences. No doubt he has noticed that, in the natural sciences, one very commonly uses ethical comparisons, in order after a fashion to bring nearer to the domain proper to human knowledge matters which are strongly distant from it; so it is possible that in the case of a moral situation he has more willingly taken a chemical image back to its moral sources because there exists inversely only one single and unique nature and because the kingdom of serene rational freedom is continually traversed by the indications of a compulsion of the passions which can only be effaced—and, here below, always in an imperfect way— by a force which comes from higher up.[5]

The ethical realm, the realm of the natural sciences, and the realm of a transcendent grace are here distinguished only to be joined in the concept of a single and unique "nature" where all work together, even if not always harmoniously. What Goethe says seems to confirm unequivocally the interpretation of the novel grounded in a totalizing ontology I have so far proposed.

Nevertheless, there are aspects of *Die Wahlverwandtschaften* which do not seem to be fully accounted for in this interpretation and which seem disturbingly at variance with it, even at variance with the interpretation Goethe seems to give of his own novel. These features of the text lead to an entirely different reading of it. They make of *Die Wahlverwandtschaften* another demonstration of the self-subverting heterogeneity of each great work of Western literature. This heterogeneity of our great literary texts is one important manifestation of the equivocity of the Western tradition generally. This equivocity is present in the languages we have used to express ourselves in that tradition, and in the lives we have led in terms of those languages. Life incarnates language, embodies it, for man the sign-making animal, as Ottilie, Edward, Charlotte and the Captain incarnate the laws of language expressed most barely and literally as the ratios of the elective affinities.

In the case of the topic of this essay—interpersonal relations, the presentation of them in narrative, and the analysis of narrative from the point of view of the assumption that interpersonal relations are essential in it—there are two entirely incompatible notions in our tradition and in the human experience the tradition records or has generated. One sees selves as inalienable preexisting substances, securely grounded in transhuman "being," for example in the Being of God. Interpersonal relations are then lines of connection drawn between selves so conceived, lines which fulfill the selves, perhaps, but do not essentially alter or determine them.

The other notion of interpersonal relations sees selves as nothing, or as nothing but a locus traversed by fleeting elements which have the

J. Hillis Miller

sad nature of signs, to be indications of absence rather than of presence. Such selves seek to ground themselves in others, by drawing others to themselves, but each such self succeeds only in experiencing its solitude. The model narrative in our tradition of this self-emptying relation of the self to itself is that melancholy story of Narcissus trapped within his prison house of language, able to see and love himself only, able to hear only echoes of his own voice, in a dialogue always with himself. It is my hypothesis that novels in our tradition are most often the dramatization of the crisscross or interference of these two assumptions about interpersonal relations. Interpretations based on only one or the other are pre-judging the text and likely to miss something essential. Moreover, interpersonal relations as such can never be the adequate ground, the beginning and end, of the interpretation of a work of fiction, since they are always encompassed and superseded, in one direction by ontological questions which are the proper domain of metaphysical rather than of ethical considerations, and in the other direction by the linguistic questions of which the story of human relations is the allegorical representation.

The importance of the apparently casual motif of the reading over one's shoulder, introduced three times, at widely spaced intervals, in *Die Wahlverwandtschaften*, is that it defines the mode of existence, for Goethe here at least, both of subjectivities and of intersubjective relations. To read is to exist. I exist because I read. I come into existence when I read. The act of reading is, for Goethe, the universal originating moment of subjective life and therefore of whatever relations there may be between subjectivities. The metaphorical extension of the act of reading to cover all human activities, perceptions, social relations, all acts of making sense of the world, changing it, or using it, is made explicitly at several points in the novel.

The most important of these follows just after a passage in which Edward flashes out in anger against his wife when she reads over his shoulder. In a tactful attempt to appease his anger she explains that she had lost the thread of what he was reading and had looked over his shoulder to get it right again. She had been misled by a pun, a double meaning latent in language which switched her mind from one track to another. "I heard you reading something about Affinities [*Verwandtschaften*], and I thought directly of some relations [*Verwandten*] of mine, of two cousins who are just now occupying me a great deal" (31); ["Ich hörte von Verwandtschaften lesen, und da dacht' ich eben gleich an meine Verwandten, an ein paar Vettern, die mir gerade in diesem Augenblick zu schaffen machen"] (29). Edward's response makes a generalization which forms the basis of an interpretation of *Die Wahlverwandtschaften* which might be called linguistic or semiotic rather than ontological. The semiotic reading, the reading by way of the emblem of reading, is not imposed on the text from the outside. Like the ontological reading, it is woven into the text, articulated there, a black thread intertwined with the red one. The text is heterogeneous. The novel's lines of self-interpretation contradict one another. The meaning of the novel lies in the necessity of this contradiction, in the way each of these readings generates its subversive counterpart and is unable to appear alone, as Narcissus lives confronting his left-handed mirror image.

"It was the comparison [*eine Gleichnisrede*] which led you wrong and confused you," Edward explains to Charlotte. "The subject is nothing but earths and minerals" (31); ["Es ist eine Gleichnisrede, die dich verführt und verwirrt hat, sagte Eduard. Hier wird freilich nur von Erden und Mineralien gehandelt. . . ."] (29). The literal subject of the book Edward reads is, he explains, nothing but the behavior of earths and minerals. The implication might seem to be that these are without ambiguity, something literally there which can be described in literal language, *buchstäblich*. Charlotte, however, has, as Edward says, been misled by the "comparison." The German word here, *Gleichnisrede*, contains one of the usual words for metaphor, figure or parable: *Gleichnis*. It is impossible to be sure whether Edward means she has been misled by taking the word *Wahlverwandtschaften* to refer to human relations, whereas it is actually a technical term, a *Kunstwort* referring to chemical affinities, or whether he means, as is perhaps more probable, to call attention to the fact that the *Kunstwort* is actually a metaphor borrowing a term for human relations to describe impersonal chemical reactions. Charlotte has been misled by taking the word literally, as though it were a "woman's word," a word used as it might be in ordinary domestic life. The female penchant for taking words literally plays a crucial role in determining the circumstances of Ottilie's death. It is the *Kunstwörter* which are metaphorical, an illicit projection from the human realm to what is outside it, a reading into nature of what is only human.

The particular form of *Gleichnis* in question here is personification, the projection of human qualities on natural objects which are not persons at all. Ruskin was a few years later of course to condemn this as the pathetic fallacy. The technical Greek rhetorical term for personification is *prosopopoeia*, which means, literally, giving a human face or mask to the inhuman, to abstractions, or to inanimate objects, and by extension inventing speech for something or someone absent, imaginary, or dead. *Prosōpon* is Greek for face, mask, dramatic character, and *poiein* is "to make," the root in "poetry." *Die Wahlverwandt-*

schaften could be described as an extended allegorical investigation of *prosopopoeia* in the form of a "realistic story" of marriage and adulterous passion. Such an allegory is of course an example of what it investigates, since it gives human faces or masks to what are impersonal laws of language. The novel is the genre which most systematically and most covertly does this, since personification or impersonation is its basic presupposition, its founding convention, as when the narrator speaks for the characters in indirect discourse, giving a face and a voice to the imaginary, the absent, or the dead. One reason for the power and importance of *Die Wahlverwandtschaften* among other major Western novels is the way it brings to the surface this fundamental law of the genre. This novel foregrounds the conditions of its own being.

The law in question is most explicitly formulated in the sentence which just follows Edward's remark to Charlotte that she has been misled by the comparison. "But man," he says, "is a true Narcissus; he delights to see his own image everywhere; and he spreads himself underneath the universe, like the amalgam behind the glass" (31); ["aber der Mensch ist ein wahrer Narziss; er bespiegelt sich überall gern selbst; er legt sich als Folie der ganzen Welt unter"] (29).

It is impossible, as I have said, to be sure whether Edward means this as a reproach to Charlotte for interpreting what he has been reading as applying to her own preoccupations with her troublesome relations, or whether we are to take it as a reproach to the scientists who project human terms into inanimate objects. In fact what he says can and must apply to both. The scientists use *prosopopoeia* to construct their *Kunstwörter*. The metaphors behind these terms are then forgotten, and the words come to be taken as literal, as *Wahlverwandtschaften* is the proper technical term for the special preferential affinities certain chemical elements have for one another. This "literal" word is then metaphorically projected again into human relations in a *prosopopoeia* in reverse which is a regular feature of such a play of figure, for example in the way George Meredith personifies nature in his poetry but then in his novels borrows terms from nature to define the subjectivities of his characters. Each of these operations, that of the scientist, that of Charlotte, appears to be grounded in the literal referentiality of the other, but the other, when examined, turns out to be already a figure drawn from that realm into which it is now being re-displaced. No unambiguous literal reference can be found in the use of language on either side, as Edward's definition of the way man is a true Narcissus recognizes.

The peculiarity of this definition lies in the way it sees man as an absence, as the neutral possibility of taking on this or that image, rather than as a fixed, pre-existing shaped self. Man is a true Narcissus who loves to see his own face everywhere in the mirror of the world. He "delights to see his own image everywhere," as the translation has it. Goethe's German is *er bespiegelt sich überall gern selbst*, literally: "he himself is reflected willingly everywhere." *Spiegel* is "mirror" in German. Man does this, however, by spreading himself behind things like the thin layer of "amalgam" behind a glass which makes it a mirror. The German word here is *Folie*, "foil," with an overtone playing from one language to another of folly, and of foil, in the sense of fencing foil, in the sense of frustrate or impede, as in "foiled again," and in the sense of fold or leaf, as in "folio," the fold of a book, or as in the leaf put behind a jewel to set it off, or as in the gold leaf used as the background of a medieval painting. Far from being fixed self or substance which can see its own image in the mirror of the world, as Narcissus saw his face in the water, man, in Goethe's definition here, is without face or figure. He is neutral, invisible, without fixed image or character, like the invisible foil behind the mirror. He puts this non-entity under the whole world, including other people, as if he were the world's substance or ground. The image of himself he sees everywhere is made of the figurative transfer to himself of all the objects he confronts, as for example, in the rest of this chapter of *Die Wahlverwandtschaften*, but those objects are already in themselves examples of *prosopopoeia*, masks, figures. Edward, Charlotte, and the rest name human relations in a figure drawn from the behavior of chemicals. Man sees himself in rocks, trees, and water. If man reads the world in human terms, personifies it, in turn he reads himself in terms of inanimate objects. He has no images for himself but those generated by his reflecting of himself everywhere, and no terms for inanimate objects but those illicitly projected from the human realm. As the Captain says, "That is the way in which he treats everything external to himself. His wisdom and his folly, his will and his caprice, he attributes alike to animals, plants, the elements, and the gods" (31); ["so behandelt er alles was er ausser sich findet; seine Weisheit wie seine Torheit, seinen Willen wie seine Willkür leiht er den Tieren, den Pflanzen, den Elementen und den Göttern"] (29). This passing back and forth is the substitution of figure for figure in a constant interchange without literal ground, naming objects with figurative transfers of human terms which are already themselves figurative transfers of natural terms, in a ceaseless coming and going.

"Animals, plants, the elements, and the gods"—this odd hierarchy moves down only to leap up at the end, as though the gods were chthonic, beneath the elements, and, as they exist for man, as much a projection of human qualities on what is without them, as much a *prosopopoeia*, as are personifications of elements, as in the term "elective affinities." What is missing in this slightly twisted version of the classic great chain of being is of course man himself, who has now become the colorless ground or foil for the whole chain.

There are many examples in the novel of the projection of human qualities into animals, plants, elements, and gods, but the most important case of projection or "reading into" is not named here. It is rather manifested in the passage itself and in the novel as a whole. This is man's Narcissistic reading of his own qualities into other people in "interpersonal relations," for example in love. The passage describing man as a true "Narcissus" gives the key to the interpretation of the novel, but the key must be displaced metaphorically, turned to fit the reading of one person by another as well as man's reading of animals, plants, elements, and gods.

If the drama of elective affinities among the four principal characters of *Die Wahlverwandtschaften* is taken as an allegory of the crisscross substitutions in a metaphorical ratio, Ottilie, the last added and necessary fourth, is also the one who ruins the ratio. She is the unidentifiable final term, silent or absent, neither literal nor figurative, therefore not "properly" nameable. She is the "O" which deprives the proportion of its reasonable ground in the distinction between literal and figurative and therefore takes it outside the safe confines of Occidental metaphysics. Her silence and effacement make the relations among the four principal persons like one of those dangerously subversive metaphorical equations Aristotle allows for in the *Poetics*. This is that form of figurative proportion in which one of the four terms is missing or incomplete. The examples he gives include the sun, traditional symbol of the *logos*, ground of all other metaphorical substitutions of figurative for literal. The sun is the basic means of transfer, as in all those figures for man, for example the Sphinx's riddle, which describe the journey of man's life as like the diurnal trajectory of the sun. Since the sun cannot be looked in the eye, its radiance cannot be named properly or literally. Proper or literal naming depends on seeing what is so named in the presence of the present. Any name for the radiance of the sun is therefore a catachresis, neither figurative nor literal. It is, for example, something drawn from the natural world of engendering and applied literally to the father-no-father, engenderer of all metaphors, what Wallace Stevens calls "the furiously burning father-fire."[6] The sun therefore is the base of any metaphorical equation into which it enters, and at the same time it always subverts that equation:

By metaphor formed on the basis of analogy (or proportion) [says Aristotle] is meant the case when a second term, B, is to a first, A, as a fourth, D, is to a third, C; whereupon the fourth term, D, may be substituted for the second, B, or the second, B, for the fourth, D. . . . Hence one will speak of *the evening* (D) as the *old age* (B) of the day—as Empedocles does; and of *old age* (B) as *the evening* (D) of life—or as "the sunset of life." In certain cases, the language may contain no actual word corresponding to one of the terms in the proportion, but the figure nevertheless will be employed. For example, when a fruit casts forth its seed the action is called "sowing," but the action of the sun casting forth its flame has no special name. Yet this nameless action (B) is to the sun (A) as *sowing* (D) is to the fruit (C); and hence we have the expression of the poet, "*sowing* a god-created flame."[7]

Ottilie plays the same role in the proportion among the four characters of *Die Wahlverwandtschaften* as the missing term for the sun's act of casting forth its flame does in Aristotle's example. She is the blind spot in the novel, invisible from excess of light, silent, a kind of black hole into which everything disappears. Edward, dazzled by Ottilie's beauty, imagines that she is his missing other half, to whom he is drawn by a special elective affinity justifying the substitution of her as his figurative wife for Charlotte, his proper lawfully wedded wife. She is the D substituting for his B. She is the counterpart in a changed sex which matches him exactly and will complete what is lacking in him, make him whole, do him the little service of picking up the gold knob on his cane if he should happen to drop it, as in the example from the life of Charles I Ottilie gives to excuse her habit of picking up things for people. Edward's desire is to possess his own pleasure as the pleasure of another, or to possess the pleasure of the woman as his own pleasure. Does she not have headaches on the left side, as he on the right? Does she not imitate his handwriting exactly? And does not the magic goblet which does not break at the dedication of the new house have their initials, E and O, intertwined on it as a prophetic emblem of their indissoluble unity?

Edward presents Mittler with a series of figures for his sense of this unity when Mittler comes, in another example of his failure as a mediator, to try to persuade Edward to give up his "foolish frantic passion" for Ottilie. "And so she is present," says Edward, "in every dream I have. And whatever happens to me with her, we are woven in and in together. Now we are subscribing a contract together. There is her hand, and there is mine; and they move one into the other, and seem to devour each other" (124). Goethe's German in fact says, "And so her image (*Bild*) mixes itself in each of my dreams"; ["Und so mischt sich ihr Bild in jeden meiner Träume"] (102). Edward's relation to Ottilie is the relation of an object to an image, like his own face in the mirror, or like a figure in a dream. His relation to that image is like the weaving together of two strands to make a single rope or fabric, ["Alles was mir mit ihr begegnet, schiebt sich durch- und übereinander"] (102), or like the drawing together of two hands, names, and signatures in a written contract: ["Bald unterschreiben wir einen Kontrakt"] (102). The autonomous "drawing together" or "contracting" of two persons when they underwrite a joint document, in a performative promise to act as one, substitutes for the naturally and supernaturally based attraction (*Bezug*) apparently described in the chapter on the elective affinities. Goethe's German (unlike the English translation) plays the double meaning of the word *Hand*, as part of the body and as handwriting. As one meaning of the word slips into the other, so Otto's hand and Ottilie's hand become their names and the names are superimposed, merge, and devour one another; ["da ist ihre Hand und die meinige, ihr Name und der meinige, beide löschen einander aus, beide verschlingen sich"] (102). The relation between the two is mutually destructive, like the drowning of Narcissus in his mirror-image.

Edward's prophetic dream means more than, and differently from, the meaning he gives it. The dream echoes similar images elsewhere in the novel, the matching hands matching the matching headaches, the motif of handwriting reminding the reader again that what is involved in this kind of interpersonal relation is not persons as such, but signs, images, forms of writing. Edward and Ottilie exist, both for themselves and for each other, as images or as writing, as Edward is the image of Ottilie which hovers always before him, and as Ottilie is presented most intimately, most from the inside, in the selections from her diary. Far from having the quality of subjectivity and inwardness one might expect from a young girl's diary, these entries are surprisingly impersonal. They are made up of quotations, citations, maxims, and reflections such as Goethe himself composed and published elsewhere. If the "selves" of the two lovers are images or handwriting, names, these names have the capacity to move into one another, overlap, merge, and, in an ominous figure, devour one another like particle and antiparticle, leaving nothing behind, the "O" they share and which it is their destiny to become. This is worked out most fully in the emblem of the drinking glass:

My fate and Ottilie's [Edward tells Mittler] cannot be divided, and shall not be shipwrecked. Look at this glass; our initials are engraved upon it. A gay reveller flung it into the air, that no one should drink of it more. It was to fall on the rock and be dashed to pieces; but it did not fall; it was caught. At a high price I bought it back, and now I drink out of it daily—to convince myself that the connection between us cannot be broken; that destiny has decided. (126)

[Mein Schicksal und Ottiliens ist nicht zu trennen und wir werden nicht zu Grunde gehen. Sehen Sie dieses Glas! Unsere Namenszüge sind darein geschnitten. Ein fröhlich Jubelnder warf es in die Luft; niemand sollte mehr daraus trinken; auf dem felsigen Boden sollte es zerschellen, aber es ward aufgefangen. Um hohen Preis habe ich es wieder eingehandelt, und ich trinke nun täglich daraus, um mich täglich zu überzeugen: dass alle Verhältnisse unzerstörlich sind, die das Schicksal beschlossen hat.] (104)

The glass is in fact broken after Ottilie's death, broken casually and off stage by his servant, who substitutes a nearly identical one, to Edward's dismay. The reader may see his dismay as a momentary recognition that the meaning of the first glass was a matter already of metaphorical transfer or substitution, another case of "reading into," not a literal reading of what is "really there." There is, as the novel everywhere indicates, no such thing as a literal or *buchstäbliches* reading of signs. All reading is *bildlich* or figurative, a reading of signs made into *Kunstwörter*. Or rather, the only true literal reading is no reading, the blank silence and death-like sleep of Ottilie. The passage just quoted begins and ends with the notion of a "destiny" (*Schicksal*) which binds Edward and Ottilie together and makes them one. The destiny, however, is Edward's reading of Ottilie's image as the reflex of his own, just as he reads the letters "E" and "O," which are his own initials (his names are Edward and Otto), as joining his name Edward with Ottilie's name.

All four of the principal characters have the same name or a variant of it. There seem not enough names to go around in this novel. All the characters are already undermined by the zero or absence which Ottilie brings into the fourfold proportion, making it not A is to B as C is to D, but A is to B as C is to O. The O works back to cancel all the others and make it a null equation: O is to O as O is to O. The Captain's name is also Otto, and Charlotte contains the name of course as part of itself. When the Captain sees in the drowned body of little Otto "the stiffened image of himself" (239); ["sein erstarrtes Ebenbild"] (194), he is also seeing the "image" of Charlotte, of Ottilie, of Edward, of all four in their strange relation of double adultery or double crisscross cancelled figuration. Little Otto is the extension of Edward's genealogical line which Ottilie has tried to pick up and save, as Mary cherished the Christ child in the Christmas pageant Ottilie enacts, but which she has instead lost, ending the line in silence and death.

Ottilie is the odd person out in the system of substitutions. As such, she undoes that system, making the "little circle of three," Charlotte, Edward, and the Captain, into a square with a missing fourth side, thereby disintegrating the figure. Ottilie is neither the literal nor the figurative, or rather she is an impossible embodiment of both. She is an incarnation of the figure called catachresis. She is the beautiful unattainable aesthetic surface which spreads a powerful erotic glow over the whole novel, a glow which has been projected as a veil over what she "really is" by Edward's Narcissistic love for her as his metaphorical "image," his double of the other sex. He cannot possess her pleasure as his own. That pleasure remains discrete, elsewhere, unattainable, occurring always too early or too late, somewhere and sometime else.

Ottilie is the mute letter, not the aesthetic spirit. She is the *Buchstabe* which undoes Edward's projected love. As the literal, Ottilie is unattainable in another sense, since the letter is silent, unnameable, unapproachable, the darkness of death, about which nothing can be said.

This double existence of Ottilie is admirably figured in the description of her beautiful corpse beneath the glass-covered lid of her coffin. As the incarnation of the literal, Ottilie cannot enter into relations, not even relations with herself. She is the literal in the paradoxical sense of being the letters, the senseless matter, marks or sticks, of which written language is made, and at the same time she is the absence of any ground in matter or beneath it for the meaning which is spread over matter by a process of substitution and sideways superficial transfer. In this she is not the staff or *Stab* of the *Buchstabens*, but the O of death. The death she represents is not transcendence or sublimation, but death as absence, as the literal "thing" behind all language of which nothing can be said except in metaphor. Such metaphors are veils over the "X ignotum" which is left untouched. Or rather, since absence implies presence, Ottilie is that which never was or could be present. She is neither present nor absent, but simply the blank, the unapproachable, the zero about which nothing can be said except in the Narcissistic falsehoods of figure.

Ottilie's vow of silence, which presages her death, comes, as she writes to her friends, from taking "too literally, perhaps" (258); ["vielleicht zu buchstäblich"] (210), her promise not to speak to Edward. Ottilie writes: "Against his own will he stood before me. Too literally, perhaps, I have observed my promise never to admit him into conversation with me. My conscience and the feelings of the moment kept me silent toward him at the time, and now I have nothing more to say. . . . Do not call in anyone to mediate; do not insist upon my speaking; do not urge me to eat or to drink more than I absolutely must . . . leave me to my own inward self" (259); ["er stand selbst gegen seinen eigenen Willen vor mir. Mein Versprechen mich mit ihm in keine Unterredung einzulassen, habe ich vielleicht zu buchstäblich genommen und gedeutet. Nach Gefühl und Gewissen des Augenblicks schwieg ich, verstummt' ich vor dem Freunde, und nun habe ich nichts mehr zu sagen. . . Beruft keine Mittelsperson! Dringt nicht in mich, dass ich reden, dass ich mehr Speise und Trank geniessen soll, als ich höchstens bedarf. . . . mein Innres überlasst mir selbst"] (210). Ottilie allows herself to write, but no longer to speak. This makes clear the alignment of writing with silence and with the absence of what is implied by speaking, namely consciousness, personality, selfhood, the presence of the ego to itself. This opposition functions throughout the novel, for example in the striking impersonality of Ottilie's diary.

The best emblems of Ottilie's identification with silence, however, even before she lies silent in death within her glass-lidded coffin, are the two times when she appears to be asleep but in fact can hear though not speak. One of these has occurred in her childhood, before the novel begins, as she lay, apparently asleep, but actually in a kind of speechless trance, listening to Charlotte describe the unfortunate circumstances of her orphan life. The second time repeats the first and occurs on the night after she has caused the drowning of little Otto. The passage is one of the most important to an understanding of the novel:

. . . this is the second time that the same thing has happened to me [says Ottilie to Charlotte]. You once said to me that similar things often befall people more than once in their lives in a similar way, and if they do, it is always at important moments. . . . Shortly after my mother's death, when I was a very little child, I was sitting one day on a footstool close to you. You were on a sofa, as you are at this moment, and my head rested on your knees. I was not asleep, I was not awake: I was in a trance. I knew everything which was passing about me. I heard every word which was said with the greatest distinctness, and yet I could not stir, I could not speak; and if I had wished it, I could not have given a hint that I was conscious. On that occasion you were speaking about me to one of your friends; you were commiserating my fate, left as I was a poor orphan in the world. . . . I made rules to myself, according to such limited insight as I had, and by these I have long lived. . . . But I have wandered out of my course; I have broken my rules; I have lost the very power of feeling them. And now, after a dreadful occurrence, you have again made clear to be my situation, which is more pitiable than the first. While lying in a half torpor on your lap, I have again, as if out of another world, heard every syllable which you uttered. I know from you how all is with me. I shudder at the thought of myself; but again, as I did then, in my half sleep of death, I have marked out my new path for myself. (242–43)

[zum zweitenmal widerfährt mir dasselbige. Du sagtest mir einst: es begegne den Menschen in ihrem Leben oft Ähnliches auf ähnliche Weise, und immer in bedeutenden Augenblicken. . . . Kurz nach meiner Mutter Tode, als ein kleines Kind, hatte ich meinen Schemel an dich gerückt: du sassest auf dem Sofa wie jetzt; mein Haupt lag auf deinen Knien, ich schlief nicht, ich wachte nicht; ich schlummerte. Ich vernahm alles was um mich vorging, besonders alle Reden sehr deutlich; und doch konnte ich mich nicht regen, mich nicht äussern, und wenn ich auch gewollt hätte, nicht andeuten, dass ich meiner selbst mich bewusst fühlte. Damals sprachst du mit einer Freundin über mich; du bedauertest mein Schicksal, als eine arme Waise in der Welt geblieben zu sein. . . . Ich machte mir nach meinen beschränkten Einsichten hierüber Gesetze; nach diesen habe ich lange gelebt. . . . Aber ich bin aus meiner Bahn geschritten, ich habe meine Gesetze gebrochen, ich habe sogar das Gefühl derselben verloren, und nach einem schrecklichen Ereignis klärst du mich wieder über meinen Zustand auf, der jammervoller ist als der erste. Auf deinem Schosse ruhend, halb erstarrt, wie aus einer fremden Welt vernehm' ich abermals deine leise Stimme über meinem Ohr; ich vernehme, wie es mit mir selbst aussieht; ich schaudere über mich selbst;

J. Hillis Miller

aber wie damals habe ich auch diesmal in meinem halben Totenschlaf mir meine neue Bahn vorgezeichnet.] (197)

When Ottilie writes the letter explaining her vow of silence, she speaks again of the chosen course of her life, but this time with a difference. The rules she made for herself in her first trance-like state were a willed or elected plotting of the course of her life, not a destiny imposed on her by either malign or benign spiritual powers, though she may have chosen a course which seemed justified by the Christian values of renunciation and quiet obedient devoted work for women in which she has been brought up. Now once again she is making rules which, it seems, will put her back on her track after the detour of her passion for Edward. In her letter, however, after her renewed encounter with Edward, and after her discovery that her passion seems irresistible, a true elective affinity, she recognizes that she can never again recover her path: "I have stepped out of my course, and I cannot recover it again. A malignant spirit which has gained power over me seems to hinder me from without, even if within I could again become at peace with myself" (258); ["Ich bin aus meiner Bahn geschritten und ich soll nicht wieder hinein. Ein feindseliger Dämon, der Macht über mich gewonnen, scheint mich von aussen zu hindern, hätte ich mich auch mit mir selbst wieder zur Einigkeit gefunden"] (209–210). That "malignant spirit" is, the reader knows, Ottilie's metaphysical personification of her projection of herself into Edward, reflex of his Narcissistic love for her. Beneath any rules she makes for herself, any course she lays out, beneath even the red thread of her love for Edward, Ottilie is a trance-like silence, a half-sleep of death. This silence cannot love or be loved. It cannot relate itself to anything or to anyone. It cannot speak. It cannot trace a visible trajectory or line. Therefore it cannot be understood by another person or, in its representation, by the reader of the novel. It remains mute, discrete, effaced. It fulfills itself in the final impenetrable silence of her death. In death she becomes what she has been all along: hidden, untouched, mute, mere body, the letter, but therefore infinitely desirable in her unattainable beauty. In the same way the novel, clothed in that extraordinary beauty of which Benjamin speaks, can never be penetrated and made transparent in any interpretation. It always exceeds and escapes any reading of it.

Die Wahlverwandtschaften seems at first to invite a reading in terms of a notion of intersubjectivity as a relation between two independent selves, each of which, in his true love for the other, can function as the ground of that other. This notion of interpersonal relations, the novel shows, is inextricably tied to a tightly knit system of philosophical and linguistic notions, the system in fact which makes up the fabric of Western metaphysics, for example the distinction between metaphorical and literal uses of language. The novel presents this system, dramatizes it in a text of masterly beauty. At the same time, however, the novel also unravels the system in its presentation of what is in fact unpresentable: the silence of Ottilie, the missing fourth term in the crisscross of elective affinities. This undoing of the line, the breaking of the red thread by the black which can not be outlined, is always latent in the system itself, not least in that part of it involving notions of selfhood and interpersonal relations. This *Die Wahlverwandtschaften* admirably shows. It is a characteristic of realistic fiction as a genre, however, both to show selfhood as dependent on intersubjective lines and at the same time to show the impossibility of securely founding a self on the bond to another self. This is the end point reached by following Ariadne's thread through the corridor in the labyrinth labelled *Anastomosis.*

NOTES

1. Walter Benjamin, "Goethes *Wahlverwandtschaften,*" *Illuminationen* (Frankfort: Suhrkamp Verlag, 1969), p. 126; my translation.

2. This essay is drawn from "Ariadne's Thread," a book in progress on the use of line imagery in works of fiction and in the interpretation of works of fiction. It comes from a chapter on interpersonal relations in fiction entitled "Anastomosis."

3. Johann Wolfgang von Goethe, *Elective Affinities,* trans. James Anthony Froude and R. Dillon Boylan (New York: Frederick Ungar, 1962), p. 139; *Die Wahlverwandtschaften* (Munich: Deutscher Taschenbuch Verlag, 1975), p. 115. Numbers in parentheses after citations refer to pages in these editions.

4. This is discussed by Heinrich Nüsse in *Die Sprachtheorie Friedrich Schlegels* (Heidelberg: Carl Winter, Universitätsverlag, 1962); see especially Chapters 6–8, pp. 68–97.

5. Cited by Benjamin, "Goethes *Wahlverwandtschaften,*" pp. 134–35, my translation. The German is as follows: "Es scheint, dass den Verfasser seine fortgesetzten physikalischen Arbeiten zu diesem seltsamen Titel veranlassten. Er mochte bemerkt haben, dass man in der Naturlehre sich sehr oft ethischer Gleichnisse bedient, um etwas von dem Kreise menschlichen Wissens weit Entferntes näher heranzubringen; und so hat er auch wohl, in einem sittlichen Falle, eine chemische Gleichnisrede zu ihrem sittlichen Ursprunge um so eher zurückführen mögen, als doch überall nur Eine Natur ist und auch durch das Reich der heiteren Vernunftfreiheit die Spuren trüber leidenschaftlicher Notwendigkeit sich unaufhaltsam hindurchziehen, die nur durch eine höhere Hand, und vielleicht auch nicht in diesem Leben völlig auszulöschen sind."

6. "The Red Fern," 1. 12, *The Collected Poems of Wallace Stevens* (New York: Alfred A. Knopf, 1954), p. 365.

7. Aristotle, *On the Art of Poetry,* trans. Lane Cooper (Ithaca, N.Y.: Cornell University Press, 1947), p. 69.

TWO

RECOGNIZING CASAUBON
Neil Hertz

ABOUT half-way through *Middlemarch*, after having described one more manifestation of Mr. Casaubon's preoccupying self-concern, the narrator goes on to add a more general reflection:

Will not a tiny speck very close to our vision blot out the glory of the world, and leave only a margin by which we see the blot? I know no speck so troublesome as self. (307)[1]

The remark is characteristic of George Eliot in a number of ways, most obviously in its ethical implications: egotism in her writings is almost always rendered as narcissism, the self doubled and figured as both the eye and the blot. But equally typical is the care with which a particular image is introduced and its figurative possibilities developed. The speck blots out the glory of the world: that in itself would have enforced the moral. But the trope is given a second turn: the glory of the world illuminates the margin—the effect is of a sort of halo of light—but only so as to allow us all the better to see the blot. The intelligence at work extending a line of figurative language brings it back, with a nice appropriateness, to the ethical point. This is an instance of the sort of metaphorical control that teacher-critics have always admired in *Middlemarch*, the sign of a humane moral consciousness elaborating patterns of action and imagery with great inventiveness and absolutely no horsing around. Many a telling demonstration—in print and in the classroom, especially in the classroom—of the extraliterary value of formal analysis has been built around passages like this.

But what about that blot and its margin? Is the figurative language here so firmly anchored in a stable understanding of the moral relations of the self that it can't drift off in the direction of other margins and other blots?

I have in mind two specific citations, both associated with Mr. Casaubon early in the novel. At one point George Eliot's heroine, Dorothea, is seen in her library "seated and already deep in one of the pamphlets which had some marginal manuscript of Mr. Casaubon's" (28); at another, Casaubon's pedantically accurate memory is compared to "a volume where a *vide supra* could serve instead of repetitions, and not the ordinary long-used blotting-book which only tells of forgotten writing" (19). It might be objected that the blot we've been considering is clearly not an inkblot, the margin clearly not the margin of a printed page; that indeed it is only by ruling out those meanings as extraneous to this particular context that we can visualize the image at all—this image of vision, of obstructed vision, of some small physical object coming between one's eyes and the world. Of course: the image, to remain an image, must restrict the range of figurative meaning we allow to the words that compose it. And, given that restraining function, it seems all the more appropriate that the image here is operating to clarify an ethical point about the self, just as it is appropriate that the tag "the moral imagination" has been so popular a way of referring to George Eliot's particular powers as a writer.

And yet, between themselves, those words *blot* and *margin* work to encourage just such a misreading of the image they nevertheless define and are defined by: *blot* helps us hear a rustle of paper in *margin*, *margin* makes *blot* sound just a bit inkier. And both, as it happens, are easily drawn out of their immediate context by the cumulative force of a series of less equivocal allusions to handwriting, printing, writing-in-general, all clustered about the figure of Casaubon. One character refers to him as a "sort of parchment code" (51), another wisecracks "Somebody put a drop [of his blood] under a magnifying glass, and it was all semi-colons and parentheses" (52), his own single lugubrious attempt at a joke turns on "a word that has dropped out of the text" (57), and there are more serious and consequential allusions of the same sort. Early in their acquaintance, when Dorothea is most taken with her husband-to-be, George Eliot writes: "He was all she had at first imagined him to be: almost everything he had said seemed like a specimen from a mine, or the inscription on the door of a museum which might open on the treasure of past ages" (24). Later, in Rome, after the first quarrel of their marriage, Dorothea accompanies him to the Vatican, walking with him "through the stony avenue of inscriptions" and leaving him at the entrance to the library (150). Back in England, in their own library, after another quarrel, Mr. Casaubon tries to resume work, but "his hand trembled so much that the words seemed to be written in an unknown character" (209).

In the past, when critics have directed attention to such passages it has been either to comment on the general appropriateness of these images to Mr. Casaubon—who is, after all, a scholar—or on the particular finesse with which one image or another is adjusted to the unfolding drama of the Casaubons' marriage. More recently Hillis Miller, citing a pair of similar passages, both about Dorothea's wildly mistaken first impressions of her husband, has stressed the non-dramatic value of these allusions: Casaubon, he notes, "is a text, a collection of signs which Dorothea misreads, according to that universal propensity for misinterpretation which infects all the characters in *Middlemarch*."[2] Miller is right about Casaubon, but the point he would make is still more inclusive: he is arguing for a reading of the novel that would see every character as simultaneously an interpreter (the word is a recurrent one in *Middlemarch*) and a text available for the interpretations (plural, always partial, and often in conflict) of others. It is with reference to Lydgate, he could have pointed out, and not to Casaubon, that George Eliot writes that a man may "be known merely as a cluster of signs for his neighbors' false suppositions" (105).

Miller's argument is persuasive, and the reading of the novel he sketches is a bold and attractive one: he takes *Middlemarch* to be simultaneously affirming the values of Victorian humanism which it has been traditionally held to affirm—for example, a belief in the consistency of the self as a moral agent—and systematically undercutting those values, offering in place of an ethically stable notion of the self the somewhat less reassuring figure of a focus of semiotic energy, receiving and interpreting signs, itself a "cluster of signs" more or less legible. Miller's movement towards this poised, deconstructive formulation, however, is condensed and rapid, and may still leave one wondering how those two notions of the self are held in suspension in the novel, and what the commerce is between them. In the pages that follow I propose to take up that question by dwelling on the figure of Casaubon, and by asking what it might mean, if *all* the characters in *Middlemarch* may be thought of as texts or as clusters of signs, for the signs of textuality to cluster so thickly around one particular name. Or, to put it another way, why is Mr. Casaubon made to seem not merely an especially sterile and egotistical person, but at moments like a quasi-allegorical figure, the personification of the dead letter, the written word? Personifications exist somewhere in the middle ground between realistically represented persons and configurations of signs: that would seem to be ground worth going over. But I want to approach it obliquely, by first considering some passages where it is not Casaubon, but George Eliot herself—not the blot but the eye—around whom are clustered the signs of egotism and of writing.

Reading through George Eliot's early letters one comes across—not on every page, but often enough to catch one's attention—a particular kind of apology. In one, for example, written when she was nineteen, she concludes with these lines:

I have written at random and have not said all I wanted to say. I hope the frequent use of the personal pronoun will not lead you to think that I suppose it to confer any weight on what I have said. I used it to prevent circumlocution and waste of time. I am ashamed to send a letter like this as if I thought more highly of myself than I ought to think, which is alas! too true. (I, 23–24)[3]

And then, beneath her signature, as a second-thought, a post-script:

In reading my letter I find difficulties in understanding my scribble that I fear are hopelessly insurmountable for another. (I, 24)

Typically, apologies for what she fears may seem like egotism are accompanied by apologies for her handwriting:

I . . . hope that you will be magnanimous enough to forgive the trouble my almost undecipherable letter will give you. Do not, pray, write neatly to me, for I cannot undertake to correspond with any one who will not allow me to scribble, though this precious sheet has, I think, an extra portion of untidiness . . . . (I, 8)

I have written an almost unpardonably egotistical letter to say nothing of its other blemishes . . . . (I, 52)

Tell me if you have great trouble in making out my cabalistic letters; if you have, I will write more deliberately next time. (I, 134)

The feeling behind these apologies need not be either particularly strong or particularly sincere: often they're perfunctory, or positively comical, as in this passage, where jokes about handwriting oddly prefigure the language that will be associated with Casaubon thirty years later:

You will think me interminably loquacious, and still worse you will be ready to compare my scribbled sheet to the walls of an Egyptian tomb for mystery, and determine not to imitate certain wise antiquaries or antiquarian wise-acres who "waste their precious years, how soon to fail?" in deciphering information which has only the lichen and moss of age to make it more valuable than the facts graphically conveyed by an upholsterer's pattern book. (I, 64)

What's curious is the stress not simply on the messiness of what she calls her "scribble," but on its cabalistic or hieroglyphic indecipherability. The point might be that language turns opaque and resistant when it is too purely in the service of the self, when self-expressive scribbles replace legible communicating signs. In that case these apologies for sloppy handwriting might be read as slight nervous displacements of the apologies for egotism they accompany. But there is more going on here than that: writing, like the self-doubling of narcissism, is disturbing not simply because it may seem "self-centered" but because it is both that and self-dispersing at once.

When handwriting is legible it becomes not only available to others but transparent—and attractive—as self-expression, seemingly adequate in its relation to whatever it is the self would exteriorize. At such moments one's sense of the distance between one's self and the signs one produces can be cheerfully ignored or even enjoyed. And in fact an instance of just such enjoyment—narcissistic through and through, and thoroughly engaging—can be discerned in what is, by a happy accident, the earliest bit of George Eliot's writing to have survived. It is to be found on the cover of a school notebook she used when she was fourteen, a notebook which contains some arithmetic exercises, an essay on "affectation and conceit," the beginnings of a story in the manner of Sir Walter Scott, some poems she'd copied out, some drawings, and so forth. But on its cover, in a large, flourishing, ornate script, is a date—"March 16th 1834"—and a name: "Marianne Evans." It is her signature, but not quite her name, for she was christened Mary Anne, not Marianne. Gordon Haight, who reprints parts of the notebook in an appendix to his biography,[4] remarks that she was learning French at the time, as well as being trained, as was the custom in girls' schools, in elegant penmanship: the combination seems to have produced this striking emblem of a writer's beginnings, the schoolgirl's slight, slightly romantic alteration of her name, written out large and with care, there to be contemplated on the cover of her book, the space of musing revery opening up between herself and her signature, a space in which a certain play of transformation becomes possible.

Sometimes that space is welcomed as "breathing-space," or, in a favorite image of George Eliot's, as "room" into which she can "expand"; at those moments the writing which structures that space stops being "scribble" and becomes what she likes to call "utterance," drawing on the Pentecostal associations of that word:

It is necessary to me not simply to *be* but to *utter*, and I require utterance of my friends . . . . It is like a diffusion or expansion of one's own life to be assured that its vibrations are repeated in another, and words are the media of those vibrations. How can you say that music must end in silence? Is not the universe itself a perpetual utterance of the One Being? (I, 255)

But these moments of expansive utterance, where neither the distance between the self and its signs, nor the difference between selves is felt as a problem, are commonly followed in George Eliot's texts by moments of anxious "shrinking" and remorse:

I feel a sort of madness growing upon me—just the opposite of the delirium which makes people fancy that their bodies are filling the room. It seems to me as if I were shrinking into that mathematical abstraction, a point—so entirely am I destitute of contact that I am unconscious of length and breadth. (I, 264)

This alternation between exuberance and apology, expansion and shrinking, utterance and scribble, was to govern George Eliot's literary production throughout her life: she lived it as a rhythm of fluctuating excitement and discouragement while she was working on her novels, followed by deep gloom when each was completed. More interestingly, she inscribed that alternation into her novels, but curiously transformed. At a number of climactic moments the play of expansion and shrinking reappears, but the rhythm is broken, lifted out of the interior life of a single character and distributed to a pair of characters, one of whom is seen expanding in loving recognition of the other, who is commonly figured as shrunken or shrinking from contact. Late in *Middlemarch*, for example, when Mrs. Bulstrode, humiliated by the revelations of her husband's past, but loyal to him nevertheless, goes to join him, we are told that "as she went towards him she thought he looked smaller—he seemed so withered and shrunken" (550). Elsewhere in the novel, when Dorothea touches her husband's arm, only to be horrified by his unresponsive hardness, the narrator adds: "You may ask why, in the name of manliness, Mr. Casaubon should have behaved that way. Consider that his was a mind which shrank from pity" (312).

These are instances of a distribution of attributes operating within the fictional world of the novel: images that we have seen George Eliot, in letters, applying to her own inner life are attached, as in a medieval psychomachia, to separate characters in her narratives. But at times this distributive activity may be seen operating across the boundary that separates the lives of the characters—the ways they conduct themselves and engage with one another—from the sensed activity of an author, the ways George Eliot conducts the plotting of her novels. For example, Dorothea's loving acknowledgement of her husband is followed, after not too long an interval, by his death; or again, when Mrs. Bulstrode goes to her husband's side, he is a permanently broken man. Within the world of *Middlemarch*, neither Dorothea nor Mrs. Bulstrode can be held responsible for the turns of fate that crush their husbands, but it is nonetheless true that certain recipients of moral generosity don't fare well in that world. Seeking an explanation, a critic might wish to read

Neil Hertz

such scenes as unwittingly playing-out their author's preoccupations in some wishful and compensatory fashion. Richard Ellmann, for example, has found in the language associated with Casaubon echoes of images linked, in an early letter, with the novelist's fears of her own erotic fantasizing. "The severity with which Casaubon is treated," Ellmann speculates, "would then derive from her need to exorcise this part of her experience. . . . To berate Casaubon, and to bury him, was to overcome in transformed state the narcissistic sensuality of her adolescence."[5] To seek an author's personal allegory behind the realistic surface she has woven is often as unrewarding as it is methodologically dubious, but in the case of George Eliot's works, because they are explicitly about the imagining of others—about the status of the image of one person in the imagining mind of another—the play between the imaginer and the imagined, between author and character, and the possibility of a narcissistic confusion developing between the one and the other, has already been thematized and made available for interpretations such as Ellmann's. If anything, his claims are too modest: what he presents as a contingent psychobiographical detail—an author's uneasiness about her own "narcissism"—may be read as neither contingent nor primarily biographical, but as part of a sustained and impersonal questioning of the grounds of fiction. Nowhere is that questioning more energetically in evidence than in the pages (in Chapters 20 and 21) that recount the Casaubons' experience in Rome. If we turn to them now, beginning with the final paragraphs of Chapter 21, we shall find another instance of the bifurcated activity characteristic of Eliot's writing:

Today she had begun to see that she had been under a wild illusion in expecting a response to her feeling from Mr. Casaubon, and she had felt the waking of a presentiment that there might be a sad consciousness in his life which made as great a need on his side as on her own.
   We are all of us born in moral stupidity, taking the world as an udder to feed our supreme selves: Dorothea had early begun to emerge from that stupidity, but yet it had been easier to her to imagine how she would devote herself to Mr. Casaubon, and become wise and strong in his strength and wisdom, than to conceive with that distinctness which is no longer reflection but feeling—an idea wrought back to the directness of sense, like the solidity of objects—that he had an equivalent centre of self, whence the lights and shadows must always fall with a certain difference. (156–57)

These lines have been rightly admired, both as a powerful presentation of Dorothea's experience and as an epitome of the moral imagination at work, a text exhibiting the links between generous conduct, literary creation and the reading of novels. For Dorothea's exemplary action would seem to be easily assimilated to the activity of a novelist and to that of a reader: to conceive Mr. Casaubon as different from oneself, and to do so "with that distinctness which is no longer reflection but feeling" sounds like a display of the same imaginative power that created the character of Casaubon in the first place, and the same power that *Middlemarch* would quicken in its readers. And indeed this view of the novel, and of the use of novels generally, was one George Eliot had already endorsed: "A picture of human life such as a great artist can give," she wrote, "surprises even the trivial and selfish into that attention to what is apart from themselves, which may be called the raw material of moral sentiment."[6] We shall want to pause to ask where Mr. Casaubon fits into this set of beliefs about literature and conduct, other than as the passive (and not altogether grateful) object of Dorothea's (and George Eliot's, and the reader's) regard. But first, let us look more closely at how George Eliot elaborates this view of the moral imagination. The notion that literature calls attention to un-noticed aspects of life, to its intricacies or simply to its variety, is certainly not peculiar to her; more characteristic, however, is the stress she places on the reader's (or the character's) reluctance to attend: in the sentence just quoted, it is the element of surprise that counts—even "the trivial and selfish" are to be shocked into noticing what is apart from themselves. Typically her plots present someone jolted into the consciousness of others, with the jolt all the more forceful because of the resistance encountered, a resistance which is generally figured as a powerfully narcissistic investment in an image of the self, the blot that obscures the glory of the world. Or—still more generally—an investment in *some* image, for the notion of narcissism in these novels is deepened to include other sorts of imaginative fascination.

Thus the "moral stupidity" which Dorothea must emerge from can be presented as a clinging to a mistaken idea of her marriage: "Today she had begun to see that she had been under a wild illusion in expecting a response to her feeling from Mr. Casaubon. . . ." Later in the novel, echoing the encompassing turn of phrase of the earlier passage—"We are all of us born in moral stupidity"—George Eliot writes "We are all of us imaginative in some form or other, for images are the brood of desire" (237). She is writing there of the old miser Featherstone, who never emerges or even begins to emerge from what she names as "the fellowship of illusion." But the repetitions of syntax and cadence suggest an equivalence: to be born in moral stupidity is to be born imaginative; and it is against the inertia of this mode of imaginative activity, the narcissistic dwelling on and in an image, that the moral imagination has to both define itself and defend itself.

Define itself first, for the differences between these two kinds of imagination—one supposedly turned outward and hence moral, the other self-enclosed and narcissistic—may not, under scrutiny, be all that clear. Both activities, whatever their outward effects, would seem to originate within the same enclosure: it becomes important to be able to distinguish them at their source, and not merely in terms of their consequences. George Eliot is here engaging the same problem that led Romantic theorists like Coleridge to insist on a sharp and essential difference between the mental activities they named Imagination and Fancy, and her solution—if we now look back at the paragraph on moral stupidity—will be seen to resemble theirs. For what is most remarkable in that passage is the fact that Dorothea's exemplary action, the acknowledgement of an irreducible difference between persons, is accompanied by—is accomplished in—the flashing reduction of another sort of difference, that between "reflection" and "feeling," "idea" and "sense." To recognize Casaubon as possessing "an equivalent centre of self, whence the lights and shadows must always fall with a certain difference" is, for Dorothea, to overcome not merely her own egotism, but also what another Eliot has called a "dissociation of sensibility," a troublesome interior difference. And, oddly, what she achieves is made to sound very much like what Mr. Casaubon, at another point in the novel, is pitied for never having experienced, that "rapturous transformation of consciousness" into "the vividness of a thought, the ardour of a passion, the energy of an action" (206–7). If we now ask what Mr. Casaubon is doing in this scene, we can see that he is presented both as a character, another person, the object of Dorothea's recognition, and as a figure, an exteriorized embodiment of a mode of imagination threateningly antithetical to hers—and to George Eliot's. For Dorothea to recognize him "as he is" is, for the author, to cast out what he may be taken to represent.

But what, exactly, may he be taken to represent? At times he would seem to be the personification of the written word, at others the personification of the narcissistic imagination; the connection between the two can be made in a more systematic way in terms of an economy of anxiety, by suggesting that the dislocation implicit in narcissism, the doubling of the self into an eye and an image, an eye and a blot, is a more manageable and comforting fiction than the more open and indeterminate self-dispersion associated with a plurality of signs or with the plurality of interpretations that writing can provoke. In Chapters 20 and 21 of *Middlemarch* one can follow a movement towards the more reassuring fiction. They begin with the superb paragraphs in which Mr. Casaubon is associated with a vision of Rome as "stupendous fragmentariness" (143), an unintelligible plurality that baffles Dorothea with "a glut of confused ideas" (144); they then move through a complicated and uncertain grappling—on George Eliot's part—with the threat of narcissism, the threat that her own imaginative activity is nothing but narcissistic, to the exteriorization of that disturbing possibility in the figure of Casaubon, a personification now no longer of "writing" but of "narcissism" who can be "recognized" and banished from the novel. We shall follow that movement in Chapter 20 more closely in a moment, but first we should take note of some texts that bear on another mode of imagination commonly attributed to George Eliot and held to be at work in the paragraphs on Rome, the "historical imagination."

In 1856, in a review entitled "Silly Novels by Lady Novelists," George Eliot commented on the current vogue for historical fiction in language that reads like a program for the writing of *Romola*:

Admitting that genius which has familiarized itself with all the relics of an ancient period can sometimes, by the force of its sympathetic divination, restore the missing notes in the "music of humanity," and reconstruct the fragments into a whole which will really bring the remote past nearer to us, and interpret it to our duller apprehension,—this form of imaginative power must always be among the very rarest, because it demands as much accurate and minute knowledge as creative vigour.[7]

Her own work on *Romola*, which she began five or six years later, involved her in months of painstaking research in reconstructing the fragments of Renaissance Florence. But the emphasis on "accurate and minute knowledge" in this passage is common to most of the essays and reviews she wrote in the 1850s, just before she turned to fiction. Knowing the names of things, getting things right becomes, for an intellectual journalist, not just a criterion of success, but a moral criterion as well: the attention to detail required by research into any subject, but particularly into historical questions, is referred to as an escape from self, a salutary counter to the narcissism implicit in a vague and wishful relation to the things around one. Yet here a characteristic problem asserts itself: it is in the nature of historical research, even of the most rigorous and self-effacing kind, that the energies caught up in it are far from disinterested. Curiosity about the past, a wish to reconstruct the fragments into a whole, may indeed be a move beyond a casual, lazy or provincial self-complacency, but it draws its powers from a more fundamental wish to reconstruct an original mirror of the self, a totalization of history which will be a history of one's own origins. In a bizarre scene in *Romola* George Eliot's sense of the willfulness informing attempts at historical reconstruction is dramatized in a striking and pertinent way.

Romola is both a Victorian humanist's effort to reconstruct a moment in the past and the story of a similar effort, that of the Florentine humanists, to piece together the fragments of classical

Neil Hertz

civilization. One of the characters, Baldassare, is presented as someone who has been betrayed by his son into captivity and the loss of his fortune; as a result of his sufferings, we learn, he has lost his memory, too, and with it his ability to read Greek. Making his way to Florence, he attempts to rehabilitate himself and to reclaim what's due him—to recapture his skills as a classical scholar and to avenge himself on his son. George Eliot has constructed the plot so that these two motifs inter-lock in a peculiar scene. The son comes to visit Baldassare, who recognizes him and leaps at him with a dagger; but the dagger breaks, his son escapes him and he is left alone, impotent to avenge himself and still incapable of making out the Greek text that he had been puzzling over earlier:

He leaned to take up the fragments of the dagger; then he turned towards the book which lay open at his side. It was a fine large manuscript, an odd volume of Pausanias. The moonlight was upon it, and he could see the large letters at the head of the page:

(and here George Eliot prints out the Greek capitals in a large open space on her own page before continuing):

ΜΕΣΣΗΝΙΚΑ. ΚΒ'
In old days he had known Pausanias familiarly; yet an hour or two ago he had been looking hopelessly at that page, and it had suggested no more meaning to him than if the letters had been black weather-marks on a wall; but at this moment they were once again the magic signs that conjure up a world.

Excitedly he takes up the book and reads, then goes out to walk about the city, feeling "the glow of conscious power":

That city, which had been a weary labyrinth, was material that he could subdue to his purposes now: his mind glanced through its affairs with flashing conjecture; he was once more a man who knew cities, whose sense of vision was instructed in large experience, and who felt the keen delight of holding all things in the grasp of language. Names! Images!—his mind rushed through its wealth without pausing, like one who enters on a great inheritance.[8]

The fragments of the dagger that had failed him are replaced by the no longer fragmentary Greek letters, once plural, discontinuous and indecipherable—mere black marks—now capable of reconstitution into a text that is at once the mirror of Baldassare's re-integrated self (hence the excited exclamations: "Names! Images!") and the instrument of his vengeance. "The city, which had been a weary labyrinth"—like Casaubon's habitual setting—is now something Baldassare can subdue to his purposes: the mastery of language here, the reconstitution of the written word into significant clusters, is seen as thoroughly imperialistic, an emblem of the willed integrity of a wrathful father. There has rarely been a neater instance of what Jacques Derrida has called "ce qui revient au père": what literally comes back to this father is his memory, his identity and with it his power to dominate. What, then, are we to make of the historical novelist's wish to "restore the missing notes in the 'music of humanity' " and reconstruct the fragments into a whole? That no longer sounds like an utterly innocent project. It is with this in mind that we can now turn to the paragraphs on Rome.

Chapter 20 opens with Dorothea in tears, with "no distinctly shapen grievance that she could state, even to herself" (143). We might wish to say that it soon becomes clear what is distressing her, that she has been hurt by her husband's cold and pedantic behavior, and over-whelmed by what she has seen of Rome, but that would be to travesty the experience of reading these paragraphs, to turn aside from the subtlety with which Dorothea's psychological state is rendered, as well as from the deft intermingling of the causes of her distress. From the chapter's third paragraph on, it becomes impossible to separate Dorothea's response to her husband from her response to the city, and just as impossible to allow the one noun—Casaubon—to stand in some flatly symbolic equivalence to the other noun—Rome. Certain likenesses are taken for granted: Casaubon is old, he is a historian and an interpreter, he is (to Dorothea, at least) a center of authority; but these paragraphs don't exactly dwell on this analogy or spell out its terms. Instead, the words associated earlier in the novel with Mr. Casaubon, the images that had been clustered around his name, are allowed to drift free of that center and to disperse themselves through the urban landscape: allusions to Mr. Casaubon himself, or to Dorothea's role as his wife, practically disappear. This disappearance, the withdrawal of Casaubon from the foreground of this prose, is marked by an odd figure, a sort of "dissolve" that displaces the couple's relation onto the seasons:

Dorothea had now been five weeks in Rome, and in the kindly mornings when autumn and winter seemed to go hand in hand like a happy aged couple one of whom would presently survive in chiller loneliness, she had driven about at first with Mr. Casaubon, but of late chiefly with Tantripp and their experienced courier. (143)

While Mr. Casaubon retires to the Vatican Library, Dorothea is left alone with Rome and with her own life, and both are figured to her as enigmas: her confused and disorganized feelings are assimilàted to the fragmentary nature of the scene around her, a scene now made up as much of the bits and pieces of language associated with Casaubon as of the "broken revelations of that Imperial and Papal city":

The weight of unintelligible Rome might lie easily on bright nymphs to whom it formed a background for the brilliant picnic of Anglo-foreign society; but

Dorothea had no such defence against deep impressions. Ruins and basilicas, palaces and colossi, set in the midst of a sordid present, where all that was living and warm-blooded seemed sunk in the deep degeneracy of a superstition divorced from reverence; the dimmer yet eager Titanic life gazing and struggling on walls and ceilings; the long vistas of white forms whose marble eyes seemed to hold the monotonous light of an alien world: all this vast wreck of ambitious ideals, sensuous and spiritual, mixed confusedly with the signs of breathing forgetfulness and degradation, at first jarred her as with an electric shock, and then urged themselves on her with that ache belonging to a glut of confused ideas which check the flow of emotion. Forms both pale and glowing took possession of her young sense, and fixed themselves in her memory even when she was not thinking of them, preparing strange associations which remained through her after-years. Our moods are apt to bring with them images which succeed each other like the magic-lantern pictures of a doze; and in certain states of dull forlornness Dorothea all her life continued to see the vastness of St. Peter's, the huge bronze canopy, the excited intention in the attitudes and garments of the prophets and evangelists in the mosaics above, and the red drapery which was being hung for Christmas spreading itself everywhere like a disease of the retina. (143–44)

I have quoted this passage at length both in order to recall its intensity and to draw attention to its organization. The persistent emphasis on the scene's at once soliciting and resisting comprehension, linked to the rhythms in which these sentences accumulate layer on layer of plural nouns, until that accumulated charge is released in a "shock," a "glut of confused ideas which check the flow of emotion"—these elements mark this experience of Dorothea's as an experience of the sublime, in the specific sense that term took on in the writings of Kant or of Wordsworth. I mention this not simply to identify a literary tradition—though I have enough of Casaubon in me to take an intense, bleak pleasure in interrupting a passionate moment with a scholarly gloss—but because to recognize the rhythm of the sublime in these sentences is to anticipate where the text might go from here, what one might expect to follow after that abrupt shock. At one point, for instance, Kant describes the feeling of the sublime as a pleasure that arises only indirectly, produced "by the feeling of a momentary checking of the vital powers and a consequent stronger outflow of them."[9] Elsewhere, explaining the "bewilderment or, as it were, perplexity which it is said seizes the spectator on his first entrance into St. Peter's in Rome," he writes: "For there is here a feeling of the inadequacy of his imagination for presenting the ideas of a whole, wherein the imagination reaches its maximum, and, in striving to surpass it, sinks back into itself, by which, however, a kind of emotional satisfaction is produced."[10] We might, with this model in mind, ask if there will be an outflow of vital powers in this passage, or a sinking back of the imagination into itself. Or, if what we have in mind is the language of "Tintern Abbey," we might wonder if

Dorothea will be released from "the burthen of the mystery," the "heavy and the weary weight of all this unintelligible world," and allowed to "see into the life of things." One way or another, a reader may be led to expect some resolution, and, indeed, his expectations are rewarded, although—and this too is characteristic of the sublime—not in quite the form he may have anticipated.

For the movement of these pages seems to issue in not one but three moments that qualify as "resolutions," partly because of their position in the text, partly because of the level of their diction and the nature of the metaphors of which they are composed. One of these, the last in the sequence, I have already described in some detail: it is the paragraph with which Chapter 21 concludes, the paragraph beginning "We are all of us born in moral stupidity." For if it is the "dream-like strangeness of her bridal life" that Dorothea is confronting in the opening pages of Chapter 20, the baffling disparity between her sense of whom she was marrying and the realities of living with Mr. Casaubon, then her acknowledging that she had "been under a wild illusion" can be thought of as one response to the shock she registered in the previous chapter, a response that is deferred chiefly for reasons of dramatic verisimilitude, because it takes time to adjust to such new awareness. Here the sequence of sublime checking followed by some resolution underlies the ethical scenario we noticed earlier, where a character is jolted out of moral stupidity into the recognition of something apart from the self.

But the intensity of Dorothea's feelings, as they are presented in those opening paragraphs, as well as the scope of George Eliot's rhetoric, are far in excess of anything that could be resolved dramatically: she has been shown attempting to come to terms not simply with her husband, but with the heterogeneous assault of Rome, with a collection of signs that may be "summed up" in a verbal formulation (e.g., "all this vast wreck of ambitious ideals") but which neither Dorothea nor the author is in a position to render as a totality. The resolution of *this* aspect of Dorothea's experience is to be found in the sentences immediately following those on the checking of the flow of emotion, and in one sense it is no resolution at all: it takes the form of a compulsively repeated set of images, fixed in Dorothea's memory for life and unexorcisable. The plurality of unmasterable fragments is converted into a repetitive series of painful tokens. This is a dark sublimity, beyond the pleasure-principle for Dorothea, and sufficiently at odds with the values of Victorian humanism to be distressing to George Eliot as well. The later paragraph, in which Dorothea recognizes Casaubon, may be read as, quite literally, a domestication of the anxiety associated with this earlier moment.

Neil Hertz

If one wanted to demonstrate that *Middlemarch* offers a reader two incompatible systems of value, conflicting views of the interpretation of history, of the possibilities of knowledge, of the consistency of the self, few passages in the novel would provide better evidence. One could contrast the sublime of repetition with that of recognition, then read the first as an undermining of moral and metaphysical categories, the second as the recuperation of those same categories. But what, then, are we to make of still another moment in these pages that is bound to strike a reader as "sublime"? It is to be found in the paragraph immediately following the description of Rome, and it has been cited, admiringly, perhaps as much as any other passage in George Eliot's works:

If we had a keen vision and a feeling for all ordinary human life, it would be like hearing the grass grow and the squirrel's heart beat, and we should die of that roar which lies on the other side of silence. As it is the quickest of us walk about well wadded in stupidity. (144)

We might begin by noticing that these sentences, although they share with the other "resolutions" a sense of high-powered epistemological confrontation, are not about Dorothea's response either to Rome or to Mr. Casaubon; they are, rather, about how "we"—the reader and the narrator—might respond to Dorothea, and indeed they come at the end of a paragraph that had begun with a slightly awkward wavering of tone, as the narrator seemed to back off from the intensities of Dorothea's experience:

Not that this inward amazement of Dorothea's was anything very exceptional: many souls in their young nudity are tumbled out among incongruities and left to "find their feet" among them, while their elders go about their business. Nor can I suppose that when Mrs. Casaubon is discovered in a fit of weeping six weeks after her wedding the situation will be regarded as tragic.

One of George Eliot's most acute contemporary readers, Richard Holt Hutton, was struck by the oddness of these lines, and bothered by what he heard as a "bitter parenthetic laugh" at the expense of those souls tumbled out "in their young nudity."[11] I think it *is* an odd moment, but that the tonal irony seems less directed at the "souls"—that is, at Dorothea—than it does at some imagined insensitive reader: the "Nor can I suppose" is somewhat heavy-handedly reminding the reader of the limits of his perception of the tragic, of the limits of those powers of sympathetic imagination which would enable him to discern the tragic in "the very fact of frequency." Still more puzzling, however, is the combination of this sardonic diction with the note of high assurance the narrator strikes in the sentences about "the roar . . . on the other side of silence."

What is going on in this passage makes more sense once we learn that it is dense with self-quotation, with allusions to George Eliot's earlier fiction. Those "souls in their young nudity," for example, "tumbled out" and left to " 'find their feet' " would seem to be a rendering as a figure of speech of what was once, in a story called "Janet's Repentance" (one of the *Scenes of Clerical Life*), a piece of dramatic action: there the heroine is literally thrown out of her house by her drunken husband, and her situation is described in these terms:

> The stony street, the bitter north-east wind and darkness—and in the midst of them a tender woman thrust out from her husband's home in her thin night-dress, the harsh wind cutting her naked feet, and driving her long hair away from her half-clad bosom, where the poor heart is crushed with anguish and despair.[12]

Also to be found in "Janet's Repentance" are lines which echo in the squirrel's heartbeat:

> Yet surely, surely the only true knowledge of our fellow-man is that which enables us to feel with him—which gives us a fine ear for the heart-pulses that are beating under the mere clothes of circumstance and opinion. Our subtlest analysis of schools and sects must miss the essential truth, unless it be lit up by the love that sees in all forms of human thought and work the life and death struggles of separate human beings.[13]

In still another story, "The Lifted Veil," the hero discovers in himself a power that torments him and which he describes as a "diseased participation in other people's consciousness": "It was like a preternaturally heightened sense of hearing," he relates, "making audible to one a roar of sound where others find perfect stillness."[14]

The validity of the novelist's imagination of others, whether it is seen as a saving gift or as a curse, is what is at stake in this paragraph in *Middlemarch*. Placed between Dorothea's failure to reconstruct the fragments of history and her success in recognizing her husband as someone with an "equivalent centre of self," this passage seeks language adequate to a slightly different task, that of stabilizing the incommensurable relation between an author conceived of as somehow "outside" (but uncertainly outside) her creation and a privileged (but fictitious) consciousness within that imagined world. The allusions to earlier works of fiction, the reappearance of those evocations of pathos or of imaginative power, are accompanied by the reversal of their original meanings: what had seemed pathetic reality in "Janet's Repentance" has been transformed into a metaphor, and the "fine ear for heart-pulses," the ability to hear "a roar of sound where others find perfect stillness"—these are precisely the faculties that a reader is now told he does not possess. The wavering, then steadying of tone in which the narrator addresses the reader may be read as one way of readjusting to the felt instability of the author's relation to her character, to the unsettled sense that it was through an intense identification with Dorothea's experience in Rome that the magnificent previous paragraph had been written, but that the burden of that paragraph was the fictitiousness and the willfulness of such identifications. The sublimity of the image of the roar on the other side of silence emerges from this thoroughly negative insight.

Behind this language about the limits of perception is still another text, one with a long history in eighteenth- and nineteenth-century writing about the sublime: it is the passage in the *Essay Concerning Human Understanding* in which Locke is praising the aptness with which the human senses are scaled to man's position in the hierarchy of creatures:

If our sense of hearing were but a thousand times quicker than it is, how would a perpetual noise distract us. And we should in the quietest retirement be less able to sleep or meditate than in the middle of a sea-fight. Nay, if that most instructive of our senses, seeing, were in any man a thousand, or a hundred thousand times more acute than it is by the best microscope, things several millions of times less than the smallest object of his sight now would then be visible to his naked eyes, and so he would come nearer to the discovery of the texture and motion of the minute parts of corporeal things; and in many of them, probably get ideas of their internal constitutions; but then he would be in a quite different world from other people: nothing would appear the same to him and others.[15]

Locke's language converts a scaled continuum into an opposition between the ordinary world of sensation and sociability and the "quite different world" in which the man with microscopic vision would find himself. To allude to that language in *Middlemarch* is to stress that discontinuity at the moment when the incommensurability between an author and the creatures of her pen is under consideration. Suppose, to draw out the turns of this figure, one *were* to hear the roar which lies on the other side of silence. Possibly one might not die of it; instead— and this may not be the preferable alternative—one might become like Locke's man, moving nearer to the discovery of the texture and motion of things, but in a quite different world from other people. If, for example, one were to bring a drop of Mr. Casaubon's blood into focus, one might see nothing but semi-colons and parentheses. That is the possibility that is written into *Middlemarch* in the idiom of the sublime; it is clearly not a possibility to be steadily contemplated by a working novelist—it must be repressed if books like *Middlemarch* are to be written at all. One sign of that repression is the recognition and exorcism of Casaubon.

NOTES

1. George Eliot, *Middlemarch*, ed. Gordon S. Haight (Boston: Houghton Mifflin, 1956). Page numbers are given in the body of the text.

2. J. Hillis Miller, "Narrative and History," *ELH* 41 (1974): 466. Miller's account of the novel is further developed in "Optic and Semiotic in *Middlemarch*," in *The Worlds of Victorian Fiction*, ed. Jerome H. Buckley (Cambridge, Mass.: Harvard University Press, 1975), pp. 125–45.

3. *The George Eliot Letters*, ed. Gordon S. Haight, 7 vols. (New Haven: Yale University Press, 1954–55). Volume and page numbers are given in body of text.

4. *George Eliot: A Biography* (New York and Oxford: Oxford University Press, 1968), p. 552. The notebook itself may be seen in the Beinecke Library at Yale.

5. "Dorothea's Husbands," in *Golden Codgers: Biographical Speculations* (London: Oxford University Press, 1973), pp. 28, 38.

6. In "The Natural History of German Life" (1856), reprinted in Thomas Pinney, ed., *Essays of George Eliot* (New York: Columbia University Press, 1963), p. 270.

7. Pinney, pp. 320–21.

8. *Romola* (Edinburgh and London: Blackwood, n.d.), Chapter 38 ("The Black Marks Become Magical"), pp. 291–92.

9. Immanuel Kant, *Critique of Judgment*, trans. J. H. Bernard (New York: Hafner, 1951), p. 83.

10. Kant, p. 91.

11. Review of Book 2 of *Middlemarch*, *Spectator*, 3 February 1872, repr. in *George Eliot: The Critical Heritage*, ed. David Carroll (London: Routledge, 1971), p. 291.

12. "Janet's Repentance" in *Scenes of Clerical Life* (1858) ed. David Lodge (Harmondsworth: Penguin, 1973), p. 343.

13. "Janet's Repentance," p. 322.

14. "The Lifted Veil" in *Silas Marner—The Lifted Veil—Brother Jacob* (Edinburgh and London: Blackwood, n.d.), p. 301.

15. *An Essay Concerning Human Understanding*, ed. Alexander Campbell Fraser (1894; rpt. New York: Dover, 1959), 1, 403.

THREE

THE DEATH OF *ACEPHALE* AND THE WILL TO CHANCE: NIETZSCHE IN THE TEXT OF BATAILLE
Allan Stoekl

MORE THAN any other theoretician, except perhaps Blanchot, Bataille presents the reader—and the potential critic—with a dilemma. Are we to *repeat* what Bataille has already written, appropriating aspects of a coherent "theory of waste"? This might have a certain value if we are applying those theories to other texts or political constructs. If, however, we return to read Bataille, it seems unlikely that we can formulate anything about "spending without return" (*dépense*) that will be more incisive than what Bataille himself wrote. At best we can summarize or schematize.[1] Yet summarizations or schematizations will be the inevitable result if we approach Bataille's writings as a kind of homogenous body of work. Is there in fact one Bataillean "theory"? To our knowledge, no such unity has ever been demonstrated.

Another approach dismisses (overtly or covertly) any possibility of a Bataillean "totality," only to privilege certain aspects or periods of Bataille's work over others. *Tel Quel* in the early seventies, for example, stressed certain of Bataille's political texts from the thirties which, in some ways, are quite compatible with a Maoist dialectic.[2] The problem with readings of this kind is that, in stressing a single period, the critics who would appropriate Bataille ignore his subsequent writings which might, in fact, be critiques of the positions they are using. They therefore ignore the possibility of an effective Bataillean critique of their own positions.

Nietzsche in the Text of Bataille

Both of these approaches neglect the *specificity* of texts within Bataille's *oeuvre*. If Bataille is a repetition of both Hegel *and* Nietzsche (as Denis Hollier and Jacques Derrida have argued),[3] the interrelation of periods and positions in Bataille must be seen from both a dialectical and a transgressive point of view. This interrelation will be dialectical in the sense that succeeding positions attempt to take into account the failures of preceding texts, and try to successfully work out new positions. On the other hand, it will be transgressive to the extent that the new positions taken will not attempt to be successful formulations of an absolute knowledge, but rather of a nonknowledge, an impossible "durable orgasm" (as Bataille refers to it in "L'Oeil pinéal (1)" [2, 25]). The position of the commentator will then both be necessary and impossible. Necessary because an overview will reveal a coherence in Bataille's works that up to now has remained unexplored (and will remain so if the *oeuvre* is seen simply as a collection of texts that present a unified theory), and impossible to the extent that awareness or self-reflexivity of this development will reduce it to the status of a simple dialectic, conflating it with Hegel and entirely losing Nietzsche in the process. Bataille himself was "aware" of this problem, not in relation to a commentary on his works, but in the possible interrelation of his texts as a dialectic leading to a simple endpoint. It became necessary for him to confront any dialectical movement, no matter how transgressive, with another series, or side, of texts that would work to forget that dialectic. That very forgetting, in its all-pervasiveness, would therefore seek to devalorize any systematic reading of Bataille. Ironically, however, that process of total forgetting (which constitutes the major intervention of Nietzsche in Bataille) has its own dialectic of development, which inevitably indicates the necessity of our critical intervention.

I
FROM *Acéphale* TO "LE RIRE DE NIETZSCHE"

Bataille's relation to Nietzsche is as complex as his relation to Hegel. We must, in fact, separate two main periods (whose interest for us is less historical than conceptual) in Bataille's rewriting of Nietzsche. The first period can roughly be associated with the *Acéphale* group, and ends with the beginning of World War II. The second starts at the beginning of the second world war, and culminates in *Sur Nietzsche* (written 1944, published 1945). In an unfinished project for a preface (written in 1960) to *Le Coupable*, Bataille recalled the crisis that ended the *Acéphale* project:

I had spent the preceeding years with an untenable preoccupation; I had resolved, if not to found a religion, at least to head in that direction. What the history of religion had revealed to me gradually excited me. . . . And even though such a whim [lubie] might seem utterly stupefying, I took it seriously. (6, 369)*

In another manuscript, written about the same time:

I even find a little pleasure in evoking the bitter memory of the faddish notion [velléité] that I had some twenty years ago, of founding a religion. I want to make it clear now that my stalemate, the fact of which appeared more clearly to me with each passing day, is the origin of this Summa [somme] that today is on the point of being completed. It was at the very moment that my efforts proved to be vain that I started Le Coupable. (It was consequently with Le Coupable that, on September 5, 1939, I started this disconnected [décousue] work. . . .) (6, 370)

The dream of a "religion"—and a community around it—collapsed at the outbreak of the war. A war that, needless to say, made the individual heterogeneity[4] of a subversive group or community seem petty—especially after June, 1940. The war is now a kind of heterogeneity in itself, not a tissue of political compromises and violations like those condemned by Contre-Attaque, but rather the pure heterogenous force of a tornado or some other natural disaster. Bataille is not now forced somehow to create an heterogeneity of mobs or violence. He is forced inward—he is alone—the "outer world" is heterogeneity,[5] as in the case of the noise of the battle between Germans and Americans in Bataille's area: "If there is any grandeur in these noises, it is that of the unintelligible. They suggest neither the murderous nature of the projectiles, nor the immense movements of history, nor even a danger that is coming closer," (6, 178). Of course external events play their role in an "inner emigration," and Bataille's was only one of many during the war. What interests us, however, is the inner logic that made the turn from "community" to "impossible individuality" necessary.

Nietzsche was in fact the centerpiece of the Acéphale project, and to understand what happens to Nietzsche in the switch from Acéphale to the Somme athéologique (which is composed of L'experience interieure [1943], Le Coupable [1944], and Sur Nietzsche [1945]), a clear picture of the Nietzsche of Acéphale must be grasped.

Nietzsche (and Nietzsche as "superman" [surhomme]) in Acéphale is, first of all, not clearly separable from a mythic entity, a cthonic earth deity, or a gnostic archonte: "6. The acéphale mythologically expresses the sovereignty that is vowed [vouée] to destruction, and to the death of God, and in this the identification with the headless man compounds and mingles itself with the identification with the superhuman [surhumain] which is entirely the 'death of God' " (1, 470).

* All quotes used are from the Oeuvres Complètes of Bataille (Paris: Gallimard, 1970). The first number refers to volume number, the second to page number. All translations are my own.

This headless god is associated with the *surhomme* of Nietzsche and with the position of time as an imperative object and as explosive liberty of life. A time that is radically outside a constructive, usable time (the time of Hegel's dialectic) and which is associated by Bataille with the impossible time (*sans fond*) of the eternal return. The article "L'Obélisque" which is contemporaneous with the *Acéphale* writings bears this out: "The *toxic* character of the 'return' is even of such great importance that, if it were for a moment set aside, the formal content would risk appearing empty . . . the audacious act that the 'return' to the summit of this tearing apart [*déchirement*] represents, only tears from the dead God his total strength in order to give it to the deleterious absurdity of time," (1, 510).

Despite this impossible time, the projected rebirth of gnosticism will take place on a cultural level. Unlike *Contre-Attaque*, this gnosticism will be outside of any conceivable political formulation (this " 'dionysian' truth cannot be the object of any propaganda," [1, 489]). The only vehicle left, it would seem, is the religious or mythical. But the *acéphale* (the mythical figure) is precisely a *critique* of any religious position, since he represents "the death of God." The *acéphale* in turn is inseparable from the *surhomme*, and together they enter into a metaphorical equivalency with:

NIETZSCHE DIONYSOS
The critical phase of the decomposition of a civilization is regularly [*régulièrement*] followed by a recomposition which develops in two different directions: the reconstitution of religious elements of civil and military sovereignty, leading existence to the *past*, is followed or accompanied by the birth of sacred, free and liberating figures and myths, that renew life and make it into "that which is set in motion [*ce qui se joue*] in the future" [*l'avenir*], "that which only belongs to a future." (1, 483)

Nietzsche becomes *acéphale/dionysos*, but what does that multi-headed mythical entity represent? In the first quote we examined (1, 470) the *acéphale* was "voué à la destruction." He was primarily being put forward as an entity that represented pure negativity. That destructiveness was in turn associated with an "eternal return" that was not seen as related in any way to a passage of time, but instead was presented as "toxic." At the same time, however, once that "toxicity" was manifested on a social plane, history would somehow end, at least the constructive notion of history put forward by Hegel: "the fall of the return is *Final*" (1, 511). Already another time scheme—another finality—contradicts the temporal model of Hegel. A kind of anti-history (manifesting itself historically) is therefore being posited. How can it be implemented?

This is where "Nietzsche Dionysos" attempts to advance a solution.

It first mentions the "regular" "decomposition" of a society ("est regulièrement suivie . . .") that manifests itself in two different "directions." One of these "directions" is the "reconstitution" of a civil and military society. This is basically the process outlined in two of Bataille's essays written in the early thirties, "La vieille taupe" (2, 93), and "La structure psychologique du fascisme" (1, 339). In these essays, what was seen originally as an heterogenous tendency is immediately reappropriated by the same bourgeois forces that initially were threatened. Society's "excess" is channeled not into nonproductive orgiastic or sacrificial waste, but is instead rerouted back into the military for war. Bataille (in "Nietzsche Dionysos") then posits a point of articulation, where the reappropriation into civil or military areas is "followed or accompanied by the birth of sacred figures and myths." This second possible direction is manifested by "figures" that are seen as "renewing" and which "only belong to a future." This direction is presumably associable with the pure "toxicity" mentioned elsewhere in connection with the mythic, acephalic figure.

The first thing that we must note is the uncertainty in the nature of the temporality of the second part of this paragraph. The "or" of "followed or accompanied by" is important, for it indicates a lack of clarity concerning the positioning of the "sacred figures." Will they disrupt the new civil-military regime? Or will they follow it, stepping into a gap caused by its self-destruction? Finally, how "toxic" will they be if they are only agents in a "renewal" of society?

The contradiction of an historical "anti-history" is thus accompanied in the *Acéphale* texts by a contradiction pertaining to the position and nature of that "final" stage of anti-history. If it "regularly" follows the "decomposition of a civilization" how can it be "final" or "belong only to a future"? How can it break away definitively (and be pure destruction) if it is always again recomposition? Does it indeed follow the stage of reappropriated negativity or does it occur at the same time? If it follows, does it break away from or destroy that previous stage? If on the other hand it occurs at the same time, how can it be an epoch that is radically different and "final"?

The same kind of contradiction and uncertainty applies to the problem of "myth" that applied to the problem of temporality. In fact the two are related. In the same section of "Nietzsche Dionysos" Bataille writes: "Nietzsche knowingly avoided even the word religion which alone lends itself to a confusion that is almost as unfortunate [*néfaste*] as the confusion between the Nietzschean Dionysus and fascism," (1, 483). As long as an anti-myth representing the "death of God" can be separated from a traditional, "appropriated" mythology, Bataille can argue that Nietzsche, and eventually Bataille's own sect, escapes a "religion." The very notion of an acephalic figure, however, is the conjunction of a concept that is totally outside any anthropomorphic model (representing not only the "death of God" but also the lie of signification, grammar, and the notion of the "human") with what is, finally, an anthropomorphic *figure*. Rather than being any sort of pure "toxicity" or destruction, this mythological figure represents in fact a reinsertion of the toxicity into a comprehensible human model. This contradiction—the anti-mythical myth—is compounded by the temporal nature in which it is framed. The "death of God" implies a prior existence of God. What is its status? Was His existence a mere fiction, now definitely discredited, or will it return? Was at least the mythical (or fictional) representation of a coherent God necessary? That representation would, in fact, be a religion, and its existence would be congruent with a "civil and military" civilization ("the reconstitution of religious elements of civil and military sovereignty"). Once this problem is introduced, the uncertainty we saw in the problem of an "anti-temporality" returns as well. Will the definitively anti-mythical myth replace the religion? If so, will that anti-myth be part of a "recomposition"? Will it follow or be contemporaneous with a different type of myth? If it is contemporaneous, how will it guarantee its *autonomy* from the other "civil and military" myth? Will it not in fact then lend itself (if it is not autonomous) to reappropriation by *fascism*? (That is precisely the "unfortunate confusion" that Bataille saw threatening the "recomposition" of Nietzsche [1, 483].) Will another "critical phase" have to be posited later in which that myth (as "recomposition") is in turn "decomposed"? Once again we have a contradiction (anti-mythical myth) accompanied by uncertainties as to its social and historical implementation.

These uncertainties manifested themselves in the indecisiveness of the (nonpolitical) political activity undertaken by the *Acéphale* group. How to implement a mythologically oriented sect that would neverthe-less bring about a radical change in society? It was necessary to avoid conventional political moments—communism because it inevitably enters into compromises with the bourgeoisie (the critique of Stalin made explicit by *Contre-Attaque*), fascism because it represents a violent social "effervescence" that is immediately "put back to work."[6] The *Acéphale* group had ritual meetings in a woods outside Paris, where lightning and its penetration into the earth (symbolic of blinding light on high and its rending fall to earth) were revered.[7] There was even talk of a human sacrifice being performed.

All this was an attempt to inscribe socially and temporally move-ments that were impossible, that radically exceeded those categories. The *surhomme*, the *volonté de puissance*, and *Dionysos*, were seen as phenomena worth establishing as radical alternatives to the political and social dead-end of the thirties. The problem—and the uncertainty—was in implementing them. Bataille hoped that somehow the fervor of a human sacrifice performed by the *Acéphale* group would unleash an heterogenous force that would cause society to erupt.[8] How that transformation was to take place was never clear; in any case, *Acéphale* was unable to find a victim, or a sacrificer, or both.[9]

We know that this "religious" movement breathed its last in September, 1939 (6, 484). When the problematic surfaces again, in "Le rire de Nietzsche" (The laugh of Nietzsche) (6, 307), a transitional text published in 1942, the problem of the *surhomme* remains, but the *acéphale*, the mythic "deity" around which a "sect" established itself, has been dropped. The problematic is now a *personal* one.[10] It involves "one" man's radical experience (the *expérience intérieure*), and the experience of Nietzsche is posited in relation to that. The *surhomme* is less a mythical entity than he is instead the individual "seeker," who is at the same time the narrator, the "author." The experience of the narrator (rather than society) has become the place of the *surhomme*, the point of the positing of the "will to power":

What I am here and now is the totality [*somme*] of the possible: what I am is impossible, and I know it; I put myself at the height of the impossible: I render the impossible possible, or at least accessible. The virtue of non-salvation [*la non-élusion*] is to *first* give salvation, to *not* make it the endpoint but instead the trampoline [*le tremplin*] of the impossible. The eternal return opens the abyss, but is the summons to jump [*mais est la sommation de sauter*]. The abyss is the impossible and remains so but a jump [*un saut*] introduces into the impossible the possible that it is, vowed [*voué*] from the first without the slightest reserve to the impossible. The jump is the superman [*le surhomme*] of Zarathoustra, and is the will to power [*volonté de puissance*]. The slightest cutting back [*compression*] and the jump would not take place. (6, 313)

The role of the *surhomme*, then, is to posit a "leap," an activity in the *possible* that enables the "impossible" to take place. ("But if I pose the possible at the outset, really at the outset? By this I only open the way to the impossible" [6, 313].) The "impossible," being beyond the human will or acts of violation, cannot be reached through activity. That is the province of the slave of Hegel's dialectic. Instead, a certain state can be reached *through* the volition, through a purposeful activity. Then, beyond that, the *abîme*, the abyss, will open up to the *surhomme* (who is also the narrator): "First of all, I succeeded in making a great silence inside myself. That became possible just about each time I wanted it. In this silence, often dull [*fade*] and exhausting [*épuisant*] I evoked all possible lacerations [*déchirements*]. Obscene, laughable, funeral representations followed each other," (6, 299).[11]

The activity of the *surhomme* consists therefore in preparing himself for the *expérience intérieure*. Understanding lies in making the interior experience (*expérience intérieure*) a jump, it is "jumping" (6, 313). The experience itself then is *one individual's*, and it is at least related to certain individual meditative practices. Yet this meditation is not on any anthropomorphic deity, nor is it the communal disciplined experience of the Zen monk (cf. Bataille's comments in *Sur Nietzsche*, 6, 90–91). It is the meditation of an individual who distrusts (or laughs at) organizations or "sects" precisely because they impose a "form," a "discipline," they make a *project* of the experience. (That again leads to the work of the slave.) On the other hand, Bataille's self-imposed project in this text is to act only to the extent that he contemplates what radically escapes the act, in other words, he contemplates what escapes any coherence. As soon as the "discipline" of the *surhomme* becomes discipline as such, his attention is diverted from obscenity and destruction. It will then be diverted from what will enable him—or cause him—to explode beyond his limits. His attention, in that case, is focused merely on another project, albeit "mystical."

This "project," then, remains in some ways similar to the *Acéphale* project, but at the same time is an implicit critique of it. Any "sect" will impose an external discipline on the experience itself, therefore turning it into nothing more than a task. The "experience" in "Le rire de Nietzsche" is still reached by an "activity," to be sure, but that activity is a simulacrum of a disastrous, mortal or obscene experience (such as the execution of the Chinese man by dismemberment [cf. 5, 139]) that can offer no comfort or social reinforcement. And once the social element drops away from the problem of the radical experience (along with the notion of a project, a teleology), the "temporal" problem, the problem of the interrelation of the radical experience and *time* (which is constituted by work, the job or discipline) will wither away as well. In fact we see the final "activity" is not of the slave, but of the trampoline (*le tremplin*) whose *rebound* (which "causes" the "leap" into the impossible) is *outside* the time of preparation and anticipation. Possible time or the act is valorized only insofar as it can be totally *escaped*.

In order to grasp the difference between the *Acéphale* position and that of "Le rire de Nietzsche," it is perhaps first necessary to understand Bataille's use of the word "impossible" in "Le rire de Nietzsche."

In "Le sommet et le declin" (the second part of *Sur Nietzsche*) the problematic of the "radical experience" is retained. In *Sur Nietzsche*, as we will see shortly, the notion of "effort" is criticized even more systematically than in "Le rire de Nietzsche." It is worth noting in the following quote from *Sur Nietzsche* how the terms "impossible" and "inaccessible" are used:

Like Kafka's castle, the summit in the end is only the inaccessible. It escapes from us, at least to the extent, that we continue to be men (*d'être hommes*), to speak. . . .

The summit is not "what must be attained," the decline "what must be suppressed."

Just as the summit is only, in the end, inaccessible, the decline, from the beginning, is inevitable.

The summit in essence is the place where life is impossible to the limit. . . . (6, 57)

The "summit" (*le sommet*) here represents the kind of experience Bataille was grasping at in "Le rire de Nietzsche." The act of *working* for the summit causes it to elude one's grasp. At the same time the very act of grasping is *human*. To "attain" it then, we must cease to be thinking, speaking "men." But if we are not men, then what are we?

Two alternatives to being human in Bataille are being an animal and being dead. Needless to say, neither simple animality nor simple death are what Bataille means here by "the summit." One must be *at the same time* human, consciously acting and still recognizing interdictions, *and* not human (not a speaking, acting, conscious subject). One must somehow be human and dead (or human and an animal, like Bataille's erotic subjects) at the same "instant." This experience is therefore "impossible" according to a logic that forbids contradiction, and is from that point of view "inaccessible."

If "the summit" were purely inaccessible, if it were something that definitively could not be experienced, Bataille would not be justified in speculating about it. The important point comes, in fact, when he admits that the "inaccessible" is accessible, the impossible is possible: "I only attain [the summit], to the very feeble extent that I attain it, in spending my forces without counting," (6, 57–58).

The contradiction between human and non-human, between thought and animality, is precisely the impossible which must somehow be experienced, and which therefore must be possible. "What I am here and now is the totality of the impossible. What I am is impossible . . . I put myself at the height of the impossible . . ." (6, 313). This is a kind of second order "possible," however, in that it indicates a reaching of the impossible not through work—the constructive activity of the slave in Hegel—but through some process that succeeds in escaping work. Only to the extent that it escapes the "possible" of labor, language, and finally the civil/military and religious state, does the "impossible" become *possible*.

Where does this leave the *Acéphale* position? The very stress that

Bataille places on the possibility of the impossible in "Le rire de Nietzsche" indicates a problem in the earlier *Acéphale* version of Nietzsche. We saw that there was a "contradiction" in those earlier positions—a "contradiction" that might be associable with a kind of "impossibility." A temporality outside of time, an anti-mythical myth are, in fact, identical to the non-human human experience posited in "Le rire de Nietzsche." The problem is not in *resolving* these contradictions, of appropriating their negativity—in fact the problem is just the opposite. How can one *implement* the negativity of the "impossible" relation—how can that negativity be torn from an abstract, uncertain manifestation, and its concrete, *possible* manifestation be seen (without at the same time denying its impossible status)? In this light, the *Acéphale* positions had to be "left behind" for the simple reason that the implementation (the possibility) of their "impossibility" was uncertain—it remained abstract and theoretical. It could not be experienced for the evident reason that Bataille could not conceive how the coercive totalizing nature of a social entity (be it communism, fascism, democracy, or any theocracy ever created—Bataille had criticized each formation) could at the same time embody a "toxicity" and "empty" "destruction." His only model was eventually a regressive one: the return to the human sacrifice of "primitive" cultures. Yet there was no mechanism for preventing the inevitable appropriation of "destruction" that took place in those cultures, nor were there ways, in Bataille's project, of applying a "primitive" model to "modern" society. Finally, incapable of seeing a concrete manifestation of this negativity on a social plane, and uncertain of guaranteeing it (and indeed uncertain whether a guarantee of the permanence of the experience was necessary or not) the social model had to be replaced by a personal one. An idealized, empty impossibility, "minor" to the extent that it was immediately appropriable by fascism or religion (its negativity risking the destruction of nothing) was replaced by an—at least provisionally—"major" impossibility, whose negative force could actually manifest itself on an experiential level.

1939, 1942; a crisis occurs in Bataille's Nietzsche. We saw in the pre-1939 Nietzsche temporality opposed to abyss (eternal return), rite and myth opposed to the absence of God. Now the tables have been turned; the sect has been disbanded, the experience itself transpires in an impossible "time" that is not the simple result of a project, but is an unplanned offshoot of its taking place in an "instant." That offshoot sneaks up on the *surhomme* from behind, so to speak, and "happens." The "end" is a trampoline, something that eludes the control of the subject and then acts on him. The "impossible" becomes "possible" only to the extent that the "possible" plays its part (and to that extent it is retained) and then falls away, is forgotten, leaving only the impossible, the experience of pure contradiction. On the rebound, the "trampoline" catapults the subject somewhere else (some "where" radically other), whether he wants it to or not.

But to what extent is this shift justified in Nietzsche's own writing? And to what extent is the contemplation (even if it is of *horror*) still an activity? Is the impossible in fact still a function—a *product*—of the possible?

II

NIETZSCHE: "MAIS LAISSONS LÀ M. NIETZSCHE . . ." (6, 26)

A brief consideration of a few of Nietzsche's texts themselves, specifically those dealing with the social implementation of the term *surhomme*, might be instructive at this point. In this context, it is pertinent to recall that the *Acéphale* group saw as a major aim the refutation of the fascist reading of Nietzsche, and the denial of fascist ideology as a continuation of Nietzsche's thought.[12] We recall also the refusal of *Acéphale* to take part in the politics of "compromise" (or just plain "politics," which was seen as synonymous with "compromise"). At the same time, however, Nietzsche "himself" (in his own text) was forced to posit a social—if not political—implementation of his "ideas." Otherwise they would remain sterile, unknown. Although space does not permit an in-depth study of Nietzsche here, we might point to a few of his texts in which a certain problem appears. We read:

There is a necessity of proving the importance of a countermovement [*Gegenbewegung*] in relation to an ever more economical expenditure [*Verbrauch*] of human existence, and in relation to an ever more narrowly confined machinery of interests and realizations. I designate this a counter-movement insofar as it is a secretion [*Ausscheidung*] of a luxurious excess [*einer Luxus-Überschusses*] of humanity; in it, a stronger, more elevated type must step into the light. This type must have other conditions of formulation and conservation than the average man [*Durchschnitts-Mensch*]. My concept [*Begriff*] my allegory [*Gleichnis*] for this type is, as is known, the superman [*Übermensch*]. (1887; Fragments: 10[17], 150)[13]

Escaping from a society based on "interests," the "superman" is seen as a luxurious excess. In opposition to the settling of accounts and the equalization by the man of *ressentiment*, the "superman" is capable of positing himself in relation to luxury and waste (excess). Bataille at a certain point (in "La vieille taupe" and in the texts of *Contre-Attaque*) reversed this Nietzschean devalorization of the slave. In those texts, the proletariat—or the mob (the distinction is somewhat blurred)—was portrayed not as a force of conservation, production, and peaceful socialization (Hegel's version of the slave) or as revenge (Nietzsche's) but rather as an embodiment of pure waste and destruction. The mob decapitates the king, but not out of revenge. In this act of luxurious excess, the epitome of a waste in which the embodiment of excess—the king—is himself wasted, prevented from becoming homogenous, the revolutionary mob is seen to be closer to a Nietzschean "sacrifice of the notion of God itself" than is a Nietzschean social elite that would inevitably become a tool of the homogenizing bourgeoisie (a bourgeoisie that would stop all waste, "use" negativity, etc.). Realizing, however, that pure mob negativity was not clearly separable from fascism (cf. 7, 461: "If one wants to understand what was true [in *Contre-Attaque*], in spite of the radically contrary intention of this paradoxical fascist tendency, one must read *L'Oeillet rouge* of Elio Vittorini . . . ."), *Contre-Attaque* disintegrated in 1936. *Acéphale*, founded later that year, sought to avoid *that* trap of fascism, and embraced a more straightforwardly Nietzschean version of heterogenous social forces. The only problem was that following the Nietzschean text more "closely" led to certain other problems. The *surhomme*, seen on a social level (as a social force) separated from an incarnation as the proletariat, (or as the "masses") naturally rises to the status of a somehow privileged elite.

We continue our reading of this passage of Nietzsche:

In the era of this diminution and of this adaptation of human beings, to a specialized utility (*spezialisiertere Nützlichkeit*) there is a need for an inverse movement, the creation of a human being who synthesizes, totalizes, and justifies, for whom this mechanization (*Maschinalisierung*) of humanity constitutes an understood, agreed upon being (*Daseins—Vorausbedingung*). This being can be used as an undercarriage (*ein Untergertell*) on which he can invent his higher form (*seine höhere Form*) of being. He especially needs the rivalry between the masses of the equalized (*der "Nivellierten"*), and the feeling of distance in relation to them: he stands on them (*er steht auf ihnen*), he lives off them (*er lebt von ihnen*). This superior form of aristocratism (*aristokratism*) is that of the *future* (*der Zukunft*). (1887; *Fragments*, 10[17] 150)

In Nietzsche's text, then, the "higher form of being" in its social and temporal manifestation, is possible only through the support of the "mechanization of humanity." This alone makes the superman possible— but at the same time the superman "synthesizes, totalizes and justifies." The base exploitation by the capitalist results only in a diminution and a general pointlessness and leveling. The reign of the superman, while not stopping utility, puts it into a relation that gives it a grandeur it previously did not have: that grandeur is in relation to the "excess of force" that justifies man and gives him his meaning:

. . . . the necessity of the digging of a trench (*Kluftaufreissung*), the necessity of a distance, of a hierarchy, (*Distanz, Rangordnung*) are given. . . .

This equalized species (*ausgeglichene Species*), as soon as it will be realized, needs a justification: this lies in serving (*Dienste*) a higher, sovereign kind (*souveränen Art*), which stands on (*auf ihr steht*) the equalized ones and it is only if it is based on those that it can raise itself to its own duty (*Aufgabe*).

Not only a race of masters (*eine Herren-Rasse*) whose task will be exhausted with governing, but a race having its own sphere of life (*Lebenssphare*), with an excess of force (*einen Überschuss von Kraft*) for beauty, courage, and culture . . . an affirmative race (*eine bejähende Rasse*) which can permit (*gönnen*) itself every great luxury (*Luxus*). . . . (*1887; Fragments*, 9[153], 105)

There is a moment of waste in Nietzsche, of squandering; but in order for there to be waste there has to be accumulation and work. In order for there to be rupturing (transgression, heterogeneity) there has to be a moment of sense or coherence (interdiction, homogeneity) that is ruptured. The problem is this: what form will the future (*die Zukunft*) have? In other words, what form is the interdiction to take? And the transgression?

Although the latter terms are foreign to Nietzsche's text (they come, of course, from the Nietzschean anthropology that Bataille derived from Mauss and Caillois), a problem nevertheless arises. In the texts we have cited, the work of the slave is still seen as a necessary moment. The "mastery" of that moment, however, is radically different. Unlike the (implicitly) bourgeois boss who can offer no "meaning" whatsoever for the process of work, the superman, on the other hand, *affirms* life (and therefore "justifies" and "totalizes" it) rather than worrying about its waste or expenditure. What has happened, then, is that the rationalization for the "mechanization" of life has passed from an ideology whose main concern is "governing" to *another* ideology (or "sphere of life") which gives it a more affirmative meaning—but at the same time that "mechanization" (the rationalized moment) itself has not changed. We are not at this point criticizing Nietzsche for *not* taking up the task of changing it. Why should he? If he *were* to change it, he would become involved in the "settling of accounts" aspect of life, the superman himself would be caught up in a task—and in so doing would lose sight of the affirmative life of luxurious excess that constitutes his higher form of being. At the same time, however, in *not* questioning the form that that "mechanization" takes, the "superman" does not radically *change* life. He does not question the rationalized forms he has inherited from his predecessor. He is therefore a *continuation* of his predecessor's "rule." In isolating himself from the realm of production and rationalization, the "superman" has created a "pure" abstract realm that cannot be tainted by considerations such as what form the "moment" of "sense" or "mechanization" (or "interdiction," "recuperation," etc.) should take.

This argument begins to look familiar; it is Bataille's critique of the "eagle," the "surrealists," in his essay "La vieille taupe," and his critique of the fascists in "La structure psychologique du fascisme." In those texts, however, the "homogenous" world of the workers (as Nietzsche would have it) was not considered as such, but rather as a heterogeneity in relation to the formerly heterogenous "masters," who have now revealed themselves to be fully homogenous. The noble, the "master," the surrealist, originally heterogenous in their escape or separation from the day to day world of production and use, by constituting themselves as "purely" heterogenous, simply erect a new realm that is homogenous within itself—a "transgression" which cannot be "trangressed" thus becomes interdiction (in a similar context, Bataille speaks of the necessity of "transcending transcendence" [6, 173]). Indeed, the essay "La vieille taupe" contained one of the few disparaging references to Nietzsche in Bataille (2, 101). (The article draws correspondences between the *surhomme* and the idealist "surrealists," and the association of Nietzsche with both positions.) At the same time, however, the consequences of the essay "La vieille taupe" can be seen in the *Contre-Attaque* group, just as the emergence of that *pure* revolutionary (mob) negativity can. That (again) "pure" negativity constituted itself entirely against forms of rationalized compromise— the result being that that violence was eventually seen as "paradoxically" related to fascism. But *Acéphale also* ran the risk of fascism.

It seems that we are caught in a vicious circle, then, from *Acéphale* to *Contre-Attaque* and back again. But there might be a "way out." This would be to consider the moment of rationalization as "heterogenous" in relation to the hierarchicalized *surhomme*, but that "heterogeneity" could remain so only if, paradoxically, it interrogated its "rationalized" status. Once it shuns that rationalization, it is removed from the threat of identification with that rationalization (or work, social formation, and so on) but only at the risk of becoming a "paradoxical fascism," a purely homogenized heterogeneity. The status of the "rationalizing" sphere must then be rationalized and criticized, in light of its relation to the "sovereign kind." By this we mean that an heterogenous activity can be precisely the investigation of the other "side" (or "part")—that is, the one that is "rationalized" or "homogenous." The forms of that side are not "neutral" or of "no concern" and their re-formation and destruction is a function of a radical heterogeneity that develops itself through a self-critical, dialectical process. If we admit a gulf separating these two realms, we must nevertheless posit their manner of interaction and mutual transgression. That development through transgression (and the critique of the specific forms of the homogenous) will become clear when we examine in the next section the transition from "Le rire de Nietzsche" (1942) to *Sur Nietzsche* (1944).

It might be objected that Nietzsche himself ironizes the superman. Bataille was fond of what has been called the "laughing Nietzsche": "Neither say yes nor no to reality, unless it is only from time to time, in order to tap it with your toes, like a good dancer . . . stick a comic tail onto the most sacred things. . . . (March-July, 1888; quoted in *Sur Nietzsche*, 6, 78)

If Nietzsche ironizes his own status as a "philosopher" (or even as "superman") (cf. *Ecce Homo*, "Why am I fatality": "I require no 'believers,' it is in my opinion that I am too full of value to believe even in myself and I never address myself to the masses [*ich rede niemals zu Massen*] I am horribly frightened that one day I will be canonized." He can only ironize (or "waste" in a kind of intellectual potlatch) what he has already established as the "truth." That is, he can risk only the stable model of a social order in which those who affirm life, who reject the "decline" of the morality of the slave, will be separated in a hierarchy from the "masses." (*Ecce Homo* also contains the vision of a political prophet whose works will inspire a war that establishes an era of the superman: "The concept of politics will then be elevated [*ausgegangen*] entirely into the realm of spiritual warfare [*Geisterkrieg*]. . . . Only from my time will politics on a large scale exist on earth").[14]

At this point, our analysis of the problem of the "homogenous part" shifts—as it did in "La vielle taupe"—from the rationalized life of workers to the idealized realm of the *surhomme* itself. We perceive now in Nietzsche (at this level of our analysis) not the *surhomme* radically going beyond the realm of the "masses"—the opposition of heterogenous "luxury" to homogenous work—but instead the opposition of heterogenous irony to the homogenous but necessarily ironized doctrine of the *surhomme*. The question now is, by what criteria is this homogenous moment to be established? (". . . what possible can be introduced into the impossible?" 6, 310). Even if it *is* ironized, what are the criteria for judging the acceptability of a given homogenous "part" that enters in relation with an heterogenous "part"? Nietzsche can laugh at himself, but how can we make any evaluations of the acceptability not of the laughter or ironization "itself" (which we affirm) but of what he is laughing at *within his text*?

III
SUR BATAILLE

The rending (*déchirante*) question of this book.
(*Sur Nietzsche*, 196)

We have already seen Bataille's dilemmas in first positing a purely destructive proletariat *surhomme* (in *Contre-Attaque*), and then in recognizing the limits of that, being forced to develop a more conventionally mythological Nietzsche (in *Acéphale*) that would go beyond both a political (leftist) dead end and a cooptation by a fascist "Nietzsche." This latter Bataillean Nietzsche reaffirmed "sect" (as opposed to "mob"), reaffirmed "myth" and "rites" (but not "religion") opposed to some sort of political action that would be in some sense "effective." To be political was to "compromise." Although *Acéphale* as well saw its acts as a turning point of history, they were not seen in a "political" sense—they were not associated with class struggle. Contradictory relations therefore appeared between "myths" and things that destabalized or escaped from myth; and between "time" (associated with the constructive development of history) and a "future" in which a radical break with history would appear. These contradictory or "impossible" relations that characterized Bataille's position on Nietzsche in the late thirties are associable with community, its formation, and social change. At a certain point (after 1939) he dropped them; the mythical *surhomme* and his community were no longer an acceptable manifestation of an homogenous moment that impossibly conveyed its own undermining.

We posed, at the end of the last section, a question concerning the criteria for acceptable "homogenous" "sides" in oppositions of this nature. We know that Bataille, when he again wrote on Nietzsche after the beginning of the war ("Le rire de Nietzsche"), had by this time dropped the social, mythic, and temporal aspects of Nietzsche. We inferred that these were dropped because a simple homogeneity (or abstract impossible) always devolved out of the heterogeneity that they posited. Nietzsche, by 1942, had become, then, a purely "internal" phenomenon, outside of social, temporal, or mythical "moments" in which he would inevitably play what would appear to be an homogenous, stable role. In that transitional text of 1942, there was still a certain clinging to terms associated with the *Acéphale* "mythology"—such as *surhomme* and *volonté de puissance*—but by then the only possible act was an individual contemplation of horror that would in turn, without the subject's effort, lead him out of any act or individuality. That horror was still a function of "contemplation"—the "rebound" of the "trampoline" could not be imagined without contemplation (a goal-oriented gesture). "Nietzsche," in "Le rire de Nietzsche," was still the manifestation of an activity and still embodied a *possible* in relation to an *impossible*. "Nietzsche" at that point was still not entirely heterogenous; he was a manifestation of homogeneity, rather than being the most general force of heterogeneity or (major) impossibility (as opposed to the self-cancelling, abstract "minor" type we saw earlier). "Nietzsche" (in Bataille) after 1942 breaks away from his moorings in possibility (the contemplation of horror) because they indicated a point where the laughing Nietzsche had to take himself seriously. Giving this form (of effort, of "method of meditation") to Nietzsche would simply make him another possibility.

The final transformation in Bataille's Nietzsche occurs in 1944–45 with the writing and publication of *Sur Nietzsche*.

The reason for the collapse of *Acéphale* can be seen clearly in Bataille's approach to Nietzsche in *Sur Nietzsche*. Through *Sur Nietzsche*, we will also be able to understand the criteria for evaluating the "homogenous" "part" in a text (like Nietzsche's, or Bataille's) that thematizes heterogeneity (loss, excess, waste/force, etc.).

The "solution" is quite simply to strip Nietzsche of the homogenous part that haunted Bataille throughout the thirties and into the forties. We read in *Sur Nietzsche*:

The weakness of Nietzsche: he criticizes in the name of *moving* values whose origin and end—evidently—he could not grasp.

To grasp isolated possibility, having a particular end, which is only for itself an end, is not this in the end to risk oneself [*jouer*]?

It might be that the interest of the operation is in the risk [*le jeu*], not in the chosen end.

The narrow end is lacking? Risk [*le jeu*] will nonetheless order one's values.

The superman [*surhomme*] or Borgia sides are limited, vainly defined, in the face of possibles having their essence in the going beyond [*dépassement*] of oneself.

(*This takes nothing from the upheaval* [*la bousculade*], *the great wind, upsetting all the old satisfactions* [*suffisances*].) (6, 119–20) (Italics added)

A full reversal from *Acéphale* has taken place: it is now the *surhomme* who is criticized. The experience of "excess" is going beyond oneself, and beyond the limits of oneself. If, for example, sexuality is the experience of breaking open the limits of the body and of the self, the rupture of the limited being that constituted the self, then any attempt at fixing an identity of the self (other than as a momentary "end in itself" that does not take part in the totalizing process of the dialectic) will prove to be a failure.

In *Sur Nietzsche*, above all, Bataille seeks to avoid "defining" or limiting the nature of this experience. The very project of the *Somme athéologique* is the embodiment of this distrust of formulation, of limiting the text itself to a single mythology or to an internal or external teleology ("Working [writing] badly, in disorder, is the only way, often, of not becoming a function" [6, 154]). It was, of course, the writing of the first part of *Le Coupable* (the first book written of the *Somme*) that led Bataille away from the goal of starting a religion (which he could no longer differentiate, to his own satisfaction, from a sect), or away from a coherent mythology and community—away from a *project*.[15]

What can replace the *surhomme*? (Or, put another way, how can the *surhomme* be left empty—how can the dialectic be completely avoided yet the experience of impossibility still be a possibility, that is, more than an empty impossibility?) We recall that, in the *Acéphale* writings, the *acéphale* (the mythical personage, who was associable with the *surhomme*, Dionysos, Nietzsche) was seen as an embodiment of the "death of God." Within the "death of God" a moment of God must still be posited. A moment of *limits*—of the existence of God—must be posited in order for it (those limits, that divine existence) to be transgressed. That transgression must somehow be continuous (but not "permanent" or "stable"), since once God was "definitely" transgressed, a new "proof"—the "proof" of His death—would simply take His place. Already before 1939, Bataille, in "Le labyrinth" (1, 433, written 1935–36) posited what was clearly identifiable as Christ in a moment of death: "The universal God destroys rather than supports the human agglomerations [*agrégats*] which raise the old phantom up [*soulevent*]. He is himself only death: either a mythic delirium proposes him for worship as a cadaver covered with wounds, or by his very universality he becomes, more than any other, incapable of opposing the gradual destruction [*la déperdition*] of being with the cracked partitions of selfhood [*les parois felées de l'ipséité*]" (1, 439).

Christ is stripped of the accretions of morality and knowledge—the aspects of Christianity that Nietzsche criticizes in the *Genealogy of Morals*. All that remains is a "universal" dying God. The "essence," then, of Christianity is seen to be not redemption or eternal life, but a "universalized" destruction. This is the "kernel" of Christ, so to speak, anterior to his "reversal" and elevation as the source of all interdiction. At the same time, Christ as nothing but a bloody cadaver is still "universal." This implies a definite advance over the "primitive" religions that Bataille wrote about, through Mauss and Caillois. Those "religions," we see in "La notion de dépense," were limited by the fact that they were dependent on a given local area's manifestation of "potlatch" (ritual waste and destruction) (cf. 1, 313–14). The primitive lord or chief could be intensely hated for his abuses of potlatch by the "miserable" natives, who are impoverished by his waste. To that extent, the "greedy" "jealous" nature of the "chiefs" or religious leaders was just as pronounced as the "jealousy" (the homogenizing tendency, the selfishness and hypocrisy concerning waste) of the bourgeoisie—only the primitive chief was more *open* about the process of waste. Just as in the case of the bourgeois, then, the chief could misunderstand the process he was acting out; he could suture it over and see it as nothing more than an aid to his power. Potlatch was still a localized, piecemeal, individualized operation, not universally seen as a total waste. The advantage of Christ as a sacrificial victim, then, is that He is "universal" not in "saving" people but rather in that He *is* waste—permanent, absolute waste for all, a waste that is "absolute" and "eternal" (to the same extent that the "eternal return" was "final"). Christ's death is not limited by specific events of a single ritual or sacrificial (destructive) event. Christ disrupts social forms and does not solidify them; he is the embodiment of potlatch *in general*. He in that sense strips heterogeneity of primitive rituals, and of the possible homogenization that would accompany their diversity. Christ is "a monster lightly taking on many crimes" (1, 441), but *not* a monster redeeming them. Unfortunately, like the primitive practitioners of potlatch, Christ, on assuming His purely heterogenous position, is immediately transformed into an *homogenous* force. This homogenization is the church, and organized "religion."

Christ represents a *progress* over the earlier primitive religions. The transgression takes the piecemeal sacrifice and potlatch, which could easily be misrepresented as having to do with personal power and gain, and transforms it into a universal. But in the act of making sacrifice universal, Christianity makes that sacrifice more abstract and therefore easily appropriable. Christianity, therefore, "forgets" sacrifice's *true* nature, just as the primitive chief forgets his.

How to *combat* this process of institution of homogeneity in place of the heterogenous? The answer in *Sur Nietzsche* is the confrontation of Christianity with Nietzsche. Bataille quotes Nietzsche:

And moreover we want to be the inheritors of Christian meditation and penetration. (*Will to Power* [Volonté de puissance] 2, 371)

. . . to go beyond all Christianity by way of hyperChristianity, and not to be content with merely undoing it. (*Will to Power*, 2, 374)

We are no longer Christian, we have gone beyond Christianity, not because we have lived too far from it, but too close, and above all because we have come out of Christianity; our simultaneously more severe and more delicate piety today forbids us from still being Christian. . . . (*Will to Power*, 2, 329) [6, 152]

Nietzsche, then, is the splitting or tearing apart of Christ. He is "hyperChristian," even *more* Christian than the Christians who merely participate in a morality of "ressentiment" and salvation. "Christ" or "God" then, is only a destabilizing force that *ruptures* any coherent or rationalized social, political, or productive (philosophical) system: "God tearing apart the night of the universe with a cry [the *Eloi! lama sabachtani?* of Jesus]—is not this a summit of malice? God himself, addressing himself to God, cries 'why have you abandoned me?' In other words: 'why have I abandoned myself?' Or more precisely: what is going on? Have I forgotten myself to the point where I am risking myself [*M'être mis moi-meme en jeu*]?" (6, 151).

Nietzsche goes *beyond* an elimination of the state of doubt on the part of Christ. Christ's followers somehow forget His doubt—and He is reappropriated within an homogenous temporal and social order, within an absolute knowledge. Nietzsche splits the worshipped Christ and becomes more like Christ—hyperChrist—to the extent that Nietzsche remembers himself, remembers forgetting or doubt, does not allow himself to be reappropriated the way Christ was.

But Nietzsche, in the very act of remembering, of guarding himself from being reappropriated as Christ was (in avoiding a morality of the slave or producer) sets himself up as an alternative Christ, establishes a new kind of formalized knowledge on the basis of the necessity of that remembering, of that self-reflexivity. Nietzsche then was appropriable (in one way or another) by the fascists—as the Bataille of *Contre-Attaque* and *Acéphale* became aware. This was a Nietzsche who took himself *seriously*. Nietzsche therefore had to be split, just as Christ was. In the preface to *Memorandum*, a collection of Nietzsche quotes compiled by Bataille at about the same time as *Sur Nietzsche* was written (and deserving a separate detailed study) Bataille states: "The distance of sovereign [*souverain*] men from the masses can—and in my opinion *must*—have nothing in common with political differences separating classes during the feudal epoch. Moral liberty wins [*gagne*] (it wins in liberty) in effacement, in lightening [*allégrement*], in profound immanence. This goes against Nietzsche's insistence and the useless worry he had about new political authorities" (6, 251).

Bataille, then, who often stated that there was no "possibility" of his being an "original" philosopher, ("nothing is more foreign to me than a personal mode of thought") and that he had nothing to "add" to Nietzsche,[16] takes something away from Nietzsche. He suppresses a part of Nietzsche. That "suppression" is the suppression of Nietzsche's suppression of chance (or the forgetting of Nietzsche's forgetting). In emphasizing *force*, Nietzsche is still emphasizing *power*: the willful establishment, high on the "hierarchy," of the "superman," to the *exclusion* of others. Bataille states in a posthumous note of *Sur Nietzsche*: "The limit of Nietzsche: assigning a form to chance: it is necessary to risk [*jouer*]: and to accentuate the part of the future—exaggeration of "passeism" [*passéisme*]—it is impossible to predict in advance the forms of sovereignty [*souveraineté*]" (6, 425).

There is a double condemnation in this passage. A condemnation of a notion, in Nietzsche, of "effort" and of the possibility of predicting the future. It is, then, a condemnation of a dialectic that would attempt to posit a human will, precisely a will to power; Bataille, rewriting Nietzsche, subtitles *Sur Nietzsche* "will to (or *of*) chance" (*volonté de chance*) and therefore posits a "will" that is outside the sphere of human activity—a will that is not "human," but simply a manifestation of *chance*, an activity that cannot be used to form. Chance is posited in place of power: redefining "will" as "chance," the earlier trampoline of "Le rire de Nietzsche" is therefore implicitly criticized, since it was still posited in relation to an *activity*—even though that activity became a simulacrum of pure chance. Here simulacra or forms are not enough; it is chance itself that is at stake.

Bataille, then, must split Nietzsche apart and play him against himself, as Nietzsche did Christ. *Why* one side of Nietzsche is so firmly tied to a reactionary "dialectic" is of little interest to Bataille. In the notes to *Sur Nietzsche* he posits: "many contemptuous thoughts have a meaning in relation to the poverty of 1880" (6, 425). Bataille must be to Nietzsche what Nietzsche was to Christ. Nietzsche broadens ("universalizes") the death of God (Christ's death) into a death of *all* totalities (morality, philosophy, etc.). Bataille broadens the death of all totalities into a death of Nietzsche. Bataille must be "hyperNietzsche" or *Sur Nietzsche* (or *surnietzsche*). He must strip away or kill the last totalities (or dialectical, feudal endpoints) that Nietzsche posits. Nietzsche then becomes pure death, rupture, or chance in which any positive "side" is removed from the "impossible" relation "interdiction/ transgression."

Bataille, then, is the culmination of an "historical" process that goes from primitive cultures through Christianity and then through Nietzsche. Each stage is an advance over the earlier—a preserving (of the element of loss, of pure heterogeneity) and a negation (of each succeeding form, which proves itself in the end to fall back into homogeneity—in the case of Nietzsche, a fall back into a dialectical form, and a dialectic, which ends in feudalism, that Hegel himself has gone beyond). Nietzsche ("stripped" of his "feudal" side) for Bataille by 1944 is then a pure heterogenous moment, refusing any compromise with any established order, not dealing with any philosophy until having laughed at it twice, sacrificing the very notion of God itself.

"Bataille," going beyond Nietzsche, is the pure expression of this total rejection of a rationalized, dialectical, "homogenous" moment.

Sur Nietzsche embodies this rejection through its contingent form. At the same time, however, this *development* or progression in heterogenous moments implies a certain temporality. Each "sacred" moment (by this we mean Bataille's definition of the "sacred"—that which escapes all rationalized (or even comprehensible) societal or temporal forms, which indeed is their *rupture*—and which, when homogenized into a supportive role for the stabilized culture or social order, becomes *religion*),[17] is a progression over the last. Each "stripping" of a new phase in the series (potlatch/Christ/Nietzsche/Bataille) posits a new configuration in unity with an heterogeneity that in turn must be "stripped" on a higher level. "Stripped" in the sense of stripping clothes *and* skin—for the rupture of limits through eroticism and violence is central to Bataille's notion of the sacred. What is "stripped" always remains essentially the same—"pure" heterogeneity with no affiliation with any homogenous form. If this is a dialectic, it is a stripped dialectic; the endpoint is not the effacement of some negativity and the "sublation" of it into a positivity (in which the negativity is given its meaning and in which its action of negation ceases) but rather a telos from which the positive (stable social, cultural) forms have been removed and all that remains is negativity in its purest form. That "pureness," strangely, is made possible by a self-reflexivity—by the *awareness* that the previous forms of heterogeneity had somehow been compromised. "Bataille," the endpoint of this development (the guarantor of this purity, turning it back on Nietzsche himself), is the "awareness" of the "compromise" of Nietzsche.

But *within* Bataille we must establish two separate moments; Bataille's Nietzsche and Bataille as *surnietzsche*. Bataille's Nietzsche is the stripped down form of Nietzsche, freed from his medieval dialectic; Bataille as *surnietzsche* is the author of the autobiographical journal in which that stripping takes place. Bataille is the text that posits the relations of the series that extends from potlatch to *surnietzsche*, but which does so *problematically*. In other words, we can deduce the final moment of this dialectic but at no point does Bataille directly state—or become clearly, self-reflexively aware of—his position in that dialectic. "Nietzsche," then, in Bataille is a radical self-forgetting, a loss; "Bataille" is the agent of that loss, just as Nietzsche is the agent of the "loss" to Christianity, the remembering of the "pure" loss. At the same time, however, Bataille is problematically an awareness or remembering of that loss, its positioning at the end of a temporal nexus.[18] "Bataille," is a radical break at the end of "history" ("history" being here the history of forms of rejection of previous homogeneity—heterogeneity freeing itself from any ties to homogeneity), affirming loss or expenditure and beyond any homogenous manifestation. At the same time, since Bataille

Allan Stoekl

is both the narrator and *surnietzsche*, eccentric to the pure negativity of "Nietzsche," there will always be a "minor" dialectic; this development cannot be kept out of the text that is Bataille (since *Sur Nietzsche* is autobiography, an oblique chronicle of Bataille's experience in occupied France). This "dialectic"—or development of forms of heterogeneity to its purest state—is glossed over, *forgotten*, by the state of Nietzsche, the intensification of that state that Bataille effects. This state is "major" —in the sense that the state (problematically) forgets or ignores (as the "masters" in Nietzsche have "forgotten" the *"ressentiment"* of the slave—hence its *major* aspect) the problem of that development, and its status as endpoint. The aspect of the dialectic is minor, since it is a stripped teleology already, culminating not in any knowledge but in pure loss or heterogeneity. This stripped dialectic—which corresponds to the purely textual *community* Nietzsche/Bataille ("my book is this community" [6, 33]), though minor, nevertheless disrupts or ruptures the purity of the heterogeneity that was for Bataille "Nietzsche." That minor disruption, and major affirmation, are what must go under the name "Bataille."

There is, however, a different kind of reflection between a dialectic and forgetting, one which can be called "Hegel/Marx" (Bataille's Hegel/Marx). Bataille's Nietzsche (and its "minor" dialectic) is not the only "side"[19] of Bataille's *oeuvre*. Another side, that of Hegel/Marx, in the post-1939 writings, is associable with the progressive social dialectic of the three volume *La Part maudite* (1949–54). (It is important to stress that, although *La Part maudite* was only written after the war, the project itself was started as early as 1941—under the title "La limite de l'utile." Thus it is contemporaneous with the *Somme*.) While "Nietzsche" is first stripped, becomes "pure" loss, "pure" negativity, then is reinscribed as "Bataille" and "acquires" another (minor) dialectic, at the same time another "side" of Bataille is evident. This is the "Hegelian" and "Marxist" side which "goes beyond," and parodies Hegel and Marx, where an historical dialectic is major, but where an "active forgetting" is nevertheless in a minor position. Bataille here is Hegel/Marx.

These two sides of Bataille—"Nietzsche" and "Hegel/Marx"—do not result in a higher textual synthesis (or do so problematically . . . perhaps only here, in my writing). In fact, they constantly risk and transgress each other, denounce the lie of the other, and devalorize each other's position.[20] Yet at the same time each is contaminated by the other, each contains a minor residue of the other. Already in *Sur Nietzsche* Bataille poses the *necessity* of a project such as that of *La Part maudite* while refusing to carry it out. He recognizes, in advance, the alteration that the *La Part maudite* project would work on the *Somme athéologique*, precisely by exteriorizing it: "Insidiously, I have wanted to show what exterior significance my question could take. I must, it is true, recognize that situated in this way—on the plan of economic calculations—the question loses in acuity what it gains in completeness [*ampleur*]. It is, in fact, *altered*" (6, 60).[21] (Italics added)

The problematic of "Nietzsche" therefore stands alone. Stripped of any positivity, "Nietzsche" in Bataille becomes a philosophically "coherent" radical negativity that can enter into relation with and defy any positivity that that text can present to it. It will not, however, mistake an homogenous simulacrum of itself for the heterogeneity of its own process. Except, of course, when it takes its own heterogeneity to be somehow untainted by a mere homogenous simulacrum.

NOTES

1. Alain Arnaud and Gisele Excoffon-Lafargue, *Bataille* (Paris: Seuil, 1978) is a good example of this approach.

2. See Jean-Louis Houdebine, "L'ennemi du dedans," and Julia Kristeva, "Bataille, l'experience et la pratique," both in *Bataille* (Paris: 10/18, 1973).

3. Denis Hollier, "De l'au-delà de Hegel à l'absence de Nietzsche" *Bataille* (Paris: 10/18, 1973); "Le dispositif Hegel dans la bibliotheque de Bataille" in *L'Arc* 38, and Jacques Derrida, "De l'Economie restreinte à l'économie générale" in *L'Ecriture et la différence* (Paris: Seuil, 1967). A text that deals with Nietzsche in Bataille is Jacques Chatain, *Georges Bataille* (Paris: Seghers, 1973). Chatain's approach, however, both conflates very different texts by Bataille (for example he postulates a consistency between the *Contre-Attaque* texts and the *Somme athéologique* [p. 101] that would be quite difficult to demonstrate) and separates them without seeing any internal significance or motivation behind that separation (he ascribes the supposed increase in interest in the *Aufhebung* in the postwar years to the growing influence of Kojève [p. 102]—despite the fact that Bataille had attended Kojève's lectures already in the mid to late thirties).

Hollier's essay, "De l'au-delà de Hegel . . ." while presenting a convincing model of a Bataillean repetition compulsion (the repetition Hegel/Nietzsche) has some difficulties in explaining the modalities of the notion of "community" in Bataille (pp. 103–4). Once again, attention to the *specificities* of texts would help explain what otherwise appears to be an arbitrary valorization on Bataille's part of either an anti-social or individualistic conception of "communication," or a more generalized concern with political entities or secret societies ("community").

4. In this essay, the terms "heterogeneity" and "homogeneity" will be used in a specifically Bataillean sense. The clearest exposition of these terms —and their difference—is to be found in the essay "La structure psychologique du fascisme" ("The Psychological Structure of Fascism") (1, 339–71). Homogeneity refers to utilization, production, and above all to the conservation of limits:

> The base of social homogeneity is *production*. Homogenous society is productive society, in other words useful society. All useless elements are excluded, not from total society, but from its homogenous part. . . .
>
> Each man, according to the judgement of homogenous society, is worth what he produces, which is to say that he ceases to be an existence

for itself: he is no longer anything more than a function, ordered within the measurable limits of collective production. (1, 340)

This homogeneity can refer to personal and psychological limits (and personal activity) as well as social.

Heterogeneity, then, is any element or force that serves to break open those limits, that introduces elements that cannot be reappropriated by either personal or social utility: ". . . heterogeneity defined as non-homogenous presupposes the knowledge of homogeneity which delimits it by exclusion" (1, 344).

5. cf. 6, 147: "A wave of airplanes arrives, the siren . . . it is without a doubt nothing, but again, everything is risked [*est en jeu*]."

6. In this context, see "La structure psychologique du fascisme." Bataille in the end saw *Contre-Attaque* as, ironically enough, a reappropriation of negativity (in the form of a "paradoxical fascism")—the very thing *Contre-Attaque* had sought to avoid by positing a non-directed mob violence. As an alternative to the "politics" of *Contre-Attaque* (which nevertheless saw the mobs actively revolting against political institutions, making the mobs themselves participators in a political process) Bataille posited *Acéphale* which was to substitute the experience of the negativity of myth and sacrifice to that of mob violence: ". . . *Contre-Attaque* having dissolved, Bataille decided immediately to form . . . a "secret society" which would turn its back on politics, and which envisioned nothing more than a religious end, but an anti-christian one, a Nietzschean one," (6, 485: From a "Fragment from an autobiographical sketch").

7. The "Instructions pour la 'rencontre en forêt'" ("Instructions for the 'meeting in the forest'") (2, 227) gives a clear idea of the kind of rituals planned by *Acéphale*.

8. Roger Caillois, in *Sub-Stance* 11:12 (1976), 63.

9. Ibid., p. 61. Caillois gives a strong portrait of the Bataille of this period, though very negative due to the conflict between the two over the nature of the "gift" in "primitive" cultures.

10. Although Bataille first introduced the notion of a *practice* of "meditation" before an ecstatic or horrible image in the fifth (and last) issue of *Acéphale* (1, 545) that is, in early 1939, at that time the "practice" of meditation was still associated with an "Eglise" and with a "guerre." The "guerre" was to take place not only *within* the subject ("Je suis moi-méme la guerre") but also between the members of the sect and those who would attempt to crush it—presumably the fascists (cf. "La Menace de guerre").

11. This text is from "L'Amitie," the text whose writing was for Bataille the decisive factor in his break with the idea of forming a "secret society" or "sect" (note that only later does he disparagingly refer to it as a "religion").

12. See, for example, Bataille's exposure of a fascist reediting of Nietzsche that turned him into an anti-semite: 1, 449.

13. *Nietzsche-Werke*, Band 8:2 [Posthumous Fragments, 1887] (Berlin: De Gruyter, 1974).

14. *Ecce Homo* (Berlin: De Gruyter, 1969), p. 363, 364.

15. Indeed *Sur Nietzsche* does work towards a climax, the liberation of August, 1944, but it is a climax that is outside Bataille as he writes his journal—the events are in fact contingent, they could have taken place otherwise, or not at all. As history, August, 1944 is a dubious "endpoint" (or "liberation"). If it is a culmination, it is less as a stabilization than as an

experience of danger, gunfire, and peripheral involvement. It is therefore less an end posited by Bataille—the narrator—than a trampoline that he posits in his journal through the very project of writing during the war—which snaps back to catapult him somewhere else, beyond any telos he could have devised.

16. "Even more than the text of Volume One of *Being and Time* . . . Heidegger's inability to finish it by writing Volume Two underlines my similarity with [Heidegger]" (5, 217).

"I am not a philosopher" (5, 218).

17. See the essay "Le sacré" (1939): "Christianity has substantialized the sacred, but the nature of the sacred, in which we recognize today the burning nature of religion, is perhaps that which produces the most ungraspable (*insaissisable*) between men. The sacred is only a privileged moment of communal unity, a movement of convulsive communication of what is ordinarily repressed (*etouffé*)." (1, 562).

18. Bataille's Nietzsche, as pure "toxicity," criticizes Christianity not because it is the previous stage in any "dialectic," but only because "it is there" (or because "it is there" is precisely what it refuses).

19. This reading of Nietzsche/Bataille seeks to push the notion of "dualism" in Bataille to its logical conclusion. Two other texts on this theme are "Le materialisme dualiste de Georges Bataille" by Denis Hollier, *Tel Quel* 25 and "Le toit" by Phillipe Sollers, *Tel Quel* 29, where the notion of "sides" (of a roof, of a text) is introduced.

20. Their coexistence is impossible: it is, in fact, the "same" impossibility that we saw working in "Nietzsche Dionysos" (1, 483)—except now, of course, it is on a "higher" level—that is, the "contents" of the "sides" of the impossible relation have been made more coherent and comprehensive—they have come to include, for example, the thematization of the text itself and its processes (the text as *surnietzsche*, "community," etc.).

21. The reader at this point might object that the "transgressive" relation of the *Somme athéologique* to *La Part maudite* is no less abstract than the "contradiction" between pure "toxicity" and a new "historical era" that was characteristic of the *Acéphale* position.

This objection would be correct, up to a point. The abstraction would remain, but it would be on a higher level, so to speak, a level of greater particularity of texts and therefore of a greater (and at the same time more significantly problematic) self-reflexivity. To expect a simple "resolution" of this problem would be, of course, to call for a total return to Hegel. One postwar approach to this problem can be seen in a chapter of the last volume of the projected three volume *Part maudite, La Souveraineté* ("L'equivalence et la distinction," 8, 365–74). It is arguable that one way of reading this chapter would be to see posited *within the subject* (the subjectivity of the leftist intellectual) the contradiction: radical negativity (refusal)/social progression (affirmation).

This "negativity" would "take place" at the same *instant* as the "positivity": in that sense it would be quite different from the Maoist dialectic (and the *Tel Quel* reading of it) in which the radical negativity is situated in a temporal, diachronic framework always overcome but always reasserting itself (the *goal* in activity still being to *overcome* negativity to the greatest extent possible). Here, however, the affirmation and refusal would be embraced simultaneously, impossibly. The concrete manifestation of this? Since Bataille is dead, that is for us, his readers, to formulate.

FOUR

UN SOUFFLE UNIQUE
Patrick Wald Lasowski

What kind of fascination does the work of Pierre Klossowski actually seek to exert on its reader? . . .

. . . We would have simply liked to call to mind that the most circuitous paths, the most subtle means are here placed in the service of a pleasure and inspiration entirely devolving upon a woman's charms; the seductive power of the text necessarily being confounded with that of Roberte; *she owes being irresistable as much to the pleasure that the artist took in going back to the source of his emotion, as to the desire to have his emotion shared by the reader, to shake him up in turn.*

. . . Consequently, can only states of juvenile rapture make us sympathetic to the profoundly exciting nature of *Pierre Klossowski's work, to the insistent succulence of his sentence, of his drawing? That's what the large paintings exhibited at the F. Petit gallery in Paris have attested to.*[1] *The imperious authority of the artist in the representation of his pleasures, the intimate conviction that supports their production, the voluptuous and quasi-palpable insistence of color, that is what stirred the forests of memory within us, forests always ready to burst into flames at the simple appearance of Roberte.*

. . . Certainly we will have had eyes only for her. Therefore let the telephone ring, the axe fall, Pierre Klossowski involves us in the mysteries of the love life of the Palais Royal, reverberating today with the seismographic trepidations of his desire "fallen into personal

fantasies"[2] *but gifted with the power to masterfully put together and take apart images.*

What is a classic work—play or novel? Above all, the concrete and material representation that one has of it: a body of signs—black-distributed in the space of a book, or of a page, according to conventions which, although tacit, are not for all that any less constraining than the strictest rules intent on fixing the limits of a genre. For the reader who first of all wants to identify the object, this recognition rests on a certain number of immediate points of reference: the design of the novel will see the purity of its features establish themselves to the exclusion of any clumsy instrumentation—parenthesis, footnotes at the bottom of the page, etc.—, but according to the frequency of capital letters—proper names, the alternation of dark masses—paragraphs—with the typographical dazzle of dashes—dialogues; according to the propensity of paragraphs to multiply in one place and elsewhere to disappear for several pages, the spacing from one point of punctuation to another—sentence, the regular presence of larger clearings—chapters, etc. Every play seeks, for its part, to oppose the transalpine grace of italics—directions—to the brutal, arrogant and titular return of capital letters—proper names—from which masses of variable extension flow up to a certain point—replies.

It will therefore be understood that it is not the writer who prolongs a description but an opaque configuration that wants to assert itself, not the narrative (*récit*) which becomes exasperated but the paragraphs that grow impatient to serve, not characters that converse but an expenditure of blank space imposing its necessity—as if from the inside, all the more disregarded by consciousness since it is the everyday pivot of the procedure.

There are innumerable writers who have not wanted to reproduce this fantasmatic representation, this ideal design limited by the average of performances, but on the contrary have wanted to rival it in audacity or eccentricity.

It would be incumbent, however, on modernity to have attempted to deliver itself from this phantom, to definitively get rid of the obsession with it. Today graphic inventions, which are like a universal manifestation of forces finally liberated, no longer count in this domain. Modernity—first and above all—records the completion of the *diagram* of the classical text. So much so, that it seems accepted that usage of the traditional canon can inevitably develop only a fable obeying the classical mentality common to this canon. Otherwise it is all the more useless to make use of it: it is better to invent—outside of any reference points—one's own expression!

For Pierre Klossowski this precisely comes down to making all

Patrick Wald Lasowski

"invention" impossible by removing any support for the compulsion that drives the artist to express himself—in the very opposition to this support. In his opinion liberation can only fail. It leads, he says, to "dropping the substance for the shadow."[3]

Even if Pierre Klossowski would insidiously compare modernity with that which one assumed was the last word in classical ambitions: creation, invention, while, for his own part preferring the filiation of "artists as interpreters," he is nonetheless the first to be conscious of the crisis that the very notion of the artist is going through today.

It is in that sense that he insists on the necessity of resorting to stereotypes. A necessity based on the incommunicability of experience in an industrial world that has lost a sense of the sacred by submitting any emotion to the laws of supply and demand. . . .[4]

Pierre Klossowski has come back to this point many times, often in pages disturbing in their subtlety—but, with such *obstinacy* that lucidity seems to have taken refuge in its most extreme explorations to the point of letting the shadow of a profound obsession be outlined. It seems that here, less by recreating himself as an anathema than by identifying himself with the subversion that he describes—insofar as he would be its last expression, Pierre Klossowski seeks to assert the path of his own destiny[5] to the extent that *the artist's destiny* is eminently bound up with his work in the least of its incidents. So that Pierre Klossowski would be the last writer whose biographical space is important to us: there where emotion or obsession is born, in this "outside" that determines the arch irradiating the text through the inevitable compromises of any disclosure. This is a space that modernity cannot recognize since, on the contrary, as if trusting to the chance of a challenge ceaselessly renewed—and soon ritualized as a result of the concept of language-work—it seeks, by always going back to already given material, to solicit in and by the text the emotion that the industrial world has made impossible in the outside, to the point of emptying the very idea of "outside" of any meaning.

That is why, contrary to what is true for the creators of the journal *Tel Quel*—where Pierre Klossowski had several excerpts of his work appear—neither Mallarmé, nor Joyce, nor Bataille serve as reference points for him, but Nerval, Barbey d'Aurevilly, Baudelaire,[6] and Kafka[7] whose works are, in his opinion, the expression of the profound perturbations born of the antagonism between two worlds. It is surprising that a century later Pierre Klossowski can participate in them with so much acuity. Would not the situation have "evolved" for a writer of our day to be able to appear bound up with it? Why such backwardness when modernity forcefully affirms that the rupture was completely consummated long ago? Can Pierre Klossowski's inspiration develop only on a foundation of depression, only by maintaining the spiritual conditions of the crisis alive within it?

The work answers the question. But that does not prohibit us from evoking at this point—with a generality that ignorance imposes—the itinerary lived by the artist.

Recommended by Rilke to André Gide[8] in order to have Gide facilitate his entrance to the Vieux Colombier, his years of apprenticeship were undoubtedly marked by an intellectual atmosphere diffused by the generation of those "bourgeois writers" who knew how to give back to literary creation that classic form of prestige which it seemed to have definitively lost. Pierre Klossowski's reflexions on Claudel, Du Bos, Gide,[9] the long study on Rilke,[10] testify to that.

The disappointing relations with Breton,[11] the frequenting of the psychoanalytic circle, the long intimacy with Bataille around *Acéphale* and the College de Sociologie,[12] and conventual experience probably altered the seductiveness of this atmosphere[13] less than did the slow degradation—sanctioned by history—of all the values implicated in it: the work of art and the transmission of a message or an emotion, Uselessness, Beauty, etc. At least a rending (*déchirement*) was again necessary, and beyond the century, lead him to affirm his sympathies so much more forcefully and to renew his ties with all the upheavals of our culture: as much the passage from paganism to Christianity as the famous industrial revolution. In the one case, it was a question of a conversion effected in opposition to a sensibility founded on idolatry *in the spontaneous adhesion of the soul to products of fabulation*, in the other, a standardization of sensibilities rendering all fabulation sterile.

"For our crudely materialistic and utilitarian era has pretensions of making any kind of fallow or brushwood disappear from the globe as well as from the human soul."[14] Thus, *Les Lois de l'hospitalité* places itself decidedly "in the shadow of that tangle of vipers" which the Forward evokes[15] and to which the text comes back many times.

Consequently André Gide's presence in Pierre Klossowski's work will perhaps be able to serve us in turn as a "guide." It is found in the character of La Montagne in *La Vocation suspendue*[16]—the homosexual always experiencing break-ins! It is also found, as if improving upon the relation between aunt and nephew—Roberte and Antoine, Diane and Actéon—with a supplementary mystification of parental ties, in Roberte's godfather, G. in *La Révocation de l'Edit de Nantes*,[17] and especially in "The Godfather of the Salvationist," The Master, The Old Man, the Prompter's Guide, that "ghost" on whom the theatre curtain falls when he has just performed in a manner as lamentable as it is pathetic: On it "one recognized a very old poster representing a man with a greenish body who, with a dancing step, was spitting fire while

Patrick Wald Lasowski

applying a thermogenic pillow to his chest."[18] A leaping allegory of Gide's demoniac in our day; what ends the smell of sulphur finds itself reduced to! Soon "a thick volume bound in black leather . . . : a sort of handbook for subway engineers"[19] replaced dear Vergil. After having seen him lodged in the basement of a railway-station by F. Jammes—in *L'Antigyde*—Pierre Klossowski raises André Gide in a delirious ascension which even includes a choir of seraphim. . . .

These few indications fully demonstrate that one can in no way speak of a gloomy nostalgia. And if we were tempted to see in Gide's presence a trace of the rending (*déchirement*) so often evoked by Pierre Klossowski—identifying himself in that case with Octave, that "survivor of the bourgeois caprices of a bygone era,"[20] then it is a trace of a rending (*déchirement*) overcome very affirmatively in the work and one is well aware, by risking the classical logic of the text: at its expense.

In any love letter, writes Kafka, the kisses that are slipped in are drunk, in long draughts, by phantoms and not by the recipient of the letter.

In the same way the industrial reign seeks to take possession of the text. What results does the reader obtain when, as a skillful censor, he has lifted out, *has frozen the most intimate part of the text*? A bloodless display sworn to commonplaces. . . . Pierre Klossowski's work is inspired by a diametrically opposed process. The writer deliberately comes into conflict with those masses of residues whose degree of acquired concreteness is precisely what interests him: fixed forms, groups of words, fragments of sentences, set situations, conventional scenes, obligatory vicissitudes, etc. Such is the stereotype—a morbid tumescence, a punctual induration which, however, menaces all of language, all of the imaginary: the entire universe of representation today finds itself encrusted, residual. But Klossowski's text seeks to defer the death of this universe by any means.

"It is really a body . . . but if it is lifeless it is not for all that a cadaver"[21] muses the Great Master in front of the hanging corpse. The stereotype is itself only "incorruptible, a lifeless [*sans souffle*] body"[22]: the artist's *inspiration* here assumes a semblance of corporality, susceptible to animation. Around these hollow petrifications—when that (*ça*) leaves its sediment—prowls a delirious madwoman seeking shelter: she takes hold of these estranged petrifications, breathes herself inside them, takes possession of them. . . .[23]

The continuous whirling of the hanging body is a figure of communication: it is only by insulting its laws that the text can again make it possible. Just as the life (*souffle*) given form by the brazen serpent springs up, so too, then, the seed of the text will spring to the eyes of the reader![24]

But although there is so much insistence on recourse to the stereotype, do Pierre Klossowski's fictions conform more or less closely to the design, the diagram, characteristic of the classical text? It seems that, in this case, to avoid frightening the reader's fantasmatic universe by the appearance of his simulacrums, by giving them an outline that is still probable according to custom—but in fact: more and more *elusive* —the artist makes his work the site of a swindle. It consists of exceeding, through the diversity of the forms solicited, the logic implicated in the respectful usage of those forms. For not only is classical logic annihilated in the delirium that this swindle engenders but, in addition, the work is never really concerned about this classical structure.

Such as it presents itself, devoid of the provocative illustrations which accompanied the first editions of *Roberte ce soir* and of *La Révocation de l'Edit de Nantes*[25]—an abandonment that we can interpret as a gesture of goodwill with regard to custom, *Les Lois de l'hospitalité* does not display the profound *agitation* which governs it. On the contrary: at first nothing is more convincing than the concern with respecting—in the midst of the worst difficulties—a certain number of habits dear to the reader, a concern with not leaving behind—no matter how imperative the "constraint" might be—the most persuasive and the most tried narrative schemas.

Thus a "forward"[26] precedes *La Révocation de l'Edit de Nantes*[27] which is composed of the entanglement of a lewd confession—"Journal de Roberte" and the diary of an old madman—"Journal d'Octave." Quickly complicated by the "(Roman impressions, first fragment)": a new serpent insinuating itself into the initial tangle.[28] To which the "continuation of a detailed catalogue of my collection"[29] corresponds as the "(continuation and end of the Roman impressions)"[30] will correspond to the "(last notes dictated from his deathbed to Vittorio)."[31]

This series of violations continues in "Roberte, ce soir."[32] Two pages without a heading are followed by "Difficultés,"[33] where the "laws of hospitality"[34] are found punctuated by a "(Note d'Antoine)" at the bottom of the page.[35] Then "I La dénonciation"[36] presents the characteristics of a play, excluding Octave's overlong "digression."[37] "II Roberte ce soir"—without a comma[38]— thoughtlessly mixes theatrical responses and novelistic dialogues. The "Intermède"[39] solves nothing. And "III Où l'on avance de qu'il fallait démontrer"[40] would in turn offer all the guarantees of a play if Victor's final invasion did not violate all its laws.

The naive and propaedeutic archaism of the structure of the "Souffleur"[41] would completely reassure us—Prologue, fourteen chapters,

Patrick Wald Lasowski

Epilogue—if Chapter Two was not equivalent to a "Lettre à docteur Ygdrasil,"[42] if the fourth did not reproduce an "article" in italics,[43] and if the astonishing Chapter Seven did not upset the economy of the whole by being virtually never-ending.[44]

Thus the reign of misinterpretation is established: as much by excess, by the irreverent multiplication of genres as by their confusion, by their very exasperation in the overextended descriptions and the overlong dialogues. It ends by making the text the object of an explosive oversaturation in the mutual betrayal of specific forms of literary communication. So that far from exhausting them as forms, Pierre Klossowski accentuates, it exacerbates the role that he assumes that derision plays in their usage, while resisting the "invention" of a form that would be specifically his own. This seems to be an ordeal for the reader: a disenchantment with regard to the traditional narrative (*récit*)[45] becomes the price one must pay to make oneself susceptible to the charms of Roberte. But it can also seem like an ordeal for the artist: it consists of including the parodic point of view without limiting oneself to it.[46]

Thus, the "Afterword" corresponds to the augural "Forward." One cannot conceive of a better simulacrum of closure: here and there italics encircle the "exterior" part of the fiction: reflexion growing impatient. The latter completes the exasperation of custom, shaking up the text itself by its disconcerting *aplomb*.[47] Does it seek to "double" the text? In effect, that is a risk Klossowski takes in his insistence on emphasizing the artist's orchestrations in the face of the obstacles that prevent him from communicating his emotion, his perspicacity before the means that will—or will not—permit the emotion, however, to be shared. Henceforth, it is less the necessity of the work that asserts itself in its magnificent challenge to the world, than the intelligence—the malice—of the artist in his obsessive design to betray it!

Is it failure in the industrial world that imposes such a penetration of commentary, as if on the lookout for the text? But what if the "Afterword" is an integral part of the fiction? Then this back side arranges a non-negligible opening in *Les Lois de l'hospitalité* inviting the reader to take possession of it from the rear: reading begins again, promised to those who, thereby, will have become Roberte's accomplices.

In one sense, that is also the lesson of *Bain de Diane* whose "Eclaircissements"—which follow it[48] and are no less a part of it— obscure the relation they are assumed to have with the text more than they do the text itself. The same applies to the "Note de la page 68"[49] dedicated to St. Augustine. This is a "Footnote" of such importance for the comprehension of antiquity, that one can easily imagine some specialist referring to it on occasion without at all attempting to worry about the rest of the text.

And if *Le Baphomet* apparently avoids any complication but, on the contrary, wraps itself in the false scruples of archaism,[50] it is doubtlessly because the hallucinatory situations of the fable escape the representative vocation of the novel to such a degree that the displacement will be born of itself: one really thinks one is dreaming: one soars.

Pierre Klossowski thus manifests the profound habitus of the reversal of usages which the law of exchange imposes in our day and age, this *reversal*—contrary to the most absolute claims of modernity—presupposes the maintenance, the most stringent identification, of customary forms of communication: letter, article, newspaper, novel, theatre, interlude, note, etc. For it is only at that price that the artist will indeed be able to inflict them with "a burning surprise":[51] by sodomizing all of them, so to speak.

In the very beautiful first pages of *L'Economie libidinale*, Jean-Francois Lyotard offers us a violent fiction—but is it really a fiction?—determinant in more than one respect: "Open the alleged body". . . .[52]

Let us on the contrary treat the conspicuousness of the so-called body with respect: one must not be hasty in deploying, exposing its violence but should take care of the smoothness of its apparent coherency. One should remain, caressing, as close as possible to its richness of form, one should admire the glorious certitude of that undeniable self-assurance. Pierre Klossowski incessantly invites us to do that.

Now, Pierre Klossowski, from whom modernity drew so much inspiration that it identified itself with the project of "forcing the lock of identity"[53] is precisely far from coming to the same conclusions about it. . . . Appearing in the journal *Tel Quel* without sharing its enthusiasms, the work of Pierre Klossowski also felt itself profoundly tied to the reflections of Deleuze, Foucault, Lyotard. And yet it seems that no one can be more alarmed than Pierre Klossowski by investigations conducted here and there stemming from what could appear as a community of minds. If—to take a trenchant example—"schizo-analysis attains a non-figurative and non-symbolic unconscious, a pure abstract figural dimension (abstract in the sense of abstract painting) flows-schizzes or real-desire, apprehended below the minimum conditions of reality,"[54] how can one not think of Octave's bitterness in the face of our modern world: "explosion itself had become a need and the gaze could henceforth only be satisfied by mutilated objects, by shattered images."[55]

Pierre Klossowski comes back to that in *Cinématograph*: "I do not understand current pictorial investigations. For me it's mathematics. It is a hate or impotence of vision, a destruction, a non-painting, a non-book. Now it is 'implosions.' "[56] He thereby joins Rilke's meditations: "What is upsetting, after the disappearance of the *subject* properly speaking is that, at present, music and graphic art are reciprocally taken as *subjects* of each other—his short-circuit of the arts unknown to nature and even to imagination is, for me, today's most disquieting phenomenon, a phenomenon which is, however, liberating. . . ."[57] Those meditations are similar to Gide's in *Quelques réflexions sur l'abandon du sujet dans les arts plastiques*[58] and to those of Klossowski himself, in *La Décadence du Nu.*[59]

In fact disjointed syntax, disintegrated space, shattered forms, broken flows, voices put to torture are just so many ruptures seeking to overthrow the order of identity—an order which itself had the menace of madness hovering over Klossowski.[60] However, in their desperate eagerness to tear apart the laws of the order of identity, these ruptures run the risk of a *pathetic* inflation. The hammering throb of the sexual lexicon, having become like an inevitable martyrology of a tortured experience, runs the same risk as do the breaks affecting the outline of the novel to the profit of an immediate vertical spatiality, of a serial programming, of a reinsertion of "waste," of a proliferation of gaps which are like the blanks in the text's memory. Modernity exalts this typographic usage as the boreal promise of a Major and Definitive Signifier.

These broken-down landscapes of the avant-garde text shape, in the midst of ruins, the impossible horizon of a subject reduced to a pulp in one place, vaporized in another. One traverses them, governed by a search for a cadaver. The author's? Mallarmé's—at the avant-garde of the avant-garde itself? The reader's? Or that of the book itself—their meeting-place? The City whose abyss the modern text is, arranges no meeting: one moves on.

To this, Pierre Klossowski opposes a relationship of accomplices. That is the meaning of the "battle of the rear-guard"[61] that he carries on alone, amidst deceptions,[62] in delights of the most dubious kind.

Eternal backslider to a 1900s style, to "sequined corsets,"[63] to "infantile historic representations of a turn of the century" Thursday,[64] to the popular serial novel whose text competes in audacity with a neighboring illustration that will triumphantly end by supplanting it. Thus, Roberte whose cape hugs the wall, moves forward, "her face disguised by a wolf mask. . . ."[65]

And even in the midst of the most powerful scenes—when uncle Florence throws himself on Mme. K.—, Pierre Klossowski lets a comical mother-in-law straight out of vaudeville[66] comment on the scene against the grain: "Uncle Florence, such things aren't done when one is visiting!"[67] And this before having recourse to that obligatory accessory of the avenues of crime—the suitcase into which the body disappears.[68]

Furthermore, the author does not hesitate to plunge us into the authentically dubious atmosphere of the most banal detective novel peopled with "a part-time informer," fat and smooth shaven and a "thickset" aggressor "in shirt sleeves,"[69] where the fatal—and disabused —whir of the fan corresponds to the clamminess of the body, to the persistent odor of skin—a scene which captures the very essence of a grade-B thriller. And the sneering "He! he's"[70] the "ha! the trollop's!"[71] that punctuate the adventures of "the old pig"[72] and the "slut":[73] "Ah! you moron, on a generous impulse, admit it, you would, like the coward that you are, deliver your wife to the Asiatic and die of enjoyment at her shame,"[74]—aren't they all inspired by a very similar atmosphere? The same could be said of the magazine romance that brings together the beautiful Swiss Red Cross nurse and the blue-eyed SS officer Von A. haloed in the most lamentable Wagnerian and Nietzschean stink.[75] It would also include the "laws of hospitality" that the sensational journal *Detective* regularly promises in its flashy titles adorned with alarmingly naked women: "he had his wife sodomized in front of him by her lover! He offers his wife to his guests! . . ."

Would Pierre Klossowski be just a "vulgar imagemaker under his apparent subtlety?"[76]

At least from the most moving *tableaux vivants* of "La Révocation" to the incredibly boring dialogues of "Roberte, ce soir," from the stupefying visions of Baphomet to the unutterable confusion of the "*Souffleur*," the reader moves from surprise to surprise lead by the logical rigor, by the compelling force of a dazzling, extravagant, and troubling rhetoric—in the same way excessive make-up throws desire into confusion. The reader is also led by the compelling force of a *spectacular* syntax that serves as a pivot for the adventures of Roberte, for her "crazy descent(s) . . . down the spiral staircase"[77]—just as the Trajan column serves as a pivot for the spiral unfolding of the Roman epic. This is a syntax that *pins* Roberte and keeps her immobilized at ankles and wrists just as do her successive aggressors. Unless it is, on the contrary, Roberte who is the means by which the syntax is pinned down until it overflows from frenzy.

And indeed, as if the text thereby tore itself away from its own fascination, the long descriptions—so scrupulously erotic that it becomes painful for the dazed reader[78]—often end with a pun whose liberating spontaneity is thus introduced into a context that is most foreign to it: for example, the famous "le député devenant pute" in "La Révocation."[79] Such plays on words are frequent. They are consternating in their bad taste and facility: the connections between

Patrick Wald Lasowski

"fourreau" and "fourré,"[80] the "suées" of the *inspectresse* of "censure,"[81] the "siège" where Sonta-Sède surprises Roberte,[82] "cécité ma fée licite,"[83] the "débordements" of Alphée,[84] the "cerf-arbitre,"[85] the "larvatus pro dea,"[86] Saint-Vit Beausseant, etc. Wouldn't classical syntax only be the formal guarantee, the readiness for the press, of an "uncontrollable stifled laughter"[87] that runs along the thread of the text? Just as a smile on Roberte's face always ends by lighting up "the seriousness of her regular features" that she maintains in the midst of pleasures;[88] just as the seams of her severe tailor-made suit always end up splitting[89] —so too the tight jacket of syntax gives in. The brazen-faced audacity of the pun encroaches upon those very impossibilities that are the "Séparez là" of the "Souffleur"[90] and "the divinity in twelve persons always making an exhibition of itself" of *Le Bain de Diane.*[91]

This foundation of vulgarity thus serves to light up the syntax from underneath.[92] It is the healthy naiveté of "an eternal schoolboy" whose voluptuous emotion surges up not only in response to a naked body, but also in response to its most troubling and suggestive accessories: garters, corset, pink silk, the straps of a bra, panties, gloves, stockings, etc. "He began by lighting up the silky curves of her leg up to the hollow of the knee, then continued along the bare flesh between the garters up to the protruding buttocks filling out the panties, when Roberte's long, gloved fingers stretched out over the bulb of the flashlight."[93] "Then, keeping one arm under her head, she brings the other to her throat, slips her fingers around her breasts and running her open palm over the roundness of her belly, her long fingers inserted into her bush, while she was lifting one of her superb thighs, her head fell back into the ivy."[94] With such "tableaux vivants," with those flowing sentences that overflow with insolence—"The rosy nipple popped up in the opening of the black silk"[95]—*Klossowski's text acquires all its volume, deploys a carnal and, properly, pulpy seduction!*[96]

Consequently, no one will be surprised if, far from current cutting up, *this voluptuous model of the text* exalts the most sumptuous finitude of bodies. Imagination wanders here, not only around a *Roberte cast into* "squeezed into her new excellently cut corset which marvelously sheathed her belly and her hips,"[97] around her "bulging bra," around the "perfect curves of her beautiful legs, and around the contour of her breasts"[98]—but also around Ogier, around "his smooth flanks and his firm buttocks," "his well-rounded testicles," around his "satin pouch," all puffed-up and soft, around "his thigh sheathed in breeches."[99] Glorious and malleable forms whose display is turned completely to the outside.

This insistence on features, *this concupiscent redundancy of outline* extols the pure expressivity of a body emptying itself thereby of any "personal reality."[100] A body that is only a fictive coherence, opened by ecstasy, offered to possession: the house of pleasure of fantasms, their delightful haunt.

In Klossowski's eyes, only the *conspicuousness of the body permits the effective liquidation of the subject* reduced to its purely spectacular nature.

Thus, lust encompasses the smoothness of the body, the polish of the marble, the curve of a leg, the shape of a buttock, the contour of a breast, the sudden erection of a sex organ. Indeed don't "Vittoria's bird" and the schoolboy's "identification papers"[101] destroy the temporal unwinding of our troubles and tribulations by means of an amazing spatiality? Tumescences from which the statue takes its inspiration, developing in the space that it creates around itself until it forms the manifest, glorious volume that moves us. "The gigantic member that points its smooth and admirably bulging gland at Roberte"[102] expresses itself in this way.

Thus Roberte, in one case, offers the protruding roundness of her buttocks, and in another—"too generously endowed by nature,"[103]—the insolence of that "Tom Thumb" whose story the text tells us with an ostentatious complacency. There is no vertiginous gaping of the female sex, but rather the liveliness of the "little errand-boy," the *quidest* "raised in all its unctuous insolence,"[104] "the honorable piece" that Malvoisie teases until it reaches "the height of passion."[105] Pleasures from childhood terrors and the gothic novel: "soon the proud dragon springs out all glowing red."[106] Roberte and Valentine—feminine as a result of a supplementary e[107]—expose their sex exclusively to sodomy, to homage and to decapitation. Only the agitation of the irascible lodged in the organs disturbs Pierre Klossowski, who is preoccupied by their visible manifestation, by their real presence, speaking to the eyes, imposing on imagination itself.

Consequently the ring that the hunchback "slips" onto "the attribute of the inspectress,"[108] the "ring sealing the anus," shuts the reader in "the path of irreversible error,"[109] the path that his own emotions will have traced at the reading of a work waiting for him from the beginning of time—and from which he can never return.

ADDENDA I
VIVAT ACADEMIA

When we consider the work of Ingres,[110] and particularly the way in which this painter, soon showered with honors, made himself, from the moment of his entry into the atelier of David, the defender of the classical ideal, to the point of maintaining—one of the last to do so

Patrick Wald Lasowski

with Delacroix—the academic hierarchy of the Subject, such as it expressed itself in Western tradition in favor of dramatic themes borrowed from mythology and history, when we consider this, how is it possible to conceive of the fact that this same Ingres from time to time was able to paint, without thereby being in any way distracted from his essential preoccupations, portraits and nudes that today continue to hold our fascinated attention?

Our attention is entirely focused on the trailing hand of Mme. Rivière, arrested by Angelique's arms and her so openly "manipulated" body, definitively troubled by that authoritative lesson in arbitrariness which the "Baigneuse of 1807" alone represents. The same effects are produced by all his "voluptuous heroines in distress,"[111] all his "beautiful posers"[112] observed in the sinuous decor of the shawls and draperies that envelop them, all his haunting nudes coming from an icy Orient. At this point the glaze of such a merciless seduction displays on canvas the necessary confusion of the beauty of women with that of painting; women deadly for the Academy and for a certain way of looking.

The point is that Ingres retains the teaching of David. Finding the opportunity to illustrate his own disgust with the works of Delacroix in the opposition Poussin/Rubens, he choses the theoretical representation of the former. Integrated with his interpretation of the feminine body, this representation will give us what Baudelaire calls "delightful and bizarre fantasies,"[113] completely marked by "a libertinage which is serious and full of conviction"[114] and which testifies to a perverse lucidity with regard to anatomy. These nude figures, so close and so naked, that offer themselves to our gluttony but exhibit only the immense flesh of their marble backs are, in effect, ambiguous.

Does our emotion stem from those anatomical slips, those distortions of the body that, nonetheless, always remain probable—so marvelously do they trade on their charms, from that subtle manipulation of feminine nudity attaining the suppleness, the docility of the most ideal *material*? . . . And doing so in the context of a maniacal meticulousness with regard to the reconstruction of decor, of the smallest detail: "Illusions" says Baudelaire, born of an "almost morbid preoccupation with style."[115]

It is necessary to ask: what is the truth of these immobilized bodies? "It is certainly not the translation of feelings, passions, or of variants of these feelings and passions, nor is it the representation of great historical scenes . . . ."[116] *Excessive pleasure of the Image* governs these "superb and insulting exhibitions: the lacquered self-reflection of representation displays its only conceit!" "It is nice to sketch a woman's eyes," said this painter who, unlike Delacroix, always took care to erase all traces of workmanship; who recalled, in reference to the primacy of the drawing, that "great painters like Raphael and Michelangelo insisted on an outline in finishing."[117] The outline, the finish, that is the movement that restores bodies to the violence of their contour and submits us to the uprooting vision of a corpulence forever arrested. The morbid precision of the drawing and the fastidious concern for detail here hollow out the figurative space at the mercy of its very conspicuousness: they instruct the subtle consistency of the image to offer us a body in the mad assumption of a spirituality finally made pulpous, triumphal and definitive: so many divinities—emotions— incarnated on canvas; beyond any expression.

The fact remains that these representations are declared aberrant only in relation to a fixed norm or in comparison to the figurative logic that Ingres adopts[118] and that will often condemn him as "gothic," but that will also help him inspire the most formal of his successors, from Cabanel to Gerome. What is a norm if not the fixed, resistant, encrusted and despotic residue of an anterior extravagance that has passed triumphantly into the public domain. The *extravagance* would involve a code, but one that it does not exactly transgress, sliding over it, then making it slip, *fall*—seducing and overturning—in its turn.

It would certainly be necessary to take Ingres' temperament into consideration here, to evoke the elusive stratagem of a sensibility that is revealed by means of the most severe molestations.

But if the extravagance of this man whose *good faith* serves as fodder for Octave's malice—an extravagance which consists in obsessively reinterpreting the female figure and culminates in that old man's reverie, "Le Bain Turc"—if this extravagance cannot in any way be considered as an act of systematic subversion, will it not have had the merit, through its *displaced* position on the academic body, of revealing that Academism itself is an aberration?

ADDENDA II
HOLLOW AND RELIEF

"Many minds are no doubt preoccupied with various techniques that will compensate for the surfeit of familiar forms. But what is the point in this—assuming that we wish to find out what a novel might be —unless first of all a ground is ascertained and clearly delineated? A story that reveals the possibilities of life is not necessarily an appeal; but it does appeal to a moment of fury without which its author would remain blind to these possibilities, which are those of *excess*. Of this I am quite sure: only an intolerable, impossible ordeal can give an author the means of achieving that wide-ranging vision that readers weary of the narrow limitations imposed by convention are waiting for.

Patrick Wald Lasowski

How can we linger over books to which their authors have manifestly not been driven?"[119]

It is that "manifestly" which is at question here. For the differences
that place Bataille's work in opposition to Klossowski's flare up in those
few lines. And yet the question of "techniques," the relation of the story
to life, of the author to the "compulsion" that governs him, are
emphasized. But the "fury" testifies to the indecency that aggression
excites. The atmosphere emerging from these reflections is itself, here
and now, "intolerable." One has the feeling that the "ecstasy" whose
scene Bataille seeks untiringly to reconstitute in his work has little to
do with the "emotion" that inspires Klossowski.

Is it necessary to compare the "difficulties" specific to "Roberte, ce
soir" to those of *L'Abbé C*?[120] The last resort offered in *L'Abbé C* by the
"Table of Contents"[121] announces, in its desperate rigor, a delusive
attempt at enclosure: *the editor's story, the story of Charles C., the
epilogue to Charles C's story, abbé C.'s notes,*[122] *the sequel to the editor's
story* tear apart the action of an impossible narrative (*récit*). The
obscene "swelling," the isolation of the fragment and the pages, the
exclamatory, interrogative, and suspensive harassment, don't all these
ceaselessly break through the overstrained canvas of the text! Spasms.

If, here and there, the problem of the impossible is raised in the
field of the same theological culture,[123] in Bataille's work, however,
voluntary ascesis-servitude leads, in a most incontestable manner, to
the reintroduction of the difficulty of reaching the point where language
is always missing: on the edges of this wound, before this yawning
abyss where the text crumbles away. At that point delight and anguish
seize being in its "nudity." This gives us that "excessively shaky" writing,
that convulsive text, "manifestly" concerned with transgressing the
limits of language and integrating the notion of sin into this transgression: therein lies the whole problem of the obscene. Attacks of vertigo.

To the textual feverishness that the erotic experience engenders in
Bataille, Klossowski opposes his use of the stereotypes—in his opinion
syntactical sin does not at all yield a superabundance of grace. In the
same way he opposes Roberte's high-buttoned blouse, its severe bodice,
to the immediate seductiveness of the very low-cut necklines of Bataille's
heroines. Just as he opposes the insolence of Roberte's "attribute" and
her admirable behind to Bataille's dark night of the feminine sex.

However, are not two fingers on the same hand, two accomplices?
Rather, one thinks of those multiple rings decorating Roman hands—
mounted in different ways: in one case intaglio, in the other cameo; in
the one case the sharp incision engraving the stone just as it works
language, inhabited by the d'Aurevillian gesture of imprinting the seal
of its burning mark on the feminine sexual organs, in the other the

glorious blooming of a simulacrum that exposes the displays of its rhetoric in relief, in the *round bulge* of its dazzling tableaux—beside which our fantasms come, indefinitely, to regild themselves.

Certainly nothing took place between André Gide's[124] conjugal trilogy and the *Lois de l'hospitalité*. There is little resemblance between the gidian demoniac—such as it is expressed in the famous phrase: "there is no work of art without the collaboration of a demon"—and "the argument of Hermes Trismégiste" so often taken up by Pierre Klossowski. And there are too many differences between *Quelques réflexions sur l'abandon du sujet dans les arts plastiques* and *La décadence du nu. . . .*

So at what point of their sensibility can Gide and Klossowski be compared? A master piece of memory, "capital of the heart and the senses,"[125] in *Le Souffleur*, Gide appears with recognizable features whereas Rilke does not. If Klossowski "spares" Rilke, the last of the true artists, for his nobility, perhaps he recognizes, on the contrary, a certain buffoonery in Gide for which he would have more than just sympathy. Moreover, isn't this writer who feeds on the pleasures of his library, passes from one book to another, and continues his sentences between two readings, essentially parodic?[126]

Tragedy is, in this case, open to the laughable, existence always subject to the burlesque. "It seems to us that we are performing a chapter of the *Caves*"[127] best characterizes, in our opinion, the literary, moral, and psychological situation of the Old Man.

There is always an "affair of a counterfeit Gide" under way.

"He received a letter which began with 'Uncle Edouard' and which must have been rather pathetic. . . . *Les Faux monnayeurs* was a revelation for this monk, he is suffocating in his convent, he has lost his faith, he is thinking of suicide, no one can help him. If his voice is heard by Gide, let Gide let him know by placing an ad in the paper *La Croix* before the 15th, the only possible way to correspond with him. Old gardener seeking a position . . . something of that kind. . . . If anyone is still interested in him, let them come to the lake at the indicated time by boat. . . . If no one comes he will execute his plans: falling in, drowning, or both in order to have it look like an accident. . . . Gide already sees himself responsible for this monk and not knowing what to do with him."[128]

Such adventures are frequent. Isn't Gide a refined scholar, a greedy homosexual, as well as being the Vampire—he manifestly posed as such in certain photos, the Ogre of the countryside, the "idiot" of the village,

Patrick Wald Lasowski

the disturbing madman which Martin du Gard's testimony gives us: "a beggar who comes to warm himself in church," a "defrocked priest perhaps?"[129]

And Gille and Gide. All the more so Gille since it is he himself who takes the trouble to reveal to us that the peasants of Cuverville call him by that name. But who is "he"? The Gide of admiring witnesses: the Gide *honoris causa* or the Godfather of the *Souffleur*. Or else the Gide of the *Journal* flirting with the polymorphism of pseudo "I," "he," "X"—until he measures himself against his own fiction: "Although he is too silent, I like to travel with Fabrice."[130]

Artist and histrion.

Deleuze—another "Gilles"—emphasized this relation very strongly. As did Pierre Klossowski by means of the drawing reproduced in the issue of *Arc* that is devoted to him.[131]

Translated by Larysa Mykyta

NOTES

1. From November 28th to December 31st, 1978. See the catalogue of this exhibition, Paris, 1978.

2. To go back, out of context—but without neglecting the ties which bind Gide to Klossowski—to an expression of Claudel's in Paul Claudel, *Correspondance, 1899–1926 de Paul Claudel et André Gide* (Paris: Gallimard, 1949), p. 220. [Unless otherwise noted all citations are translated from the French by the translator. Translater's note.]

3. Klossowski, "Protase et Apodase," *L'Arc*, 43 (1970), 19.

4. Cf. especially "Fragments de lettre à Michel Butor," *Les Cahiers du Chemin* (Paris: Gallimard, 1967), p. 98.

5. Undoubtedly as a result of that we have the current constellation of "confidences"—to which also belong the film *Roberte Interdite*, the prefaces to the books of former companions, Waldbery, Okamota, the preparations with J. M. Monnoyer of the very promising *Entretiens*. Pierre Klossowski further surrenders to these impulses sometimes in a provocative manner, sometimes in the form of testimony. But also in a manner most in conformity with any quest for origins: therefore after having lengthily emphasized its importance in the work of Balthus, *Monde Nouveau*, March, 1957, he invites us to plunge into the encompassing climate of his childhood: the 1900s. Returning to that with a deliberate insistence in the course of the interview published by *Cinématographe*: "During my childhood we had a magnificent magic lantern. . . ." *Cinématographe*, 39 (1978), 44.

6. Cf. "Preface à *Un prêtre marié* de Barbey d'Aurevilly," in *Un si funeste désir* (Paris: Gallimard, 1963).

7. Cf. the preface to *Journal Intime* (Paris: Grasset, 1945).

8. Cf. footnote 1 of "Hors des Limites" in *Critique* (1954) and "Correspondance de Claudel et de Gide" in *Un si funeste désir* to which Bataille refers.

9. Cf. "Gide, Du Bos et le démon" and "En Marge de la correspondance de Claudel et de Gide" in *Un si funeste désir*.

10. Klossowski, "Rainer Maria Rilke et les Elegies de Duino," *Critique* (October, 1946).

11. Cf. letter to Patrick Waldberg. Preface to *Demeure d'Hypnos* (Paris: Edition de la Différence, 1977).

12. Cf. the preface to T. Okamoto, *L'Esthetique et le Sacré* (Paris: Seghers, 1976).

13. Seduction (seductive power) of which the family circle, opening onto the intellectual cosmopolitanism at the beginning of the century, is the first source. Eric Klossowski, painter and art critic, author of studies dedicated to the painters of Montmartre, to Honoré Daumier—whose *Les Cahiers de la Petite Dame* in *Cahiers André Gide*, No. 4 (Paris: Gallimard, 1973), p. 123, informs us of the meeting with Gide. Baladine, inspiring P. J. Jouve who will see in her a new Lou Andreas Salomé, Rilke's friend—whose marvelous *Letters à Merline* will be read. Letters written in French, while, as if weaving a supplementary link, Pierre Klossowki *translated* the *Correspondance* between Rainer Marie Rilke and Lou Andreas Salomé for *Le Nouveau Commerce* (Spring-Summer, 1967).

Here painting, drawing, illustration (Baladine illustrated the works of Rilke) seems to be a family secret, a unique gesture, appropriate for founding a community of minds, an affinity of conspirators, whose German lakes and Swiss mountains were tutelary demons . . . .

14. Barbey d'Aurevilly in *L'Ensorcelée* (Paris: Gallimard, 1977), p. 36.

15. Klossowski, *Les Lois de l'hospitalité* (Paris: Gallimard, 1965), p. 8.

16. Klossowski, *La Vocation suspendue* (Paris: Gallimard, 1950).

17. Klossowski, *Les Lois de l'hospitalité*, p. 79.

18. Ibid., p. 180.

19. Ibid., p. 182.

20. Ibid., p. 26.

21. Klossowski, *Le Baphomet* (Paris: Mercure de France, 1965), p. 97.

22. Ibid., p. 102.

23. If the work of Pierre Klossowski rests on a fantasm of possession, his experience as a translator could have for a long time, helped to nourish it. On the one hand there is a living language: German; on the other, a *dead* language: Latin, which the first pages of *Bain de Diane* examine. But considering that one does not know it, isn't every foreign language a dead letter? So much more monumental since it is inanimate, so much more tangible since meaning has fled after being incarnated in it. Translating from one language to another, what place can one assign to the Klossowskian demon translator? Animating the first language to erect a new monumentality that corresponds to it, he leaves behind two equivalencies confronting each other, between which his infinite vacillation triumphs. But abandoning the successive skins in which he clothed himself—Kafka, Kierkegaard, Nietzsche, Rilke, Vergil and Suetonius—it is characteristic of this demon to introduce them in turn into his own text, which he thus dispossesses himself of in their favor.

Beyond possible comparisons, beyond influences exerted, beyond loving translations, what meaning can be given to the large number of authors and texts inhabiting Klossowski's work? Flaubert and *L'éducation sentimentale* are named; St. Thomas is reproduced almost textually (before being identified with the character of Dacquin and Blanchot with that of Hochheim?); Gide is represented in *Les Lois de l'hospitalité*. Descartes is mocked, Ovid and Plautus are quoted, The Acts of the Apostles are solicited, classical philology

Patrick Wald Lasowski

and eternal alchemy are spoken of ironically in *Le Bain de Diane.* Hugo and Rilke are present in *Le Baphomet.*

These are the simplest examples. We could list a thousand more. We assume that there are undiscoverable ones. A sort of social game begins at this point (who is concealed behind the Scandinavian ash-tree Ygdrasil?) where the reader is lost. Furthermore, the presence of *Roberte, ce soir* in the two parts of the trilogy that encircle it and, in the very heart of the work, the presence of *Sade mon prochain* and of *Violette* in *Les Lois de l'hospitalité,* the thesis of brother Damiens in *Le Baphomet,* all reveal the spiraled swirling of a work enclosed in the intimate circle of its own culture. Thus, a unique creative force (*souffle*) circulates between the shelves of a real and imaginary library—refusing to the gesture of writing the inaugural abruptness of a creation torn from silence, but dedicating it to the continued corruption of what it will have itself engendered! [The complex interplay between the various meanings that the words *souffle, inspiration,* and *insuffler* have, in French in general, and in Klossowski's work in particular (see especially *Le Baphomet*), is demonstrated in the body of the article and in this footnote. It is because no English equivalent could be found to simultaneously suggest all those meanings that the French title has been retained. Translator's note.]

24. Cf. *Le Baphomet,* pp. 63 and 110.

25. Pierre Klossowski, *Roberte ce soir* (Paris: Minuit, 1953), and *La Révocation de l'Edit de Nantes* (Paris: Minuit, 1959).

26. *Les Lois de l'hospitalité,* p. 7.

27. Ibid., p. 11.

28. Ibid., p. 17.

29. Ibid., p. 80.

30. Ibid., p. 88.

31. Ibid., p. 85.

32. Ibid., p. 105.

33. Ibid., p. 109.

34. Ibid., p. 110.

35. Ibid., p. 112.

36. Ibid., p. 114.

37. Ibid., p. 131.

38. Ibid., p. 137.

39. Ibid., p. 148.

40. Ibid., p. 151.

41. Ibid., p. 175.

42. Ibid., p. 194.

43. Ibid., p. 216.

44. Ibid., p. 278.

45. Also with regard to "literary creation". . . .

46. Nonetheless a doubt remains as if—in Pierre Klossowski's work—an irreducible foundation of disillusionment with regard to the act of writing could not be suppressed. From that comes the sentiment of a virtuosity which is always ironic toward itself, of an ultimate indifference as to the means which the artist will use. . . .

Thus this "oversaturation" of the texts cannot be identified in our opinion with the *affirmation* of "discontinuity" characteristic of modernity, as M. Kajman argues in his remarkable work, *Corps et Ecriture dans Les Lois de l'hospitalité* (Diplôme d'études supérieures, Université de Lille III, Juin 1971, under the direction of A. Nicolas). It is the "preliminary image" that must be called "discontinuous," not the text. The latter rather exalts in a derisive insurrection, a formal polytheism of the narrative (*récit*) in opposition to the unique, continuous, and divine diagram of the classical novel.

That's why nothing is basically more disappointing, more sterilizing, than to describe—as we rapidly do here—Klossowski's fictions. Such a description will never approach those thrilling places where the magic of the text effectively exercises itself.

47. A self-confidence that manifests itself for example in the typographic decomposition of certain sentences, pp. 344, 347, 350—as high school students see it done on the blackboard to Latin sentences.

48. Klossowski, *Le Bain de Diane* (Paris: J. J. Pauvert, 1956), p. 107.

49. Ibid., p. 117.

50. See, for example, the burlesque desuetude of "icelui". . . .

51. In *Les Lois de l'hospitalité* to revenge himself on Roberte, Vittorio uses her as he would a boy: he moves through her "from bottom to top—how to describe it—with a burning amazement," p. 69.

52. J. F. Lyotard, *Economie libidinale* (Paris: Minuit, 1974), p. 9.

53. *Les Lois de l'hospitalité*, p. 134.

54. Gilles Deleuze and Felix Guattari, *Anti-Oedipus*, trans. by R. Hurley, Mark Seem, Helen R. Lane, (New York: Viking, 1977), p. 351. See also Gilles Deleuze and Felix Guattari, L'Anti-Oedipe (Paris: Minuit, 1972), p. 421. The question of "intensity," of "loss of identity" whose importance in Klossowski's work Deleuze has emphasized from *Différence et Répétition* (Paris: Presses Universitaires de France, 1969), p. 398 on, finds absolutely no echo, for the former, in "abstract painting". . . .

Is it necessary to recall that Deleuze wrote a very fine study on Klossowski—"Pierre Klossowski ou le Corps Langage" in *La Logique du sens* (Paris: Minuit, 1969)—and that an exerpt from L'Anti-Oedipe was published in the issue of L'Arc devoted to Klossowski, L'Arc, 43 (1970), 54.

55. *Les Lois de l'hospitalité*, p. 47.

56. *Cinématographe*, 44.

57. *Lettres à Merline* (Paris: Seuil, 1950), p. 86.

58. In *Verne*, I (1937).

59. In *Almanach Letterario*, Bompiani, 1967. Without insisting here on the importance of Pierre Klossowski's graphic work nor on that of Balthus' lightly touching upon the "academic pornography of the Third Republic" we borrow these few words from Giancarlo Mormori: "Balthus e uno dei rari pittori intellettuali del noto secolo, razza in via di estinzione, addirittura massacrata dalle successive ondate dell'avanguardia anticalssica" (Nel pianeta delle bambine, in L'Espresso, 33:19 (August 1973), p. 12. It is in this article that we found part of the information that forms the content of our note on Pierre Klossowski's family milieu.

60. See a study quoted by Gilles Deleuze and Jean Decottignies, "Syntaxe et Solecisme, *Litterature* 26:6 (1977), which speaks well about a "frenzied fiction."

61. Lettre à Patrick Waldberg, p. 10. An expression which J. M. Monnoyer admirably comments on in L'Exercise plastique aux barres parallels in "Roberte au Cinema," *Obliques* (1978).

62. We don't even know if it is indeed Pierre. Cf. *Cinématographe*, 40.

63. *Les Lois de l'hospitalité*, p. 313

64. *Le Baphomet*, p. 210.

65. *Les Lois de l'hopitalité*, p. 17

Patrick Wald Lasowski

66. "Tautologie? Asks my mother-in-law. . ." *Les Lois de l'hospitalité*, p. 315.

67. Ibid., p. 317.

68. Ibid., p. 321. —one finds the ubuesque version of this suitcase in the "grave" of *Baphomet*, p. 172.

69. Ibid., p. 41.

70. *Les Lois de l'hospitalité*, p. 76.

71. Ibid., p. 191.

72. Ibid., p. 32.

73. Ibid., p. 32.

74. Ibid., p. 74.

75. Cf. "Malwyda! . . . That's my sister," p. 91.

76. Here we are reversing the terms of the judgment that Pierre Klossowski applies to the painter Tonnerre: "a subtle imagemaker under his apparent subtlety." "La Judith de Frederic Tonnerre (1865)," in *Figures*, Paris, New York, September, 1961.

77. *Les Lois de l'hospitalité*, p. 43.

78. One thinks of the reproach addressed to Flaubert by Duranty: "obstinate description". . . .

79. *Les Lois de l'hospitalité*, p. 60.

80. Ibid., pp. 59–60.

81. Ibid., p. 67.

82. Ibid., p. 138.

83. Ibid., p. 75.

84. *Le Bain de Diane*, p. 76.

85. Ibid., p. 100.

86. Ibid., p. 45. It would be necessary to quote—almost all the words enclouded in the posture of their italics. Saint-Vit and Beauséant are the names of the heros in *Baphomet*.

87. *Les Lois de l'hospitalité*, p. 18.

88. Ibid., p. 58.

89. Cf. Ibid., p. 59: "when suddenly the material tore, the seams split"; p. 139: "the gauntlet of the Colossus . . . split her bra"; p. 323: so that all the seams of her blouse split," etc.

90. Ibid., p. 219.

91. *Le Bain de Diane*, p. 48.

92. In this way the apotheosis of the crescent—when the stag "hurled himself with lowered head" into "the rear of the idol"—is worthy of the most beautiful bits of gallantry. Ibid., p. 104.

93. *Les Lois de l'hospitalité*, p. 57.

94. Ibid., p. 190.

95. Ibid., p. 140.

96. One thinks of Marcel Proust: "Albertine folded her arms behind her dark hair, her swelling hip, her leg falling with the inflexion of a swan's neck that stretches upwards and then curves over towards its starting point." *Remembrance of Things Past*, trans. I. A. Blossom (New York: Random House, 1932), p. 433. See also: *A la Recherche du temps perdu*, 3 (Paris: Gallimard, 1973), p. 79.

97. *Les Lois de l'hospitalité*, p. 69.

98. Ibid., pp. 58–59.

99. *La Baphomet*, p. 86, p. 146, p. 209 respectively.

100. *Les Lois de l'hospitalité*, p. 128.

101. Ibid., p. 68, p. 62 respectively.

102. Ibid., p. 138.

103. Ibid., p. 72.

104. Ibid., p. 72, p. 147 respectively.

105. *Le Baphomet*, p. 50.

106. Ibid., p. 206. A dragon with which Roberte is completely identified in the film *Roberte Interdite*: "There is the dragon who is lying in wait for you, my dear." *Obliques*, p. 31.

107. A salute to Albertine? or to Denise?

108. *Les Lois de l'hospitalité*, p. 147.

109. *La Baphomet*, p. 105, p. 145 respectively.

110. We were inspired by the remarkable *Ingres* by R. Rosenblum— *Ingres* (Paris: Cercle d'art, 1968), p. 138. Also see pp. 31, 47, 78, 105.

111. Same as note 110.

112. P. Courthion in *Ingres* (Geneva: Pierre Coilleur, 1918), p. 14.

113. Baudelaire, "Le musée classique 1846," in *Curiosités Esthetiques* (Lausanne: De l'oeil, 1956), p. 97.

114. Ibid., p. 98.

115. Ibid., "Exposition Universelle, 1855," p. 211.

116. Ibid., p. 210.

117. Cited in *Ingres* (Genèva: Pierre Cailleur, 1948), p. 60.

118. Outside of which he cannot paint . . .

119. In Bataille, *The Blue of Noon*, trans. Mathews (New York: Urizen, 1978), p. 153. See also *Le Bleu du Ciel* (Paris: U.G.E., 10–18, 1970), p. 11.

120. Bataille, *L'Abbé C* (Paris: Minuit, 1950). Especially since Bataille and Klossowski have each devoted an article to the other's text, mutually falling back upon the close intimacy that unites them. An intimacy haunted by tall tales, by disturbing characters who seem to be, from Roman priest to psychoanalyst, romantic products of a sensibility specific to the period between the two world wars.

121. Cf. Ibid., p. 227.

122. Notes that are themselves divided into a "Forward," "Diary," etc.

123. Cf. for example the question of Grace faced with ancient Pathos, with erotic experience.

124. Of which *Robert* is precisely the pivot. Where he is questioned about Eveline's true nature; where the havoc caused by free thinking in families. . . ." is evoked, in *Robert* (Paris: La Pléiade, 1969), p. 1323.

125. *Les Lois de l'hospitalité*, Avertissement, p. 7.

126. We were inspired by a study by Roman Wald Lasowski devoted to André Gide, parodic writer.

127. *Les Cahiers de la Petite Dame*, in *Cahiers André Gide* 4 (Paris: Gallimard, 1973), p. 87. It is a question of helping "young R. M." to escape, to cross the border by night.

128. Ibid., p. 345.

129. *Notes sur André Gide* (Paris: Gallimard, 1951), p. 12.

130. *Journal*, I (Paris: La Pléiade, 1970), p. 628.

131. *L'Arc*, 49 (1972).

FIVE

DIVINE AGONIES: OF REPRESENTATION AND NARRATIVE IN ROMANTIC POETICS
Eugenio Donato

> But for you it would perhaps be a duty since you could occupy yourself
> with awakening the dead of Tübingen. The undertakers will, certainly,
> try to harm you as much as possible. If your efforts should be in vain
> I think, of course, that it would be a self-betrayal to bother yourself with
> that species. But are you going to find a more favorable field of action
> among your Swiss than among our Swabians? That is the question.
>
> Hölderlin to Hegel,
letter of November 25, 1795, from Stuttgart.

> One has only to say the words 'College of Tübingen' to grasp what
> German philosophy is at bottom—a *cunning* theology. . . . The Swabians
> are the best liars in Germany, they lie innocently.
>
> Nietzsche

NIETZSCHE's resounding proclamation that "God is dead," by the lucid
forcefulness of its statement, may easily lead us to neglect the fact that
Nietzsche's harrowing of that event is only one episode—even if we
should eventually discover that it is the most decisive episode—in the
history of a topos that is central to the Romantic imagination. Within
the corpus of Nietzsche's writings it appears more than once. If Section
125 of the *Joyful Wisdom*, entitled "The Madman," is the most important

version of the theme, the theme reappears again in various places, particularly in *Zarathustra* and the *Posthumous Fragments*. It is not certain, in fact that, as we shall see later, we should treat all the occurrences as equivalent.

At any rate, if the theme that "God is dead" has important but unrelated historical antecedents, the topos does not become obsessive, but more importantly does not acquire significant variations until the Romantics. The young Hegel, for example, will remind his readers that Pascal had already anticipated that theme. Nevertheless, for Hegel, the theme belongs to modernity:

Formerly, the infinite grief only existed historically in the formative process of culture. It existed historically as the feeling that "God Himself is dead" upon which the religion of more recent times rests; the same feeling that Pascal expressed in, so to speak, sheerly empirical form: *"la nature est telle qu'elle* marque *partout un Dieu* perdu." By marking this feeling as a moment of the supreme Idea, the pure concept must give philosophical existence to what used to be either the moral precept that we must sacrifice the empirical being or the concept of formal abstraction. Thereby, it must re-establish for philosophy the Idea of absolute freedom and along with it the absolute Passion, the speculative Good Friday in place of the historic Good Friday. Good Friday must be speculatively re-established in the whole truth and harshness of its Godforsakeness.[1]

Anticipating for a moment, we may already note the characteristically Christian form that the theme takes in Hegel, who metaphorically connects the topos of God's death with the Christian Passion. The theme of "God is dead," in fact, grounds the birth of a certain philosophy —Hegel's—but this grounding has to follow the particular pattern set by the Gospels for Christ's death: that, in fact, God's death announces the death of religion and of a number of philosophies—specifically, Kant's and Fichte's—to be resurrected at the end of a unique process in the glorified luminous, timeless, body of Hegel's own philosophical discourse.

The double function of speculation is that of bringing back to a privileged incorruptible form of life an older philosophical discourse that died from its incapacity to overcome a corruptible materiality and to contemplate the final luminous spatial manifestation of the new philosophy. It is worth noting, however, that the basic narrative pattern that will ground the advent of the new philosophy is the Christian model of the narrative of the Passion namely death/entombment/resurrection. It is the existence of the Christian model that permits the transubstantiation of religion into philosophy and the rebirth of the old philosophy into the new.

Since the variations that the theme may take are important and significant, one must be careful not to disregard the specific aspects that the topos may take in individual poets or thinkers. Schiller, who was among the earliest of the Romantics to use the theme, in opposition to Hegel, places it in a strictly Greek context. Part of his poem "The Gods of Greece," neglected today but popular in the nineteenth century, in an awkward Victorian translation, reads:

> Beauteous World, where art thou gone? Oh, thou,
> Nature's blooming youth, return once more!
> Ah, but in Song's fairy region now
> Lives thy fabled trace so dear of yore!
> Cold and perish'd, sorrow now the plains,
> Not one Godhead greets my longing sight;
> Ah, the Shadow only now remains
> Of yon living Image bright! . . .
>
> . . . .
> All that's bright and fair they've taken too,
> Ev'ry colour, ev'ry living tone,—
> And a soulless world is all we view.
> Borne off by the Time-flood's current strong,
>
> . . . .
> All that is to live in endless song,
> Must in Life-time first be drown'd![2]

The contrast with Hegel is striking. Even though the disappearance of the Greek gods constitutes the genesis of Schiller's text—since the poem is the nostalgic evocation, the "song that mourns," inscribed by the trace (*Spur*) left by their absence—Schiller's world does not have the possibility of a resurrection; the past lost forever dooms the modern poet to a belatedness that divides history into two distinct moments: one of Gods and "golden years of nature" and one of elegiac poets and presumably art. Nature for Schiller does not belong to the same temporal category as art. We can begin to see how the choice of the versions of the theme of the Death of God organizes different narrative structures that in turn will produce different "Histories." Thus, if for Schiller belatedness conditions the idiom of the artist, for Hegel belatedness is necessarily philosophical according to a scheme that localizes art and religion in an equivalent temporal moment. At any rate, Hegel and Schiller are useful examples because they provide us with early examples of the two fundamental centers—Greek and Christian—around which the topos will organize itself throughout the nineteenth century before taking a more generic form with Nietzsche.

The two centers are not always clearly distinguishable. If Keats, in the "Hyperion" and "The Fall of Hyperion" fragments, resorts to a Greek model, in as complex a poet as Hölderlin the theme of the withdrawal of the Divine often uses the Greek model but at times, as Szondi has shown, the Greek and Christian models are indistinguishable.[3] The best known version—and certainly the most popular version in the nineteenth century—of the theme before Nietzsche is Jean-Paul's, which was translated in French by Mme. de Stael and influenced Vigny's and Nerval's treatment of the topos;[4] Jean-Paul's text was also translated more than once in English, the most famous English version of Jean-Paul's text being, probably, Carlyle's.

Jean-Paul's Christian version of the topos is particularly interesting because, in contrast to Hegel, he uses in a paradoxical fashion the Christian model to propose a non-redemptive, non-eschatological form of history. Jean-Paul's text is worth quoting at some length. In Carlyle's version it reads:

I passed through unknown Shadows, on whom ancient centuries were impressed.—All the Shadows were standing round the empty Altar; and in all, not the heart, but the breast quivered and pulsed. One dead man only, who had just been buried there, still lay on his coffin without quivering breast; and on his smiling countenance stood a happy dream. But at the entrance of one Living, he awoke, and smiled no longer; he lifted his heavy eyelids, but within was no eye; and in his beating breast there lay, instead of a heart, a wound. He held up his hands and folded them to pray; but the arms lengthened out and dissolved; and the hands, still folded together, fell away. Above, on the Church-dome, stood the dialplate of *Eternity*, whereon no number appeared, and which was its own index: but a black finger pointed thereon, and the Dead sought to see the time by it.
Now sank from aloft a noble, high Form, with a look of uneffaceable sorrow, down to the Altar, and all the Dead cried out, "Christ! is there no God?" He answered, "There is none!" The whole Shadow of each then shuddered, not the breast alone; and one after the other, all, in this shuddering, shook into pieces.
Christ continued: "I went through the Worlds, I mounted into the Suns, and flew with the Galaxies through the wastes of Heaven; but there is no God! I descended as far as Being casts its shadow, and looked down into the Abyss and cried, Father where art thou? But I heard only the everlasting storm which no one guides, and the gleaming Rainbow of Creation hung without a Sun that made it, over the Abyss, and trickled down. And when I looked up to the immeasurable world for the Divine *Eye*, it glared on me with an empty, black, bottomless *Eye-socket*; and Eternity lay upon Chaos, eating it and ruminating it. Cry on, ye Dissonances; cry away the Shadows, for He is not!"[5]

We can now observe how the topos of the Death of God is, in fact, governed in either the Greek or Christian version, by a more fundamental opposition. The topos can be used to allegorize a redemptive eschatological history grounded in a privileged narrative, as in Hegel, or on the contrary used, as in Keats or Jean-Paul, to deny the very possibility of an eschatological end, a privileged *Telos* to history, and hence to problematize the very nature of narrative.

That the theme of the Death of God, whatever else it may signify in any one particular author, allegorizes the specific temporal mode that governs narrative and hence history is made explicit by one of the more interesting and neglected versions of the topos, namely Flaubert's in *The Temptation of Saint Anthony.*

Flaubert's variant offers a number of unique characteristics. Flaubert, instead of writing of the Death of God, transforms the theme into the death of the gods. This change allows him to portray as a history, as a narrative history, a topos that deals with the temporal modes of history. Like Hegel's, Flaubert's history moves from East to West. First he describes the death of the Gods of India, then the death of those of Persia followed by those of Egypt and Greece. Unlike Hegel's, the movement of history is not a redemptive one. Instead of placing at the end of his series the triumphant appearance of a "true" philosophical or theological discourse, he situates his literary description in the belated moments of a decaying history.

The different moments of Flaubert's history are interesting in themselves. The Buddha dies within the context of a cyclic history: "And having in this last existence, preached the law, nothing now remains for me to do. The great period is accomplished! Men, animals, the gods, the bamboos, the oceans, the mountains, the sand-grains of the Ganges, together with the myriad myriad of the stars,—all shall die; —and until the time of the new births, a flame shall dance upon the wrecks of worlds destroyed!"[6] The death of the Egyptian gods ending with the death of Isis is, on the other hand, inscribed in a linear history that leaves in its wake only archeological ruins: "The breath of Typhon devours the pyramids. . . . Egypt! Egypt! Thy great motionless gods have their shoulders already whitened by the dung of birds; and the wind that passes over the desert rolls with it and the ashes of thy dead!"[7]

If, in the Egyptian context, nature becomes the antithetical enemy of history, it is this same nature that decrees the necessary non-redemptive nature of history. The death of the Greek gods is preceded by a voice which "rises, indistinct and awful like the far roar of waves, like the voice of forests in time of tempests, like the mighty moaning of the wind among the precipices" and states: "We knew these things!— We knew them! There must come an end even for the Gods! Uranus was mutilated by Saturn,—Saturn by Jupiter. And Jupiter himself shall be annihilated. Each in his turn;—it is Destiny!"[8]

The Flaubertian Greek gods, in a gesture not unrelated to the withdrawal of the Divine in Hölderlin's poetry, do not die but withdraw to leave behind the last remnants of a history whose law is one of decay and corruption. Jupiter withdraws saying: "I no longer desire to receive those [the souls] of men. Let the Earth keep them; and let them move upon the level of its baseness. Their hearts are now the hearts of slaves; —they forget injuries, forget their ancestors, forget their oaths,—and everywhere the folly of crowds, the mediocrity of individuals, the hideousness of races, hold sway!"[9]

The withdrawal of Apollo into what Flaubert calls "pure thought"—"No enough of forms! Further, higher!—to the very summit—to the realm of pure thought"—will make it impossible for the belated history, to succeed in his artistic undertaking. The final moment in the episode of the history of the death of the gods coincides with Hegel's and describes the death of the Christian god but his death places a nihilistic void at the place of, and an answer to, Hegel's triumphant philosophy: "Woe! Woe! the Holy of Holies is open, the veil is rent, the perfumes of the holocaust are dissipated by all the winds of heaven! The jackal whines in the sepulchres; my temple is destroyed; my people dispersed! . . . An enormous silence follows—the deepest night."[10] Flaubert's narrative of the death/withdrawal/disappearance of the gods is an historical narrative that, by sequentially stratifying a number of possible temporal models for history, constitutes an historical allegory with an absolute nihilistic end associated with the impossibility of a Christian redemptive history. If such an historical allegory emblematizes the belated situation of the modern artist, the latter's temporal position does not coincide with the nihilistic moment of the disappearance of the Christian God but instead with that of the withdrawal of Apollo that renders the *Idea*—Flaubert's expression for absolute form—hopelessly beyond the reach of the modern artist. As we shall see later the emblematization of the belatedness of the modern associated with the nostalgic valorization of an impossible art form, through the figure of Apollo, is not unique to Flaubert—it is, in fact, Keats who offers us the most complex version of the problem, which is significant in relationship to the Hegelian model of the topos.

Hegel's Christian redemptive scheme in the last analysis is the basis for the final dialectical sublation of history and of art as well into the domain of philosophical discourse. As the ending of the *Phenomenology* makes clear, philosophical discourse is to climax a history in which art represents a single moment. Flaubert's narrative then, on the face of it, is a parody of the Hegelian project. Like Hegel, Flaubert writes a "history" that appears to have the same orientation as Hegel's. Flaubert's "history," however, is constituted by a series of disconnected and different histories that are grounded in an artistic—and not philosophical—text. It is the Apollonian moment and not the Christian moment that makes the narrative possible. Yet the possibility opened by the Apollonian moment, by allegorizing the nonredemptive nature of the history by which it is constituted, states the future impossibility—or the impossible future—of dialectically sublating philosophical discourse.

Eugenio Donato

An appreciation of the radicality of the Flaubertian gesture could be aided by a parenthetical digression. As it is well known from his *Aesthetics*—and from the *Phenomenology* as well—Greek art represents for Hegel a supreme moment in his philosophic narrative and if there is any nostalgia in Hegel for the loss of the Hellenic past it is more than compensated by the future hope that this disappearance is a necessary movement toward the ultimate spiritual appearance of philosophy, which alone has the power to transform the material reality of nature and human history into a spiritual concept. Within Greek art one particularly privileged moment for Hegel is the statuary of Greek gods. The statuary is privileged because in it Greek art succeeds in achieving a *mimetic* moment between spirit and matter, form and content.

This shape assumed obtains its pure form, the form belonging to spirit, by the whole being raised into the sphere of the pure notion. It is not the crystal, belonging as we saw to the level of understanding, a form which houses and covered a lifeless element, or is shone upon externally by a soul. Nor, again, is it that commingling of the forms of nature and thought, which first arose in connexion with plants, thought's activity here being still an imitation. Rather the notion strips off the remnant of root, branches, and leaves, still clinging to the forms, purifies the forms, and makes them into figures in which the crystal's straight lines and surfaces are raised into incommensurable relations, so that the animation of the organic is taken up into the abstract form of understanding, and, at the same time, its essential nature—incommensurability—is preserved for understanding.[11]

Before Greek statuary, art for Hegel had two alternatives. One alternative for Hegel is a form of imitation that adheres so much to its natural objects as to be incapable of a separation that allows a reflexive identity of form and content. The threat of such art is, of course, that by being too identical with its object it will not create enough of a difference between them to allow philosophy to dialectically sublate that difference.

The other alternative is symbolical art, which, as in the case of the Egyptian pyramids—identified in the *Aesthetics* with natural crystals— can only signify by symbolizing the act of signification—such a symbolization always implying an absence. The problem, of course, is that in the *Encyclopaedia* Hegel identifies poetic language with symbolical representation. For Hegel the poetical image is inseparable qua image from an object upon which it, so to speak, grafts itself. In Hegel's words: "when imagination elevates the internal meaning to an image and intuition, and this is expressed by saying that it gives the former the character of an *existent*, the phrase must not seem surprising that intelligence makes itself *be* as a *thing*. . . ." Then in the *Zusatz* Hegel comments:

Divine Agonies

This conditioned, only relatively free, activity of intelligence we call *symbolic* imagination. This selects for the expression of its general ideas only that sensuous material whose independent signification corresponds to the specific content of the universal to be symbolized. . . . *poetic* imagination, though it is freer than the plastic arts in its use of materials, may only select such sensuous material as is adequate to the content of the idea to be represented. . . . The sign must be regarded as a great advance on the symbol.[12]

Hegel denies to poetry the abstract proprieties of signs. Symbols remain attached to objects in all their corporeity and materiality yet since these objects are used to signify they are not adequate to the reality of the objects, i.e. their essence, and hence come to represent the absence of the truth of the objects that they represent; they lack what in another context Hegel calls their "soul" and the poetical language that uses them resists the effort of philosophical sign language to "resurrect" them in the spiritual a-temporal form of the concept.

This curious identification between the Egyptian pyramids and poetical language is then, only paradoxical. In both cases the act of signification is doomed for Hegel because the absence inscribed by symbolical representation is not sublatable, or so to speak, resurrectable into a philosophic concept. In other words—and in the *Encyclopaedia* Hegel's quarrel is with his contemporary lyrical poetical idioms—poetry cannot recuperate into its language the objects it represents but can only allegorize their loss in representation, their "death" which even philosophy may not be able to resurrect in its own discourse. The privilege of Greek statuary based on a mimetic reflexive identity between form and content over Romantic poetry is understandable. For Hegel such a mimesis can offer philosophical discourse the opportunity to re-erase the distance between form and content in the spiritual unity of the concept, a possibility denied by the symbolic nature of poetry.

Let us return to Flaubert; the death of Apollo, more exactly the withdrawal of Apollo allegorizes the impossibility of any identity between form and content and disrupts any possibility of mimetic recuperation in representation. For Flaubert the artistic act can only assert its necessary failure but the failed artistic act remains privileged over a hopelessly impossible philosophical discourse. In short, for Flaubert the necessarily failed artistic act points to an epistemological nihilism that would make any philosophical discourse, in the Hegelian sense, impossible—this impossibility is inscribed in the reversal of the Christian redemptive version of the topos of the Death of God as used by Hegel.

Flaubert's version of the Death of God in many ways prefigures Nietzsche's version, which can, in fact, be read as an extreme radicalization of Flaubert's. For our purposes it would be useful to isolate the form that the topos takes in section 125 of *The Joyful Wisdom*. In spite of its length the section deserves to be quoted in its entirety particularly since it is difficult to break its narrative line.

The Madman.—Have you ever heard of the madman who on a bright morning lighted a lantern and ran to the market-place calling out unceasingly: "I seek God! I seek God!"—As there were many people standing about who did not believe in God, he caused a great deal of amusement. Why! is he lost? said one. Has he strayed away like a child? said another. Or does he keep himself hidden? Is he afraid of us? Has he taken a sea-voyage? Has he emigrated?—the people cried out laughingly, all in a hubbub. The insane man jumped into their midst and transfixed them with his glances. "Where is God gone?" he called out. "I mean to tell you! *We have killed him,*—you and I! We are all his murderers! But how have we done it? How were we able to drink up the sea? Who gave us the sponge to wipe away the whole horizon? What did we do when we loosened this earth from its sun? Whither does it now move? Whither do we move? Away from all suns? Do we not dash on unceasingly? Backwards, sideways, forwards, in all directions? Is there still an above and below? Do we not stray, as through infinite nothingness? Does not empty space breathe upon us? Has it not become colder? Does not night come on continually, darker and darker? Shall we not have to light lanterns in the morning? Do we not hear the noise of the grave-diggers who are burying God? Do we not smell the divine putrefaction?—for even Gods putrefy! God is dead! God remains dead! And we have killed him! How shall we console ourselves, the most murderous of all murderers? The holiest and the mightiest that the world has hitherto possessed, has bled to death under our knife,—who will wipe the blood from us? With what water could we cleanse ourselves? What lustrums, what sacred games shall we have to devise? Is not the magnitude of this deed too great for us? Shall we not ourselves have to become Gods, merely to seem worthy of it? There never was a greater event,—and on account of it, all who are born after us belong to a higher history than any history hitherto!"—Here the madman was silent and looked again at his hearers; they also were silent and looked at him in surprise. At last he threw his lantern on the ground, so that it broke in pieces and was extinguished. "I come too early," he then said, "I am not yet at the right time. This prodigious event is still on its way, and is travelling, —it has not yet reached men's ears. Lightning and thunder need time, the light of the stars needs time, deeds need time, even after they are done, to be seen and heard. This deed is as yet further from them than the furthest star,—*and yet they have done it!*—It is further stated that the madman made his way into different churches on the same day, and there intoned his *Requiem aeternam deo.* When led out and called to account, he always gave the reply: "What are these churches now, if they are not the tombs and monuments of God?"[13]

Nietzsche's pronouncement that "God is dead" is placed in the context of a narrative that we may describe as a sort of *Conte Philosophique* after the fashion in which de Man characterizes Nietzsche's *Truth and Illusion in an Extra Moral Sense* a *Conte Philosophique.* The two texts are, in a certain way, related. We must question, first, the necessity of the fable: in what way does section 125 of *The Joyful Wisdom* differ from the simple statement "God is dead" or from the way in which the statement appears a number of times in Nietzsche's work?

I do not intend in this context to analyze the passage in great detail, but simply question the function and the necessity of the narrative element in the passage.

Section 125 of *The Joyful Wisdom*, in spite of the apparent surface logic of the fable, is a tale about telling tales—a narrative about narrative. The fable tells about the impossible conditions of telling the tale of "The Death of God." The narrative is thus simultaneously a *"mise en abîme"* of narrative yet a *mise en abîme* that does not simply reflect the tale infinitely into itself but states the impossibility of the reflexive moment and this impossibility constitutes the very temporality of the narrative. In other words, the fable tells a tale but the tale that is told tells of the impossibility of telling the tale of the Death of God. The event always precedes the narrative moment—"we have killed him"—which states that the understanding of what the narrative tells will always follow it: "This prodigious event is still on its way, and is travelling—it has not yet reached men's ears." The narrative thus unravels its own incapacity to re-present the event it narrates.

The cosmological reference at the center of the text emblematizing the non-redemptive and non-theological nature of a history into which the impossible narrative of the Death of God is inscribed echoes the opening paragraphs of *Truth and Illusion In An Extra Moral Sense*. The two texts are more closely related than one might suspect. *Truth and Illusion* is on the surface a "philosophical" text dealing with the impossibility for re-presentation to be perceptually, linguistically, or conceptually adequate to the object it is meant to represent. In its development, however, *Truth and Illusion* develops a tale which uses a literary narrative form to undermine its status as a philosophical text. In de Man's words:

The wisdom of the text is self-destructive (art is true but truth kills itself), but this self-destruction is infinitely displaced in a series of successive rhetorical reversals, which by the endless repetition of the same figure, keep it suspended between truth and the death of this truth. A threat of immediate destruction, stating itself as a figure of speech, thus becomes the permanent repetition of this threat. Since this repetition is a temporal event, it can be narrated sequentially, but what it narrates, the subject matter of the story, is itself a mere figure.[14]

Section 125 of the *Joyful Wisdom* is a philosophical tale that confirms de Man's analysis of *Truth and Illusion*. It is a literary narrative that states the incapacity of narration to represent the event of the Death of God, making of the Death of God the allegory of this in-

Eugenio Donato

capacity. The "literariness" of Nietzsche's text consists of undercutting its own grounding, thus not allowing philosophical discourse to sublate the Death of God even in a non-redemptive nihilistic history. Nietzsche's Death of God is then doubly a critique of Hegel's version. First by its narrative form it denounces any possibility of a redemptive history but more importantly, perhaps, it prevents, by stating the impossibility of representing the event it narrates, the possibility of any philosophical discourse to dialectically sublate it.

Nietzsche in the literary strategy of his tale implicates the reader as well—"Have you ever heard of the madman. . . ."—the fable tells the reader of an event in which he is implicated that precedes his awareness of that event. Inasmuch as the reader is implied in the constitution of the signification of the text—its *Bedeutung*—there is no way in which the constitution of such a signification could temporally coincide with the event that generates it. Nor can the reader grasp the meaning of an event that is projected in an indefinite future. The text literally breaks the circle of the "hearing oneself speak" that is at the heart of the Hegelian model of the way language constitutes its significations.[15] At best the text records the memory of an event and constitutes itself into "the tombs and funerary monuments" whose voice is a temporally indefinite *Requiem aeternam deo*!

Voice is a privileged aspect of language in any recuperative scheme. Voice erases itself in its very utterance, leaving a pure meaning uncontaminated by the materiality of language. Voice in its ideal form of solitary speech gives a perfectly circular form to any utterance: such a circularity is necessary to its erasure since it does not allow for the intrusion of the otherness of the listener in the constitution of meaning. Nietzsche's narrative succeeds in breaking the circular pattern of speech and remains suspended between the narrator and his readers, the protagonist and his listeners. The breaking of the circularity of voice makes it impossible for the listener to invest any "meaning" in the sayings of the protagonist. The tale thus dramatizes, through its form, the impossibility for "meaning" to become constituted by means of the non-dialogue it narrates, hence the relationship of the reader to the narrator of the tale stages the meaning-lessness of the utterance "God is Dead." The narrative form of the statement "God is Dead" makes it impossible to invest that statement with any "philosophical meaning"—with any *Bedeutung*. If we were to follow Derrida, who reads in the Otherness introduced in the linguistic sign by any interlocutor a form of "death" inherent to language that resists sublation into a transparent meaning—then Nietzsche's tale allegorizes a form of "death" inherent to language which, in spite of Hegel, is not "resurrectable." The *Requiem aeternam deo* is also the belated memorialization of the "corpse" of language that resists all metaphysical idealities.

I am aware that my reading runs counter to Heidegger's formidable readings of Nietzsche's saying "God is dead." I cannot in this context analyze in detail Heidegger's reading; however, a few remarks are in order. Heidegger reads, as the title of one of his essays indicates— "Nietzsche's saying 'God is dead,' "—all of the instances of Nietzsche's statements "God is dead" as equivalent. This telescoping of the different instances in which the statement appears, the identification of "God" with the Christian God, the realm of values and the supersensible, allow Heidegger to equate Nietzsche's "God is dead" with a critique of metaphysics—and particularly Kantian and Hegelian metaphysics.[16] Nevertheless, it is only by treating Nietzsche's statement "God is dead" as a "philosophical" statement and making it into the emblem of the problematics of nihilism that Heidegger reads Nietzsche's "transvaluation of all values" as a metaphysical reversal of metaphysics and thus makes of Nietzsche the last metaphysical thinker, who reveals and consummates the nihilistic project implicit in Western metaphysics from the beginning. These remarks should suffice to point out that Heidegger's reading, powerful though it may be, in treating Nietzsche's discourse as a philosophical discourse never raises the question that Nietzsche's text may in fact question the possibility of having his text read in a philosophical key or *only* as a philosophical statement.

Heidegger neutralizes completely the "literariness" of Nietzsche's text, or to say it more technically Heidegger neutralizes the *Darstellung* of Nietzsche's text: yet in Nietzsche's narrative strategy the *Darstellung* is unavoidable. It may just be, in fact, that the *Darstellung* of Section 125 of *Joyful Wisdom* destabilizes the literary/philosophical opposition and that the ironic space that it opens makes it impossible for the statement "God is dead" to ground a uniquely philosophical discourse, and that the statement "God is dead" undercuts the very utterance that proclaims it.

It should be clear by now from the reading that I have given of a few examples of the topos of "God is dead" that, at least, in my view the metaphor of the death of God effectively relates the problem of narrative structure to linguistic and literary representation, as inaugurated by the Romantics. I should like now to address that problem in a more specific and direct way.

How man became more natural in the nineteenth century . . .—*not* of "return to nature"—for there has never yet been a natural humanity.

Eugenio Donato

> The scholasticism of un- and anti-natural values is the rule, is the
> beginning; man reaches nature only after a long struggle. . . .
> Nietzsche

> Romantic art is only a makeshift substitute
> for a defective "reality."
> Nietzsche

If we were to try to identify the lowest common denominator of
the poetics of the major Romantics we might easily arrive at the
conclusion that their preoccupations tend towards two sets of problems.
One deals with representation: specifically how can poetical or philosophical language account for nature and object. In Wasserman's
formulation "How do subject and object meet in a meaningful relationship? By what means do we have a *significant* awareness of the world?"[17]
On the other hand through the writings of the Romantics runs a
constant preoccupation with history—particularly the French revolution
—but this preoccupation itself reflects perhaps a more fundamental
concern with the problem of narrative in general. Hegel's *Phenomenology*, Wordsworth's *Prelude*, Keat's "Hyperion" and "The Fall of
Hyperion," and even Coleridge's *Biographia Literaria* point to the
necessity of a narrative structure to ground the representational structure of the *Lyrical Ballads*, Keat's Odes, or the epistemology of the *Logic*
or the *Encylopaedia*. Stated in this form the question assumes a
paradigmatic form in which lyrical representation and narrative structure cannot be isolated or treated independently of each other. Riddel
has identified the project of a late Romantic such as Poe in terms of a
strategic quest for a pure lyrical moment that would be a spatial
moment unaffected by any temporal mode except for the possibility of
pure repetition. In Riddel's words: "If one can call the poem an
'emblem' of the origin, it is not a representation, not secondary, but in
its way an originary repetition. Pleasure, Poe argues, derives from, or is
induced by, an 'identity' of sound and thought, or more accurately, by
the intense repetition of a sound (the *'refrain'*) that unveils the identity
of sound and thought in something that precedes reference, because
reference marks the belatedness of language to idea. Only the lyric poem
achieves this 'identity.'" Yet, as Riddel correctly points out, such a quest
for a "pure lyrical" spatialized moment is bound to fail and its temporal
component is reinscribed in the lyrical moment: "This repetition in
Poe has its own aberrational moment, its madness of "time," its own
bizarre breaking out of space, which therefore causes a perturbation
in the circle of its return. . . . The language of Poesque lyric is
momentarily out of control before it can return and close, or effect the

intensity and brevity that can only come after the word has had its grotesque trial in time."[18] If Riddel is correct, then we may well have to ask the question whether in the early Romantics a "pure" lyrical moment uncontaminated by a narrative structure was ever possible after all.

For a different statement of the problem let us return to Wasserman's article, which I quoted earlier. Wasserman sees the Romantic dilemma as an epistemological one: in what way can subject and object merge together to produce meaning. At the outset the problem might seem simple: in Coleridge's words: "A Poet's Heart and Intellect should be *combined* intimately combined and unified with the great appearances in nature" or "the object of art is to make the external internal, the internal external, to make Nature thought and thought Nature."[19] The first step, then, for a Wasserman is to resolve the problem through perception: "What we might then expect is a system identifying perception with significant cognition and resolving the divorce between subject and object by making perception an act of self knowledge."[20] The key word here is, of course, "significant." Even granting, for the time being, that the Romantics might have believed in the possibility of immediate perception the question remains how this perception is transformed into "significant cognition." Wasserman senses that perception *per se* is not enough and that between perception and poetic representation enters another mechanism, namely that of memory. On this subject Wasserman refers to Wordsworth and adds: "The stuff of the mind . . . is incorporated into memory."[21] He could have quoted Coleridge who, contrasting Philosophy and Poetry with Mathematics, writes: "Philosophy . . . concludes with the definition: it is the result, the compendium, the remembrances of all the preceding facts and inferences."[22] But, of course, perception and memory are not enough to produce a poetic image. The original perception stored in memory has to be combined with another function, namely imagination. Imagination is often read as sufficient recuperative supplement to memory. In Wasserman's argument memory remains unproblematic and only a necessary step towards the final poetical recuperation in poetry of an original perception. This view may be defensible in reading the way Wasserman does a poem such as "To a Highland Girl:" it may even be defensible in a reading of "Tintern Abbey." Nevertheless, if one locates these poems in relationship to the *Prelude* the function of memory in relation to poetical representation becomes considerably more complex. Not only does memory inscribe a necessary narrative moment within the lyrical moment but the function of narrative is to monumentalize elements that do not remain intact as they are translated through memory. The function of narrative is none other than to restitute in representation

Eugenio Donato

what of the original experience is lost through memory. In Wordsworth's
words:

> . . . The days gone by
> Return upon me almost from the dawn
> Of life: the hiding-places of man's power
> Open; I would approach them, but they close.
> I see by glimpses now; when age comes on,
> May scarcely see at all; and I would give,
> While yet we may, as far as words can give,
> Substance and life to what I feel, enshrining,
> Such is my hope, the spirit of the Past
> For future restoration.[23]
>
> 12, 277–86

Wasserman's argument is centered on the perception/memory/imagina-
tion system and understandably insofar as his ultimate implicit project
is to show that the Romantics epistemologically were successful in
recuperating what in another context de Man will call the "Natural
Object." De Man's project is, of course, the opposite of Wasserman's.
De Man, starting from the premise that a poetical representation is
necessarily a linguistic representation, convincingly demonstrates that
language cannot representionally recuperate the "Natural Object" and
hence that Romantic poetics are, in fact, centered around the nostalgia
for its loss. In his words, "Critics who speak of a 'happy relationship'
between matter and consciousness fail to realize that the very fact that
the relationship has to be established within the medium of language
indicates that it does not exist in actuality": hence, "The image is
inspired by a nostalgia for the natural object. . . . The existence of the
poetic image is itself a sign of divine absence, and the conscious use
of poetic imagery an admission of this absence."[24]

De Man does not quote Coleridge but he could have, for already
Coleridge had sensed some of the problems raised by linguistic
representation. In "On Poesy or Art," for example, Coleridge writes:

Still, however, poetry can only act through the intervention of articulate
speech, which is so peculiarly human that in all languages it constitutes the
ordinary phrase by which man and nature are contradistinguished.
. . . As soon as the human mind is intelligibly addressed by an outward image
exclusively of articulate speech, so soon does art commence . . . so that not
the thing presented, but that which is re-presented by the thing, shall be the
source of pleasure.[25]

Coleridge's ultimate gesture might be recuperative, nevertheless, his
critical strength resides in his recognizing that linguistic representation
is necessarily metaphorical and that such a representational system
introduces a set of differences irreducible to absolute identity:

It is sufficient that philosophically we understand that in all imitation two elements must coexist, and not only coexist, but must be perceived as coexisting. These two constituent elements are likeness and unlikeness, or sameness and difference, and in all genuine creations of art there must be a union of these disparates. The artist may take his point of view where he pleases, provided that the desired effect be perceptibly produced,—that there be likeness in the difference, difference in the likeness, and a reconcilement of both in one.[26]

It should be clear by now that what I shall call the "lyric moment" is a metaphorical construct based on representation that goes from the "Natural Object" to the final linguistic re-presentation via a system that combines perception/memory/imagination. I have tried to show elsewhere the problems raised by each of these terms in Romantic poetry and how in specific texts one can find the allegorization of the way each of these terms fails to maintain the mechanism of identity necessary to "re-cuperate" the "Natural Object" and how in fact each of the terms implies a tropological mechanism of re-presentation. I have also tried to show that the canonic form of the paradigm is given to us by Hegel for whom, allowing for some simplification, the system takes form: Intuition (Hegel's equivalent for perception)/Representation (*Vorstellung*)/Recollection (*Erinnerung*)/Representation Proper/Imagination/Allegory/Sign/Memory (*Gedächtnis*)/Speech/Concept. Without analysing the complete system in detail, I should like to simply underscore a few of the problems raised by some of these terms in particular and by the broader paradigm in general.

To begin with, the immediacy of the object is lost in the first of the terms, namely intuition. Intuition introduces from the beginning a temporal displacement: "In representation mind *has* intuition; the latter is *ideally present* in mind, it has not vanished or merely *passed away*. Therefore, when speaking of an intuition that has been raised to a representation, language is quite correct in saying I *have* seen this." Hegel will predictably dialectically reduce the temporal displacement to a spatial identity. Nevertheless, by translating Hegel into another language we can say a temporal narrative structure is inscribed in the spatial moment of perception. Significantly Hegel will mark this inextricable interrelationship of spatial and temporal elements in representation the very mark of modernity: "In this use of the word 'have' can be seen a sign of the inwardness of the modern mind, which makes the reflection, not merely that the past in its immediacy has passed away but also that in mind the past is still preserved."[27]

However, the more critical term in Hegel's system is *Erinnerung*, which is more akin to Wordsworth's memory than *Gedächtnis*, which is a linguistic, archival, non-subjective memory. If *Erinnerung* is central to the Hegelian system of representation *Erinnerung* is also central to Hegel's concept of history. At the end of the *Phenomenology, Erinnerung* becomes the condition by which history recapitalizes itself and transcends itself into absolute knowledge, i.e., philosophical discourse:

The goal, which is Absolute Knowledge or Spirit Knowing itself as Spirit, finds its pathway in the recollection of spiritual forms as they are in themselves and as they accomplish the organization of their spiritual kingdom. Their conservation, looked at from the side of their free existence appearing in the form of contingency, is *History*; looked at from the side of their intellectually comprehended organization, it is the Science of the ways in which Knowledge appears.

And it is no accident that at this precise point in his argument Hegel should resort again to the metaphor of the Death of God in its Christian redemptive form:

Both together, or History intellectually comprehended, form at once the recollection and the Golgotha of Absolute Spirit, the reality, the truth, the certainty of its throne, without which it were lifeless, solitary, and alone. Only
> The chalice of this realm of spirits
> Foams forth to God His own Infinitude.[28]

It is around the concept of *Erinnerung* then that narrative and representation become mutually interdependent, the paradigm of one determines the nature of the other. If the function of the Christian metaphor of Death and resurrection provides the possibility of a redemptive narrative history, that same redemptive history will make a final recuperative representational system possible. Conversely, the postulation of a non-redemptive scheme for narrative and history will radically question the recuperative possibilities of representation.

It is no accident that in the *Encyclopaedia*, in describing its representational system, Hegel's metaphors associated with *Erinnerung* should be metaphors of burial and entombment. *Erinnerung* transforms intelligence into a "night-like mine or pit" or a "subconscious mine." Hegel concludes his discussion of *Erinnerung* by stating "No one knows what an infinite host of images of the past slumbers in him; now and then they do indeed accidentally awake, but one cannot as it is said call them to mind."[29] It is interesting to note that Kojève in one of the most important commentaries to the *Phenomenology* should see in *Erinnerung* the threat of nihilism. What if the recollected should never be brought up to consciousness, what if one should forget what is forgotten or to borrow Hegel's metaphor, what if what is entombed should never be resurrected. This danger of nihilism inherent in *Erinnerung* might perhaps help us read Nietzsche's call for an active forgetfulness as a critical gesture towards Hegel, but that is beyond the scope of this paper.

With Hegel we do not have to fear the threat of nihilism. The same dialectic of sublation that permits him to resurrect history into philosophy will permit him to resurrect the representations buried by *Erinnerung* into symbol and sign and eventually the sign itself will have to be elevated to the status of philosophical ideality, a concept without body or, rather, having the transparent matter, the free status of a glorified body. In Hegel's terms a philosophical ideality is "The negation of the real which is nevertheless conserved and maintained in a virtual fashion (*virtualiter erhalter*) even if it does not exist."[30]

What one might begin to suspect is that the very model of the Hegelian dialectic is based on the Christian metaphor of death and resurrection. That which is sublated has to first be negated and maintained in its sublated form only as a negation of its original actuality. As Derrida has so forcefully stated, the Hegelian dialectic is a "theory of death," being "the thought that masters corruption and death, the determination of negativity and its conversion in the power of work and of production, the capacity to assume the contradictory and sublation as the very process of the self-conception of Truth and of the Subject." As we said earlier, the dialectical process must not only sublate Nature and History but linguistic representation as well.

To quote Derrida again, for Hegel "Natural language carries and touches in itself the sign of its own death, its body has the property to resonate and in so doing to elevate its natural corpse to the level of the concept, to universalize it and nationalize it during the time of its decomposition."[31]

It should be obvious that to question the redemptive possibility of the metaphor of the Death of God is to question the redemptive possibility of the dialectic in general. Such a critical project, be it in Flaubert or in Derrida, will necessarily consist of showing that any attempt to sublate "The Real," "The Natural Object," or "language" always erects their texts as the allegories of funerary monuments that hide the decomposing corpses that lie within them.

Let us return briefly, however, to the problem of Romantic poetics. Hegel's philosophical idealities have an equivalent in a number of statements of the Romantics regarding the function of poetic speech to transform nature into something of a spiritual nature, in Keats' words, "symbol essences," in Wordsworth's happier expression—"spiritual presences":

> . . . by contemplating these Forms [i.e., of Nature]
> In his relation which they bear to man
> We shall discern, how through the various means
> Which silently they yield, are multiplied
> The *spiritual* presences of absent things.[32]

The most striking statement about the redemptive function of poetry is Wordsworth's attributing to the imagination of the capacity to transform Nature into the

> Characters of the great Apocalypse
> The types and symbols of Eternity
> Of first, and last, and midst and without end.
>
> 6, 638–40

Wasserman may be too hasty in identifying Wordsworth's epistemological wishes with Keats' poetical enterprise. If I may digress for a moment, the lines that precede the preceding verses which describe a privileged nature in the Simplon pass are often read by critics—including de Man —as one of the most successful poetical attempts by Wordsworth to poetically recapture a transcendental nature. Wordsworth's description reads:

> ... The immeasurable height
> Of woods decaying, never to be decayed,
> The stationary blasts of waterfalls,
> And in the narrow rent at every turn
> Winds thwarting winds, bewildered and forlorn,
> The torrents shooting from the clear blue sky,
> The rocks that muttered close upon our ears,
> Black drizzling crags that spake by the wayside
> As if a voice were in them, the sick sight
> And giddy prospect of the raving stream,
> The unfettered clouds and region of the Heavens,
> Tumult and peace, the darkness and the light—
> Were all like workings of one mind, the features
> Of the same face, blossoms upon one tree;
>
> 6, 624–37

Leaving aside the fact that the lines are inspired by Milton, Wordsworth's strategy beyond imagination is to place his Nature and his Text into a transcendental voice—"As if a voice were in them"—it is the ideality of the *voice* that guarantees the ultimate identification of Poetical idiom and Nature.[33] Curiously, at the beginning of Book 2 of "Hyperion" Keats has a similar passage also inspired by Milton:

> It was a den where no insulting light
> Could glimmer on their tears; where their own groans
> They felt, but heard not, for the solid roar
> Of thunderous waterfalls and torrents hoarse,
> Pouring a constant bulk, uncertain where.
> Crag jutting forth to crag, and rocks that seemed
> Ever as if just rising from a sleep,
> Forehead to forehead held their monstrous horns;
> And thus in thousand hugest fantasies
> Made a fit roofing to this nest of woe.
>
> 2, 5–15

Keats denies light to his scene and drowns the voice of the Titans in the meaningless *noise* of Nature. The poetical rendition remains then either a vision inadequate to its object or states the incapacity of such a Nature to idealize itself in poetry. In either case, Keats' project can be read as an unintentional rebuttal of Wordsworth's poetic strategy.[34]

Wordsworth, nonetheless, is particularly interesting because, as I said earlier, his poetical enterprise is articulated around the *Lyrical Ballads* and the *Prelude*. The related quests for a lyrical moment and a redemptive narration parallel Hegel's enterprise. Like Hegel at the end of the *Prelude*, Wordsworth will have his version of the ascent of the Golgotha in his climb of Mount Snowdon. It is the climb of Mount Snowdon, which by recollecting past memories, will make the narrative of the *Prelude* possible and ultimately, though retrospectively, ground the *Lyrical Ballads*. It is also during this climb of Mount Snowdon that he discovers Nature's capacity to resurrect itself into a spiritual timeless body:

> . . . which Nature thus
> To bodily sense exhibits, is the express
> Resemblance of that glorious faculty
> That higher minds bear with them as their own.
> This is the very spirit in which they deal
> With the whole compass of the universe:
> They from their native selves can send abroad
> Kindred mutations; for themselves create
> A like existence; and, whene'er it dawns
> Created for them, catch it, or are caught
> By its inevitable mastery,
> Like angels stopped upon the wing by sound
> Of harmony from Heaven's remotest spheres.
> Them the enduring and the transient both
> Serve to exalt; they build up greatest things
> From least suggestions; ever on the watch,
> Willing to work and to be wrought upon,
> They need not extraordinary calls
> To rouse them; in a world of life they live,
> By sensible impressions not enthralled,
> But by their quickening impulse made more prompt
> To hold fit converse with the spiritual world,
> And with the generations of mankind
> Spread over time, past, present, and to come,
> Age after age, till Time shall be no more.
>
> 14, 88–111

Nevertheless, it is worth noticing that even the recuperative lyrical stance generated by a redemptive narrative produces only a "resemblance" and "emblem"—"There I beheld the emblem of a mind"—and not the "object," the "experience," their nature, or their essence.

There is no doubt that Wordsworth strives to be a redemptive poet.

Nevertheless, as I said earlier what makes him interesting is the constant insistence throughout his poetry that the poetic act may fail. Even the climb of Mount Snowdon is not without shadows. The scene takes place at night by the reflected indirect light of the moon in front of a metaphorical abyss—"A fixed abysmal gloomy, breathing-place." It could be argued, in fact, that Wordsworth's constant metaphysical assertions are a necessarily repeated answer to the constant threat of a non-redemptive history. Be that as it may, it will not be long after Wordsworth that Keats will question the status of poetical vision and ask whether the language of poetry belongs to the poet or the visionary. Minimally in "Hyperion" and "The Fall of Hyperion," Keats will dramatically question any possibility of a redemptive history and assert once and for all that "We fall by course of Nature's law."

Before leaving this subject I should like to return once more, to Wasserman's article, "The English Romantics: the Grounds of Knowledge." Wasserman begins his article by invoking Humpty Dumpty's "principle of semantic wages" and for fear that we use the word Romanticism—(at "a good deal of extra pay")—he rhetorically shies away from using the expression and declares instead his subject to be the epistemologies of Wordsworth, Coleridge, Keats and Shelley. Since the publication of Wasserman's article in 1964 we have not only learned to be less coy but, in fact—after Bloom, Szondi, Nancy, Lacoue-Labarthe, etc.—have come to realize the necessity of defining the novelty of Romanticism.

Perhaps instead of invoking Lewis Carroll Wasserman should have gone further back to the original narrative of the nursery rhyme. If the Romantics inaugurated a new literary problematic the latter is perhaps related to the belated recognition that the "Natural Object" like Humpty Dumpty "had a great fall" and remains, hopelessly, shattered in fragments. If a Wordsworth might have had the nostalgia for a redemptive history that could put the pieces of Humpty Dumpty together again, a Keats, a Shelley, or a Hölderlin point to such a redemptive history as a theological mirage leaving us with the recognition that "All the King's horses and all the King's men could not put Humpty together again."

What is important for us to understand is that the shattering of Humpty Dumpty was the necessary prior condition for his tale to be told and repeated generation after generation. That necessary repetition constitutes *our* belatedness and the most important legacy of our Romantic heritage.

[There was] . . . a time when an Egyptian priest was still reproaching Solon that "the Greeks remained forever adolescent"! And us, us more

Divine Agonies

intelligent than all those superb dead, are here having become old men.
Hölderlin

How long will this posthumous life of mine last.
Keats

If one may be allowed a bold generalization, critics have been more generous to Wordsworth, in attempting to read his poetical project by relating the *Prelude* to the rest of his lyrical output, than to Keats. Keats' project seems to have troubled critics who, on the whole, tend to valorize the Odes and dismiss the "Hyperion" and "The Fall of Hyperion" fragments as ambitious failures. Wordsworth's and Keats' projects are, curiously, similar. The "Hyperion" fragments—especially if one takes into account their relationship to an early text such as "Sleep and Poetry"—frame Keats' poetical output in the same way that the *Prelude* frames Wordsworth's. The parallel is even more striking if one considers that in both cases the longer poems are retrospective attempts to ground and justify the rest of both poets' output. The difference is not in the form of the projects but in the fact that the *Prelude*, even though in its own way a "fragment," is a "completed poem," or more exactly a "closed poem," which by a final redemptive gesture provides a genetic narrative for the rest of Wordsworth's works. In the case of Keats, "Hyperion" and "The Fall of Hyperion" not only remain fragments but raise the problem as to whether they can be "closed" in a Wordsworthian sense. Ultimately, it is easy to understand why critics have focused on Wordsworth's poetical project and read it in its intentional unity since it permitted them to use—in an explicit or implicit fashion—the redemptive scheme of the narrative of the *Prelude* to read in a recuperative key the rest of Wordsworth's poetical output. It is the same critical stance that has forced the division of Keats' canon into two distinct groups of poems the "successful" Odes and the failed "fragments." In this respect and in the context of the problem of the relationship of narrative structure to poetical representation, it would hardly be an exaggeration to say that Keats' odes have been read mainly in the perspective of Wordsworth's poetics.

The more fundamental question that could be raised is why Keats' narrative poems are fragments and if their failure at narrative closure is accidental or intrinsic to the Keatsian poetical project and, in the latter case, what are the consequences of the impossibility of a redemptive narrative scheme for the poetics of a Keats, in particular, and for the later Romantics as well. In other words, the question I wish to raise is to what extent Keats' poetical project constitutes a critical reading of Wordsworth, and more generally, to what extent the narrative exigencies of Romantic poetry rendered vain the hopes for a lyrical idiom that would embody the transparent transfigured presence of the "natural object."

"Sleep and Poetry" represents Keats' first attempt to provide a narrative ground for his poetical enterprise. The poems contain two long narrative sequences. The first relates the motif that will inspire the young poet from ". . . the realm . . . /Of Flora, and old Pan" (101–2) to the "nobler life/Where I may find agonies, the strife/Of human hearts" (123–24). The second comprises a brief history of poetry in England, where Keats, after assuming the Wordsworthian critique of eighteenth century English poetical idiom, sees hope for a new poetry: ". . . let me think away those times of woe:/Now 'tis a fairer season; yet have breathed/Rich benedictions o'er us; ye have wreathed/Fresh garlands: for sweet music has been heard/In many places" (220–23). Both narrative sequences define the young poet's belated position, nevertheless, on the surface this belatedness does not seem problematical: ". . . there ever rolls/A vast idea before me, and I glean/Therefrom my liberty; thence too I've seen/The end and aim of Poesy" (240–43). Yet even the youthful optimism of Keats does not lend itself to be read as the assertion of the possibility of a poetic idiom which will somehow generate representations adequate to their objects. At best the poet's words will "echo back the voice of thine [Poesy's] own tongue" (52), and thus become the repeated, secondary copies of an original voice. The image of poetical idiom as echo will naturally lead Keats to treat his poetical enterprise as that of copying from a book in which the natural object is *metaphorically displaced*: "if I can bear/The o'erwhelming sweets, 'twill bring to me the fair/Visions of all places: a bowery nook/Will be elysium—an eternal book/Whence I may copy many a lovely saying" (61–65). The vision of the poetical object is not an "original" one. The poet transcribes a vision which is itself a text since it is a metaphorical translation of the "natural object." It is not surprising, then, that the poem should end in a library where the visions are gathered in a portfolio: "Thus I remember all the pleasant flow/Of words at opening a portfolio" (337–38) or else to decipher the engraved visions that adorn the walls of the library. The poem in the last analysis, then, states the impossibility of grounding poetical language in or on a "natural object." The language of poetry will only be the translation of a metaphor that is itself a translation. Hence the central theme of the poem is the fact that there is no way for the poet to distinguish between the "visions" he creates and those that come to him in his sleep. The undecidability of the two types of visions will eventually constitute the opening lines of "The Fall of Hyperion."

Let us return for a moment to "Sleep and Poetry." The decisive moment of the failure of the poetic act besides being thematically stated in the poem is, in fact, allegorized in one of the central themes to which we alluded earlier. Keats compares the poetical act with the possibility of identifying with Apollo, himself being a metaphor of an original sun. The failure of the poet will be the failure of Icarus to reach Apollo. Icarus with whom the poet identifies fails as the belated son—and here one might complicate the problem further by insisting on the inevitable pun Sun/Son—attempting his father's impossible project. The poet's genealogical belatedness is redoubled since Apollo, rather than an absolute origin, will be the temporally belated Sun/Son—replacing an earlier Hyperion in a game of substitutions. Icarus is no more the proper name of the poet than the belated Apollo is the proper name for the Sun. Derrida's argument that the sun is a metaphor, i.e., the metaphor that states the possibility of metaphor, is well known.[35] The gesture of the poet will be that of attempting to grasp the original metaphorical constitution of poetical language. Such a gesture will, of course, be doomed to failure. The poet like Icarus will be burned by his proximity to the original metaphoricity of metaphor.

> Lifted to the white clouds. Therefore should I
> Be but the essence of deformity,
> A coward, did my very eye-lids wink
> At speaking out what I have dared to think.
> Ah! rather let me like a madman run
> Over some precipice! let the hot sun
> Melt my Dedalian wings, and drive me down
> Convulsed and headlong! Say! an inward frown
> Of conscience bids me be more calm awhile.
> An ocean dim, sprinkled with many an isle,
> Spreads awfully before me. How much toil!
> How many days! what desperate turmoil!
> Ere I can have explored its widenesses.
> Ah, what a task! upon my bended knees,
> I could unsay those—no, impossible!
> Impossible!
>
> (300–312)

The possibility of the Keatsian poetical idiom is rooted in this impossibility. The "natural object" will, in fact, be the constructed product that will result from the poet's death as a remembrance of his failed gesture: "If I do fall, at least I will be laid/Beneath the silence of a poplar shade;/And over me the grass shall be smoothed-shaven;/And there shall be a kind memorial graven" (277–80).[36] The failure of the poetical act, nevertheless, is more radical than the poet's incapacity to reach Apollo. If Apollo as sun represents the original metaphoricity of metaphor as Derrida reminds us, such an origin never gives itself but leaves at the origin its own death in the belated metaphors of beginnings.

Returning to the poem, the lengthy description of Apollo/Sun appears in a lengthy passage that follows one of the many resolves of Keats to undertake the writing of poetry—"Yes, I must pass them [these joys] for a nobler life" (123). As it is well known after Ian Jack's book on Keats' use of the plastic arts, the passage describing Apollo in fact transcribes Poussin's painting "The Realm of Flora."[37] Apollo/Sun then is already a pictorial representation, that is, a textual metaphor. Apollo as poetical origin has already died in a representation that the poet can only transcribe. In this sense the "Hyperion" and "The Fall of Hyperion" fragments are only funerary genealogies of an "always already" dead Apollo—which condemns any poetic idiom to the role of funerary renovation. The poet cannot escape his idiom's being this twice displaced representation of a metaphor. The confrontation of poetical language with "real things" being by definition a representational impossibility.

> The visions all are fled—the car is fled
> Into the light of heaven, and in their stead
> A sense of real things comes doubly strong,
> And, like a muddy stream, would bear along
> My soul to nothingness.
>
> (155–59)

The "muddy stream" resists being transcribed into the idiom of poetry or more exactly the otherness of the muddy stream does not allow for the vision to transform itself into poetical language.

"Sleep and Poetry" had already defined Apollo through a twice displaced metaphor as the origin of poetry and suggested the impossibility of the poet to identify his idiom with such an origin. "Hyperion" and "The Fall of Hyperion" will radicalize this question by attempting to write the narrative genealogy of Apollo. Such a narrative will be impossible because Apollo rather than an absolute origin will be only one name in an infinite series of displacements, but conversely the infinite series of displacements at the origin will render the closure of narrative impossible.

Inasmuch as the genealogy of Apollo can only be written from the standpoint of his belated appearance, the modern poet's attempt at writing an epic of origins is doomed from the start, and in at least one sense "Hyperion" and "The Fall of Hyperion" are not failures but poems about the necessary failure of a certain type of poetry and inasmuch as they state above all the impossibility of a certain type of narrative poetry their fragmentary nature is intrinsic to the poems:

> O leave them, Muse! O leave them to their woes;
> For thou art weak to sing such tumults dire:
> A solitary sorrow best befits
> Thy lips, and antheming a lonely grief.
> Leave them, O Muse! for thou anon wilt find

Divine Agonies

> Many a fallen old Divinity
> Wandering in vain about bewildered shores.
>> "Hyperion," 3 (3–9)

The new belated poetry will be the poetry of the belated God Apollo. Apollo's poetry is inextricably tied to memory—"Mnemosyne!/Thy name is on my tongue," "Hyperion," (82–83). Mnemosyne, however, is silent. Apollo's divinity like his poetry is based on the possibility of reading the "mute" memories held by Mnemosyne. In other words, the belated poetry of Apollo is the repetition, the re-memorization of a dead past that persists representationally only with the ambigious status of silent memories:

> Mute thou remainest—mute! yet I can read
> A wondrous lesson in thy silent face:
> Knowledge enormous makes a God of me.
> Names, deeds, grey legends, dire events, rebellions,
> Majesties, sovran voices, agonies,
> Creations and destroyings, all at once
> Pour into the wide hollows of my brain,
> And deify me, as if some blithe wine
> Or bright elixir peerless I had drunk,
> And so become immortal.
>> "Hyperion," 3 (111–20)

It is thus from the perspective of Apollo that the tale of the earlier God is told. As I suggested, such a tale properly told would be a genealogical narrative of origins and as such an impossible tale to tell. Hence both fragments will begin the fable of the fallen Gods with the description of an already fallen Saturn transformed into funerary statuary— ". . . postured motionless,/Like natural sculpture in cathedral caverns," "Hyperion," 1 (85–86). The poetical idiom that will describe this "natural sculpture" will be an inadequate translation of the language of mourning for a "death" that necessarily precedes the narrative. "Some mourning words, which in our feeble tongue/Would come in these like accents (O how frail/To that large utterance of the early Gods!)," "Hyperion," 1 (49–51).

The poet's attempt at forcing his idiom on such an unrepresentable event can only violently restate his necessarily belated position.

> O aching time! O moments big as years!
> All as ye pass swell out the monstrous truth,
> And press it so upon our weary griefs
> That unbelief has not a space to breathe.
> Saturn, sleep on—O thoughtless, why did I
> Thus violate thy slumbrous solitude?
>> "Hyperion," 1 (64–69)

The nostalgic possibility of a new origin and a final eschatology is raised and then rejected in the *Hyperion*—"Cannot I fashion forth/Another

Eugenio Donato

world, another universe," "Hyperion," 1 (142–43). "Yes, there must be a golden victory," "Hyperion," 1 (126).

The law of the narrative will be stated by Oceanus: "And first, as thou wast not the first of powers,/So art thou not the last; it cannot be: Thou art not the beginning nor the end," "Hyperion," 2 (188–90), thus creating an exigency for a continuous displacement without beginning or end:

> ... For 'tis the eternal law
> That first in beauty should be first in might.
> Yea, by that law, another race may drive
> Our conquerors to mourn as we do now.
> "Hyperion," 2 (288–31)

The Apollonian moment, then, is not privileged but represents only one instance in a continuous play of substitutions. The unnarratable fall of the Gods constitutes thus the impossible present of the text. Appropriately, Oceanus who states the law of the text will be called a "Sophist and sage." In "The Fall of Hyperion" this law will be stated in a more direct way through the description of the face of Moneta herself being in the later poem the text of memory.

> ... Then saw I a wan face,
> Not pined by human sorrows, but bright-blanched
> By an immortal sickness which kills not;
> It works a constant change, which happy death
> Can put no end to; deathwards progressing
> To no death was that visage; it had passed
> The lily and the snow; and beyond these
> I must not think now, though I saw that face.
> "The Fall of Hyperion," 1 (256–63)

The ambiguity of the text will stem, of course, from the fact that the non privilege of the Apollonian moment both stems and engenders the non privilege of the moment of Hyperion which precedes it. The statement of Hyperion:

> The blaze, the splendour, and the symmetry,
> I cannot see—but darkness, death and darkness.
> Even here, into my centre of repose,
> The shady visions come to domineer,
> Insult, and blind, and stifle up my pomp.—
> Fall!
> "Hyperion," 1 (241–46)

will prefigure the purely visionary nature of the belated poet's text. In a sense "The Fall of Hyperion" is, itself, a reading of "Hyperion."

If, throughout "Hyperion," Mnemosyne was "straying in the world," "The Fall of Hyperion" is constituted in great part by the poetical transcription of Mnemosyne's voice as well as by that of her belated Latin version Moneta, "The pale Omega of a withered race." Significantly, "The Fall of Hyperion" will never reach the Apollonian moment but end on the ambiguous temporal status of Hyperion.

"The Fall of Hyperion" can be read as a working out of the textual consequence of "Hyperion"—and of "Sleep and Poetry" as well. If the impossibility of a redemptive narrative makes it impossible for the idiom of poetry to be grounded in Nature or History, then what is the status of the poetical text?

"The Fall of Hyperion" begins with the question, what if any is the distinction between mere visions and poetry. At first there seems to be a simple answer: poetry is the transcription of visions. Yet the very nature of this transcription is defined by an impossible mixed metaphor:

> . . . Pity these have not
> Traced upon vellum or wild Indian leaf
> The shadows of melodious utterance.
> But bare of laurel they live, dream, and die;
> "The Fall of Hyperion," 1 (4–7)

Given the definition of poetry as the shadow of melodious utterance it is not surprising that the poet should leave open the question of deciding whether "The Fall of Hyperion" is the act of a poet or a visionary.

The poem stages this very ambiguity by transcribing a vision that takes place during the falling asleep of the narrator within another vision. Representationally, the text is the transcription of a twice displaced non-identical vision. One could complicate the problem further. If Ian Jack is right in assuming that Keats knew Bellini's "The Feast of the Gods," then the first vision describing the narrator eating the leftovers of a divine banquet, might locate the first vision in a modified version of Bellini's painting.[38]

It is not surprising then that finally the text should denounce itself as vision. Moneta addressing the poet states:

> What benefit canst thou do, or all thy tribe,
> To the great world? Thou art a dreaming thing,
> A fever of thyself. . .
> . . . .
> . . . Art thou not of the dreamer tribe?
> The poet and the dreamer are distinct,
> Diverse, sheer opposite, antipodes.
> The one pours out a balm upon the world,
> The other vexes it.
> "The Fall of Hyperion," 1 (167–69, 198–202)

One may well ask who, then, are the poets? The question is insoluble within the context of the "Hyperion" and "The Fall of Hyperion" fragments. What is important, however, is that Keats should follow the preceding verses with an attack on lyrical poets, suggesting the impossibility of a successful lyrical idiom.

> . . . Then shouted I,
> Spite of myself, and with a Pythia's spleen,
> 'Apollo! faded, far-flown Apollo!
> Where is thy misty pestilence to creep
> Into the dwellings, through the door crannies,
> Of all mock lyricists, large self-worshippers
> And careless hectorers in proud bad verse.
> Though I breathe death with them it will be life
> To see them sprawl before me into graves.
> > "The Fall of Hyperion," 1 (202–10)

At any rate, the impossibility for the belated poet grounding his representations besides being dramatically reenacted through the tale of the falling of the Gods is also thematized in a more direct textual manner. When the narrator in his vision encounters the archeological remains of Saturn's temple he is forced to look west for:

> Turning from these with awe, once more I raised
> My eyes to fathom the space every way—
> The embossed roof, the silent massy range
> Of columns north and south, ending in mist
> Of nothing, then to eastward, where black gates
> Were shut against the sunrise evermore.
> Then to the west I looked, and saw far off
> An Image. . . .
> > "The Fall of Hyperion," 1 (81–89)

the belated poet is shut off from the origin of the rising sun and his gaze has to follow the direction of history and of the setting sun.

Hegel in his *Aesthetics* saw in the sound produced at sunrise by the colossi of Memnon the origin of art. Keats will identify his Hyperion with the same statuary and his idiom with the song they produce at dusk:

> . . . Hyperion: a granite peak. . . .
> . . . .
> . . . like the bulk
> Of Memnon's image at the set of sun
> To one who travels from the dusking East:
> Sighs, too, as mournful as that Memnon's harp,
> He uttered, while his hands contemplative
> He pressed together, and in silence stood.
> > "Hyperion," 2 (367, 373–78)

The belated poet is forever excluded from the possibility of recuperating a privileged origin. In its stead, always preceding his ungrounded idiom and his interminable narrative he encounters only the glyphs of a mute, lost, inaccessible original language:

... hieroglyphics old
Which sages and keen-eyed astrologers
Then living on the earth, with labouring thought
Won from the gaze of many centuries—
Now lost, save what we find on remnants huge
Of stone, or marble swart, their import gone,
Their wisdom long since fled.

"Hyperion," 1 (277–83)

Faced with the imperative of belatedness Keats will renounce the project of writing his version of a redemptive history and instead turn to Apollo and "touch piously the Delphic harp." At this juncture we may well ask whether Keats remembered another famous fragment which stated: "The master to whom the oracle of Delphi belongs, does not speak, does not hide, he makes signs"?[39]

NOTES

1. Georg Wilhelm Friedrich Hegel, *Faith and Knowledge*, trans. Walter Cerf and H. S. Harris (Albany: State University of New York Press, 1977), pp. 190–91. Incidentally, Heidegger in his "The Saying of Nietzsche 'God is Dead' " in his *Holzwege* will remind the reader that Pascal's statement comes from Plutarch. Heidegger then notes that Pascal's statement should belong to the same metaphysical space as Hegel's and Nietzsche's but for "opposite reasons." He does not, however, analyze what the "opposite reasons" are which presumably connect Pascal to Hegel or Nietzsche.

2. Johann Christoph Friedrich Schiller, "The Gods of Greece" in *The Poems of Schiller*, trans. Edgar A. Bowring (London: J. W. Parker, 1880), pp. 74–75.

3. See, for example, Szondi's reading of Hölderlin's hymn "Friedensfeier" in *Hölderlin-Studien Mit einem Traktat über philologische Erkenntnis* (Frankfort: Suhrkampf, 1977).

4. Nerval, of course, knew Jean-Paul's text directly and quoted it in the series of poems entitled "Le Christ aux Oliviers." For a brief summary of the influence of Jean-Paul on French romanticism see Jeanine Moulin's appendix to her edition of Nerval's *Les Chimères* (Geneva: Droz, 1969).

Nerval's version is interesting inasmuch as by problematizing the temporal sequence of the news of God's death in relationship to the event he prefigures Nietzsche's version of the topos:

[le Seigneur]. . . .
. . . se prit à crier: "Non, Dieu n'existe pas!"

Ils dormaient. "Mes amis, savez-vous *la nouvelle*?
J'ai touché de mon front à la voûte éternelle;
Je suis sanglant, brisé, souffrant pour bien des jours!
"Frères, je vous trompais: Abîme! abîme! abîme!
Le dieu manque à l'autel ou je suis la victime. . . .
Dieu n'est pas! Dieu n'est plus!" Mais ils dormaient toujours! . . .

5. Thomas Carlyle, *Critical and Miscellaneous Essays*, (Boston: Brown and Taggart, 1884), vol. 2, 133–34.

Eugenio Donato

6. Gustave Flaubert, *The Temptation of Saint Anthony*, trans. Lafcadio Hearn (New York: Houghton-Mifflin, 1943), p. 65.

7. Ibid., pp. 72–73.

8. Ibid., p. 75.

9. Ibid., p. 75.

10. Ibid., pp. 81–82.

11. Georg Wilhelm Friedrich Hegel, *The Phenomenology of Mind*, trans. J. B. Baillie (New York: Harper and Row, 1967), pp. 713–14.

12. Georg Wilhelm Friedrich Hegel, *Philosophy of Mind* in *The Encyclopaedia of the Philosophical Sciences*, trans. William Wallace (Oxford: Clarendon Press, 1971), pp. 211–12.

13. Friedrich Nietzsche, *The Joyful Wisdom*, trans. Thomas Common (New York: Ungar, 1960).

14. Paul de Man, "Nietzsche's Theory of Rhetoric," *Symposium* 28:1 (1974), 43.

15. I am, of course, referring to Derrida's analysis of the constitution of *Bedeutung* in Hegel in his "Les Puits et la pyramide" in *Marges de la philosophie* (Paris: Editions de Minuit, 1972).

16. For example, in his chapter on "European Nihilism," in his *Nietzsche*, Heidegger will write: "For that nihilism the saying 'God is Dead' signifies the powerlessness not only of the Christian God but for anything suprasensible to which man could or would wish to submit himself. This powerlessness consummates the ruin of the order that had prevailed until then." I will just quote one more example, among many, that show clearly Heidegger's strategy in reading Nietzsche: "Nietzsche speaks of 'European' Nihilism. By that he does not mean the positivism that establishes itself in the middle of the nineteenth century, nor its geographical expansion in Europe; 'European' here has a temporal signification equivalent to 'occidental' in the sense of history of the Occident. Nietzsche uses the term 'nihilism' to designate the temporal movement whose kingdom he was the first to recognize for the past as well as future centuries. He briefly defined its essential interpretation by these words 'God is Dead.' Which means: 'the Christian God' has lost its power over things and on the destination of man."

On the difficult problems raised by the reading of Nietzsche by Heidegger and particularly concerning the problem of Heidegger's neutralization of Nietzsche's *Darstellung*, see the works of Philippe Lacoue-Labarthe in particular his "Typographie" in *Mimesis des Articulations*, ed. Sylviane Agacinski (Paris: Aubier-Flammarion, 1975), pp. 165–270.

17. Earl R. Wasserman, "The English Romantics: The Grounds of Knowledge" in *Romanticism Points of View*, eds. Gleckner and Enscoe (Princeton: Princeton University Press, 1962), p. 335.

18. Joseph N. Riddel, "A Somewhat Polemical Introduction: The Elliptical Poem," *Genre* 11:4 (1978), 460, 463–64.

19. Quoted by Wasserman, "The English Romantics," p. 339.

20. Ibid., p. 334.

21. Ibid., p. 337.

22. Samuel Taylor Coleridge, "On the Principles of Genial Critcism" in *Biographia Literaria*, ed. J. Shawcross (Oxford: Clarendon Press, 1907), 2, 223.

23. All references to the *Prelude* will be to the 1850 version.

24. Paul de Man, "Intentional Structure of the Romantic Image," in

Divine Agonies

Romanticism and Consciousness, ed. Harold Bloom (New York: Norton, 1970), pp. 69, 70.

25. Coleridge, *Biographia Literaria*, 2, 254.

26. Ibid., p. 256.

27. Hegel, *Philosophy of Mind*, p. 201.

28. Hegel, *Phenomenology of Mind*, p. 808.

29. Hegel, *Philosophy of Mind*, p. 205.

30. Quoted by Derrida in "Le Puits et la pyramide," pp. 104–5.

31. Jacques Derrida, *Glas* (Paris: Editions Galilée, 1974), p. 16.

32. Quoted by Wasserman, "The English Romantics," p. 338.

33. Derrida's comment on the privilege of *voice* in Hegel is particularly significant in this context:

. . . objectivité et intériorité, qui ne s'opposent qu'en apparence, l'idéalisation ayant pour ses (de Platon à Husserl) de les confirmer simultanément l'un par l'autre.

Selon une métaphore coordonnée à tout le système de la métaphysique, seule l'ouïe, qui sauve à la fois l'objectivité et l'intériorité, peut-être dite pleinement idéelle et théorique. Elle est ainsi désignée, dans son excellence, suivant le langage optique (*idéa, theoria*).

Ce concept téléologique du son comme mouvement d'idéalisation, *Aufhebung* de l'extériorité naturelle, relève du visible dans l'audible, est, avec toute la philosophie de la nature, la présupposition fondamentale de l'interprétation hégélienne du langage, notamment de la partie dite matérielle de la langue, la lexicologie. ("Le Puits et la pyramide," pp. 108–9)

34. The opposition voice/noise will appear again in *The Fall of Hyperion*. Nature may have a voice but such a voice is the belated "legend-laden" voice of a past history. Nature's voice then is memory yet even this voice to the non-poets is only "barren noise." The function of the poet is to "humanize" the memorial voice of nature by "making comparisons," i.e., creating metaphors, and it is only *through* these metaphors that the voice of nature acquires the semblance of a memorial narrative:

> Mortal, that thou mayst understand aright,
> I humanize my sayings to thine ear,
> Making comparisons of earthly things;
> Or thou mightst better listen to the wind,
> Whose language is to thee a barren noise,
> Though it blows legend-laden through the trees—
> In melancholy realms big tears are shed,
> More sorrow-like to this, and such-like woe,
> Too huge for mortal tongue, or pen or scribe.
>
> "Hyperion," 2 (1–9)

All references to the poems of Keats are to *Poems*, ed. John Barnard (Harmondsworth: Penguin, 1973).

35. In Derrida's words, from "La Mythologie blanche," *Poetique* 5 (1971), 36:

Chaque fois qu'il y a une métaphore, il y a sans doute un soleil quelque part; mais chaque fois qu'il y a du soleil, la métaphore a commencé. Si le soleil est métaphorique déjà, toujours, il n'est plus tout à fait naturel.

Eugenio Donato

Il est déjà, toujours, un lustre, on dirait une construction artificielle si l'on pouvait encore accréditer cette signification quand la nature a disparu.

36. These lines will be echoed in some of the last words spoken by Keats on his deathbed to his friend Severn:

Four days previous to his death—the change in him was so great that I passed each moment in dread—not knowing what the next would have —he was calm and firm at its approaches—to a most astonishing degree —he told me not to tremble for he did not think that he should be convulsed—he said—"did you ever see any one die" no—"well then I pity you poor Severn—what trouble and danger you have got into for me—now you must be firm for it will not last long—I shall soon be laid in the quiet grave—thank God for the quiet grave—O! I can feel the cold earth upon me—the daisies growing over me—O for this quiet—it will be my first.

From *The Letters of John Keats*, ed. Hyder E. Rollins (Cambridge: At the University Press, 1958), p. 378.

37. Ian Jack, *Keats and the Mirror of Art* (Oxford: Clarendon Press, 1967), particularly pages 176–90.

38. Ibid., p. 127.

39. *The Fragments of the Work of Heraclitus of Ephesus on Nature*, trans. G. T. W. Patrick (Baltimore: Murray, 1889). Fragment no. 93.

READING TASTING
David Marshall

XIII

XIII

1 Voller Apfel, Birne und Banane,
2 Stachelbeere. . . . Alles dieses spricht
3 Tod und Leben in den Mund. . . . Ich ahne. . . .
4 Lest es einem Kind vom Angesicht,

5 wenn es sie erschmeckt. Dies kommt von weit.
6 Wird euch langsam namenlos im Munde?
7 Wo sonst Worte waren, fliessen Funde,
8 aus dem Fruchtfleisch überrascht befreit.

9 Wagt zu sagen, was ihr Apfel nennt.
10 Diese Süsse, die sich erst verdichtet,
11 um, im Schmecken leise aufgerichtet,

12 klar zu werden, wach und transparent,
13 doppeldeutig, sonnig, erdig, hiesig—:
14 O Erfahrung, Fühlung, Freude—, riesig!

XIII

1 Full-round apple, pear and banana,
2 Gooseberry. . . . All this speaks
3 death and life in the mouth. . . . I sense. . . .
4 Read it from the face of a child

5 when it tastes them. This comes from far.
6 Does it happen to you slowly, nameless, in the mouth?

7   Where once words were, findings flow,
8   out of the fruit's flesh surprised and set free.

9   Dare to say what you name apple.
10 This sweetness, first concentrating,
11 in order, in the tasting lightly raised,

12 to become clear, awake and transparent,
13 double-meaning'd, sunny, earthy, here and now—:
14 O experience, feeling, joy—, immense![1]

> O pour moi seul, à moi seul, en moi même,
> Auprès d'un coeur, aux sources du poème,
> Entre le vide et l'événement pur . . .
> Paul Valéry, "Le Cimetière marin"

I would like to write about Rainer Maria Rilke's Thirteenth Sonnet to Orpheus, where Rilke seems to write about the experience of tasting fruit; but in a letter written to his Polish translator in 1925, Rilke complains:

To our grandparents a "house," a "well," a tower familiar to them, even their own dress, their cloak, was still infinitely more, infinitely more intimate [Noch für unsere Großeltern war ein "Haus", ein "Brunnen", ein vertrauter Turm, ja ihr eigenes Kleid, ihr Mantel unendlich vertraulicher]: almost each thing a vessel in which they found something human and into which they set aside something human. Now, from America, empty indifferent things are crowding over to us, sham things [Schein-Dinge], *dummies of life* [*Lebens-Attrappen*]. . . . A house, in the American understanding, an American apple or a grapevine there, has *nothing* in common with the house, the fruit, the grape, into which went the hopes and meditations of our forefathers. . . .[2]

Faced with this citation, how can I, an American, attempt to interpret, even describe, what Rilke seems to describe: namely, the experience of tasting a piece of fruit. As an American speaker and reader and taster who calls "apple" what Rilke calls "Apfel," can I dare say that I know or feel the experience Rilke calls "Schmecken"? Wouldn't the modern, American apple that I experience "im amerikanischen Verstande" have more in common with what Rilke calls (in the Fifth Duino Elegy) a "Scheinfrucht" (a "sham-fruit") than with the more meaningful fruit that is the object of Rilke's nostalgia? But the problem is a double one, for the loss of "Haus" is accompanied by the loss of " 'Haus' "; we are faced with a problem of language. This has been implied already by our American understanding; even if I could taste the fruit Rilke imagines his grandparents tasting, I would still read the sonnet in a foreign language. Could I translate Rilke's poem into my own language, say it in my own words, call his experience by an American name? Or could I, or even one more versed in and more familiar with the German tongue than myself, adequately enter Rilke's language to sense what he is saying? And even if one could understand the poem as a native speaker understands it, still, could one say it in one's own words?

Rilke (who lived most of his life as a foreigner) has inscribed himself within this problem, too, for he places himself in a world already afflicted by empty American things—where words, much less things, are no longer "infinitely more." Even without the expectation of an American reader, how could Rilke hope and think he could fully taste a thing called an apple and express that experience in words? For we are all in the same position, we are all in some sense American readers: we can not know the thing itself that Rilke tried to know. Reading a poem, we are faced with things that appear only as *Schein-Dinge*, that seem to be things, expressed in a language whose meaning perhaps grows alien to us, even as it grows more familiar; a language whose fullness and intimacy and ability to name things has been called into question. Can we come to know the experience, the "Erfahrung," Rilke tries to translate into words, can it be told to us, or is it something we must learn, discover ourselves? What experience must we ourselves undergo to understand the experience of the poem? Can we know that experience, and if we can, can we identify it, give it a name?

Let us continue to read the poem, with the risk that our American understanding might not rise to the occasion. We find that regardless of our language or our knowledge of apples, our understanding is threatened by a sense of incomprehensibility within the poem itself. Although we may feel we know what the poem says, the poem challenges our perception by bordering on incoherency; its borders, syntactically incomplete phrases, are barely coherent lists of words. (In a sense, we could say that the sonnet is "about" the creation of lists.) Between these boundaries are fragments, abrupt shifts, and changes in direction. More than half of the poem's lines make up incomplete phrases or sentences, most elaborately in the last five lines where we read a sentence whose intricate and suspended syntax gets lost, breaks off, and becomes a list of words—a list which is itself interrupted by another list—which is in turn interrupted and ended by the final word of the poem (which, as a formal sonnet, must inevitably, and just in time, end at this [exclamation] point).

Perhaps this can be explained by the common characterization of the inspired Rilke quickly, excitedly, and emotionally overflowing with the joys of eating fruit. On the other hand, the beginning of this rhymed, deliberate, and complex sonnet, while not quite coherent, is not at all excited or rushed. The first line and the few phrases that follow are balanced, slow, slowed down by the recurring marks of ellipsis that open up the poem and insert silences. We wonder what has been left out as one thought suddenly follows another; there is a sense that the poet doesn't know how to begin (or continue) the sonnet, that he ends by accumulating a series of false (or parallel) starts. Positions and points of view shift and hardly hold together. At first we see "Voller Apfel, Birne und Banane,/Stachelbeere. . . ." (1–2) as we would see a still-life, an arrangement of different objects juxtaposed on a surface. The next phrase, "Alles dieses spricht/Tod und Leben in den Mund. . . ." (2–3), coming out of the pause of the ellipsis, confuses us, forces us to shift perspective; for we must imagine all these fruits in a mouth, though it would be grotesque to see them there all at once. But before we figure this out, "Ich ahne. . . ." (3) surfaces out of another silence, only to disappear in a direct address to readers: "Lest es einem Kind vom Angesicht,/wenn es sie erschmeckt" (4–5).

At this point in reading the poem we are faced with more than a problem of coherency. As we begin to surmise that someone is tasting in the poem, we lose all sense of *who* is tasting. As we suspect the experience of the poem, we find ourselves at a loss to locate that experience. The appearance of a grammatical first person suggests the subject of the poem but this "ich" implicitly places the reader opposite him as a second person, a partner in dialogue; and as this is made explicit (in line four) and as the reader seems to become present in the poem, we are simultaneously confronted with a third person, a child who is tasting fruit. Part of the ambiguity lies in the impersonality of the expression "in den Mund" which is echoed in the "im Munde" of line six, where suddenly an "euch" suggests that the mouth and the tasting belong to the reader. (Then, of course, as the poem continues, it is the poet who seems to be experiencing the tasting, as if it were occuring in his mouth.)

Who is tasting here; in whose mouth is this experience happening? Does every reader addressed by this "euch" share the same experience? It seems that we are being told to read someone else's experience, to interpret what is in a person's mouth from what is expressed on his face; and within the space of four words, we seem to be having the experience ourselves. The speech (line two) of the fruit in the mouth becomes translated into the text of a face or countenance. This text expresses an inner experience and in reading it, reading seems to translate into the experience itself; and although that experience would seem to be called ours, the text (the narrative voice) seems to describe it in detail. Do we find ourselves reading the text of our own experience, looking at ourselves? Where is Rilke in all this? Who are we reading, and who is reading whom? This transformation of pronouns (what appear instead of names), preventing us from fixing the experience in any one place, is reflected even in the "es" of "Lest es einem Kind vom

Angesicht,/wenn es sie erschmeckt" (4–5). The "es" changes meaning in the time and space of dropping from line four to line five, switching designations so easily we hardly notice.

The confusion of reading and experiencing and the transformation of one into the other are implicitly suggested in the second phrase of the poem: "Alles dieses spricht/Tod und Leben in den Mund. . . ." (2–3); for it suggests that Rilke himself is a reader in this poem: a reader of a poem which describes the experience of tasting fruit, a reader of Valéry's poem, "Le Cimetière marin." Here we can see a source for Rilke's notion that life follows death ("Tod und Leben") when fruit is eaten.

> Comme le fruit se fond en jouissance,
> Comme en délice il change son absence
> Dans une bouche où sa forme se meurt,
> Je hume ici ma future fumée,
> Et le ciel chante à l'âme consumée
> Le changement des rives en rumeur.[3]

In the mouth the death of the fruit's form is a negation which transforms the fruit into *jouissance, délice, Freude*. Rilke seems to have taken this idea and written a poem about it, loosely translating Valéry's French words (along with other words from the poem I haven't mentioned) into his own German words. However, what appears as a metaphor in Valéry's poem is metamorphosed into an experience in Rilke's sonnet. The literary and the figurative seem to become literal. Rilke seems to have read a text—an expression—of Valéry's tasting and transformed it into an experience of his own, tasted fruit in his own mouth. Once again, we are confronted with someone reading (interpreting) the text of someone else's experience, someone faced with the problem of entering or taking on that experience. We can see Rilke's reading of Valéry's text as a reflection of our own reading—both in Rilke's text and of it.

The problem of reading faces is prefigured in Rilke's two essays on Auguste Rodin, written in 1902 and 1907 respectively. In these essays, we see Rilke reading Rodin's sculptures—sculptures which he describes as having been "written" so that the whole body would act as a face. He shows us products of Rodin's reading and interpretation of nature:

What was expressed in the face, the pain and effort of awakening together with the longing for this heaviness, this difficulty, was written on the least part of the body; each part was a mouth saying in its own manner.
 The life showing in the face, full of reference to time and as easily read as on a dial, was, when seen in the body, less concentrated, greater, more mysterious and eternal . . . leaving the stage of the face, it let fall its mask and stood, as it was, behind the coulisses of clothing.[4]

David Marshall

The essays are filled with such configurations of faces and their readers and spectators. Rilke shows us Rodin creating human faces just as God created Adam, and interpreting faces as if they were texts: "Thus from quietly and conscientiously repeating life, the artist in his maturity learned, at first hesitatingly and experimentally and then with an ever surer, bolder confidence, to interpret the writing [der Schrift] with which the faces were completely covered."[5] He describes Rodin preparing his study of Balzac by reading Balzac's works and looking at Balzac's characters: the world

which still believed in the existence of its creator, which seemed to live with his life and to look upon him. He saw that all these thousand figures, let them do what they would, were entirely occupied with the one person who made them. And as one can, perchance, guess from the various facial expressions of the spectators what a drama is about, which is taking place upon the stage, so he searched in all these faces for the one who was still present for them. He believed, like Balzac, in the reality of this world. . . . He lived in it as if he, too, were one of Balzac's creations. . . .[6]

In this remarkable scene of Rodin searching for the figure of Balzac, Rodin reads the texts of various people (figures in a text) to see what they are looking at; he reads from their faces what they are seeing, surmises the spectacle from the expressions of the spectators, who are themselves his spectacle; and in looking at the faces looking at Balzac, he seems to gain their position, to enact their experience. Rodin becomes a character from a text looking at Balzac, believing what Balzac and his characters believed; the experience behind (in front of) the faces he was reading seems to become his own. The faces which were the mirror of Balzac become the mirror of Rodin. (Of course throughout the description, we see Rilke looking at himself studying Rodin.) Here the displacement we observed in the sonnet, the translation of reading into the experience of the text, is made more dizzying by the multiplication of faces and the doubling of the spectator as spectacle.

But what can we read from a face? What would it mean to know what a face meant, to understand its expression? Rilke speaks about the creation of surfaces:

But let us for a moment consider whether everything we have before us, everything we observe, explain, and interpret, isn't all surfaces? [Aber lassen Sie uns einen Augenblick überlegen, ob nicht alles Oberfläche ist, war wir vor uns haben und warhnemen und auslegen und deuten?] And what we name mind and spirit and love: are not these all simply a slight change [eine leise Veränderung] seen on the small surface of a near-by face?[7]

In the moment our glance reflects on the surface of a face, could we explain it in a way that would display its inner lay-out, appropriate some truth that is its own; how can we point to the slightest change, the imperceptible transformation in which we look for meaning? Is the meaning behind (or in front of), beneath, or through the surface; if we could see what we interpret from an expression, what would we be faced with? Doesn't Rodin finally see Balzac's face? In the same passage Rilke speaks of happiness, greatness, "every spacious, transforming idea: there was a moment when these were nothing but a pursing of the lips, the lifting of the eyebrows, shadowed places on a brow: and this contour of the mouth, this line above the eyelids, this darkness on a face— perhaps they have previously existed in exactly similiar form: as a marking [als Zeichnung] on an animal, a fissure in a rock, a hollow in a fruit. . . . There is only one single surface which moves through a thousand changes and transformations."[8] Again Rilke confronts us with a face but in reading the lines describing this face we find sketched a figurative text that belongs to no particular person, that represents no apparent inner experience; a text where ideas are simply the face's gestures expressed in lines—or the hollow of a piece of fruit that absorbs us; a list of lines in metamorphosis. The lines continually create the surface but don't seem to indicate anything besides their changing form; and in the course of the passage, a line becomes a shadow—*Dunkelheit*: darkness, obscurity—on the face.

Let us continue to read the sonnet; and let me say what I haven't said: that the face in question, the child's face we are to read from, is called "Angesicht," not simply "Gesicht." The prefix adds intensification perhaps (as in "erschmeckt"), a more general sense of countenance, and a sense of proximity. It also points us to the *Bible*, where "Angesicht" is used to refer to the face of the Lord, particularly in the expression "face to face."[9] 2 *Mose* 33.11: "Der Herr aber redete mit Mose von Angesicht zu Angesicht, wie ein Mann mit seinem Freunde redet," ["The Lord spoke with Moses face to face, as a man speaks with his friend"]. 5 *Mose* 34.10: "Und es stand hinfort kein Prophet in Israel auf wie Mose, den der Herr erhannt hätte von Angesicht zu Angesicht," ["And there arose not a prophet since in Israel like unto Moses, who the Lord had known face to face"]. If, then, we who would know the experience of tasting are looking to the taster's "Angesicht," are we seeing face to face, are we escaping mediation? The alternative, *Corinthians* 13 tells us, would be to see "in a glass darkly"; but the German *Bible* (in Luther's translation) is more specific: "Da ich ein Kind war, da redete ich wie ein Kind und war klug wie ein Kind und hatte kindliche Anschläge; da ich aber ein Mann ward, tat ich ab, was kindlich war. Wir sehen jetzt durch einen Spiegel in einem dunkeln Wort; dann aber von Angesicht zu Angesicht" (I *Korinther* 13.11–12) ["When I was a child, I spoke as a child and was wise as a child and had child-like resources; but when I became a man I put away childish things. For

David Marshall

now we see through a glass darkly (through a glass in a dark, obscure word); but then face to face."] (I have quoted this line in its context to show its proximity to a memory of childhood.) The mediation through the mirror is expressed in terms of language; the darkness which veils the face, and prevents our sight, is the *Dunkelheit* of a word. Is Rilke saying "Angesicht" to tell us we can escape the mediation of language, be spoken to as Moses was addressed by the Lord: "Von Mund zu Mund rede ich mit ihm, nicht durch dunkle Worte oder Gleichnisse, und er sieht den Herrn in seiner Gestalt" (4 *Mose* 12.8) ["With him I will speak mouth to mouth, and not in dark speeches (through dark words or parables); and the form of the Lord he shall behold."]? We must respond that we can not escape that mediation because in speaking to us, Rilke has named us as readers. The *Angesicht* we are faced with must be read; if we are face to face we are still face to face with a text, with language. Rilke makes it clear that we have no alternative, that there is no unmediated vision here, that the experience we are reading about (reading for?) must be read.

That word "experience," however, raises again the problem that still confronts us: we haven't yet identified what we are looking at, looking for, trying to read from the text of the poem—the experience of the poem we can't seem to know directly but which may be happening in our mouths (having been transferred from *Mund* to *Munde* in the space of a few lines). Perhaps we can only know it through language, but then language should at least be able to tell us something. In fact, in one sense the experience of the poem is expressed in terms of language: the fruit seems to be speech in the mouth (line two); in the lines "Wo sonst Worte waren, fliessen Funde,/aus dem Fruchtfleisch überrascht befreit" (7–8), we could read "Funde" as poetic invention or inspiration flowing from words, released from the poet's "Frucht" or product. In addition, the verb "sich verdichten" of line ten contains concentrated within it the verb "to write poetry"—although its prefix suggests that it also contains the seeds of that poetry's destruction. The adjective "doppeldeutig" in line thirteen suggests that the sweetness tasted must be interpreted. Does this mean that the process narrated in the poem is the process of writing poetry? At least for the moment, we are not entitled to make that claim, or to say what it means; especially since there is a sense that the process is not contained in language. The fruit may be said to replace words in the mouth ("Wo sonst Worte waren, fliessen Funde" [7]) and most significantly, the experience happening in the mouth can't be named: "Wird euch langsam namenlos im Munde?" (6).

What is this that is nameless, that cannot be indicated by a word? It seems that the process we are reading is happening in our mouths, that faced with the tasting child our positions have been reversed (reflected) and then switched again as the poet seems to be looking at us; but this experience that we are told to read is (although read) without a name. It is without title or denomination or noun or appelation or character. It is anonymous, ineffable, unspeakable, inexpressible, unnamed, unknown, indescribable, nameless. Even the grammar of the phrase refuses to posit something there; English and French translators often resort to rendering "namenlos" as "something nameless" but the use of "werden" allows the process to be noun-less. What is there—or can we ask what is not there? Is this a translation of the "absence" Valéry names "dans une bouche"?

It would be possible to point to other instances of namelessness in Rilke's work. "Namenlos" and related terms such as "unsäglich" and "unbeschreiblich" appear frequently in the *Sonnets to Orpheus* and in the *Duino Elegies*. But what would it mean to find other namelessnesses in the language of Rilke's texts? Even if we could identify them, guess what is without a name, how would we know that what is called nameless in one place is what is called nameless in another place? However, at the risk of pointing to what is not there, looking for what can't be located, let us turn again to Rilke's writing on Rodin.

One could say that these essays were obsessed with the problem in art (forming, interpretation, expression) of naming. The reader is continually confronted with the question of names: "For who remains unprejudiced when confronted with forms that have names? Who is not already making a choice when he names something face?"[10] Both essays begin with the question: the first addressing the "misunderstandings" which surround the name of Rodin: "They surround the name, not the work, which has far outgrown the sound and border of names and has now become nameless; as a plain is nameless or an ocean, the name of which is found only on maps, in books, or among men, but which in reality, is only vastness, movement, and depth."[11] We could chart the passage of this concern through the first essay to the beginning of the second essay ("Dies kommt von weit" [5]) which was written to be delivered as a lecture. Rilke begins by explaining that he must withhold the name of Rodin: "The name, which stands like a great five-starred constellation far above us this evening, can not be spoken."[12] Instead he says he wants to speak of things; but finally he risks the name he has not dared to say: "I dare it now, to name to you the name which cannot be kept silent any longer: Rodin. [Ich wage es jetzt, Ihnen den Namen zu nennen, der sich nicht länger verschweigen läßt: Rodin.] You know it is the name of countless things."[13] Then he lists and looks at Rodin's things, including his figure of Orpheus: "And I already feel how the name dissolves [zerfließt] in my mouth, how all this is only more so the poet, the same poet who is called Orpheus when his arm, with a wide sweep embracing all things, is lifted to the strings; the same who, with convulsive anguish, clings to the feet of the fleeing Muse as she escapes; the same who finally dies, his face upright in the shadow of his voices which unceasingly fill the world with song, and so dies, that this little group is often called Resurrection."[14]

What do these passages say? That when confronted with a form we choose to call face, our word is surrounded by ellipsis, indications of what we have left out. That the forms we face change, especially, for instance, things we call Rodin's work, his sculptures: we give them names but they move out of, beyond, through our names. They will not be contained, even if their place can be indicated by a line or a word in a book, on a map. We call one figure Orpheus (the singer of *Metamorphoses* whose face we see rising in shadows of distant singing voices) but the name dissolves (loses form) in our mouths; although saying more, it speaks death and life. Some names we don't dare to say because they will not mean what we see; what is nameless seems too vast and changing to be named. Looking at a group of Rodin's figures, Rilke writes: "As so often with Rodin, one dares not to give it a meaning. It has thousands. Thoughts pass over it like shadows, and behind each of them it rises new and enigmatic in its clarity and namelessness."[15] The group of figures in question is at once incomprehensible and evident, obscure and clear, unambiguous and with many meanings. One wants to assign it significance but standing in the way of interpretation, shadowed by one's own thoughts, is a proliferation of meaning—and namelessness.

As we continue to read the sonnet, we find—what we thought we knew—that after line six, Rilke seems to go on to describe the process that can't be held in place by a name. There is almost a narrative but if we try to follow it, to trace its moves, we find that after the alliteration of lines seven and eight ("Wo sonst Worte waren, fliessen Funde,/ aus dem Fruchtfleisch überrascht befreit") which makes the words in sound blend and flow together, and the interruption of line nine, the last five lines complexly propel us from word to word with increasing speed until their sentence is lost in a list of nouns and adjectives. Words proliferate but in doing so they seem to displace the process being narrated; the more words we read, the less we can point to the experience the words seem to name. Each word seems to replace the word appearing before it, until eventually we accumulate oppositions and contradictions. The sense of "klar" as unambiguous is confronted by the surprising "doppeldeutig." If we are in the realm of *deuten*, if we must explain or interpret or point to or indicate meaning, how do we understand something which is both clear and ambiguous, which has more than one meaning? The taste (is that what we were talking about?) is both "sonnig" and "erdig" (13); its direction is both inward ("sich verdictet") and outward ("aufgerichtet") (10, 11). It is "hiesig," here and now in both spatial and temporal senses, yet we thought it came "von weit," from the past, from far. The specificity and localization suggested by "hiesig" also would seem to contradict the immensity named in the almost identically spelled word it is paired with: "riesig." In fact, localization seems to be one activity being denied by the course of the poem, from the ambiguity as to who is tasting to the overabundance of meaning which surpasses any attempts to point to it with a name. (The text is not a map, although it may leave a trail across its surface.)

The verbs which narrate this process of "tasting" are verbs of movement, suggesting a movement or change from one state or place to another: "Funde" flow (run, melt, pass) are released, set free; the sweetness concentrates (with the sense of condensation, solidification) and is raised. Movement passes in and out of forms: "Geh in der Verwandlung aus und ein" ["Pass in and out of transformation"].[16] But the most important verb in the passage is "werden." This is the action that could not be named in line six ("Wird euch langsam namenlos im Mund?"); syntactically and in meaning it is at the center—bears the weight—of the last five lines. It is the verb of metamorphosis, the poetic translation of Valéry's *changer*, what causes the words in the list to become, come to be, turn out, come into existence. "Diese Süße" (10) is in the process of becoming and, in fact, it doesn't remain "Diese Süße" very long. Ironically, "Süße" is perhaps the weakest word in the passage, and the forms of the indicator "this" in line two, line five, and line ten have only the vaguest reference. Both words, ostensibly the subject of the last lines, are lost in the dizzying metamorphosis brought about by "werden." What is called sweetness can't be named, located, pointed to by one word. Like Rodin's sculptures, its namelessness comes from abundance of meaning, its transforming movement through and beyond names. It is "transparent" if we discover in that word a new etymology: not what is seen through (Rilke didn't use the more common German word "durchsichtig") but what can *trans-parare*, what appears across, beyond, over, through.

What we are trying to taste in the sonnet defeats names yet creates them simultaneously. It speaks namelessness yet gives way to names, which both generate and undermine each other. There is a sense that the lists are interrupted only because the poem runs out of time and space. "Riesig" is a breathless gesture toward immensity, a gesture which is seemingly exhilirated and celebratory, but which could also be read as exhausted: an almost desperate sense and indication of what the thirteenth sonnet of Part II calls "the untellable sums"—"den unsäglichen Summen." The last word stands in ironic juxtaposition to the first word, "Voller," for nothing in this sonnet of transformation seems in itself full, complete, or whole—especially not an "Apfel."

So what is the point of these lists? Why write a poem where language threatens to break down, where words seem inadequate by themselves and contradictory together; where to call something apple is somehow, inevitably, to fail. We have reached the line I have not yet dared to say, a line which addresses us directly:

Wagt zu sagen, was ihr Apfel nennt. (9)

(I cannot convey how that line threatens to silence me.) We already have a notion, not least because of the many ways in which line nine stands parallel to line six, of the problematic status of *nennen*. We know that its name "Apfel" is an arbitrary designation which cannot really point to what it is that we mean when we say "Apfel" (if we really say it and don't just name it). Rilke is concerned, not with the name, but with what the name doesn't name, what the name doesn't say. "Wagt zu sagen, was ihr Apfel nennt." At the center of the line lies "was," what is "namenlos." How can we say it? What does it mean to follow this dare, this invitation to risk, with a list of words?

In the Ninth Elegy, Rilke posits a time for the tellable ("Hier ist des *Säglichen* Zeit"),[17] a time when saying seems to go beyond what naming could do to touch and even transform the things of the world. How or where this saying, this *sagen*, is supposed to occur is not spelled out; and this is not the place to attempt a reading of the Ninth Elegy. But I hope the Elegy will help us to understand the saying the sonnet is daring. After speaking of a "being here"—a "Hiersein"—and a "here and now" —a "Hiesige"—that require something of us, the narrator wonders what can be taken across—"was nimmt man hinüber" (23):

> Nothing at all.
> Sufferings, then. Above all, the hardness of life,
> the long experience of love; in fact,
> purly untellable things. But later,
> under the stars, what then? they are better unsayable.
> For the wanderer doesn't bring from the mountain slope
> a handful of earth to the valley, all untellable, but rather
> some word he has won, a pure word, the yellow and blue
> gentian. Are we perhaps here in order to say: House,
> Bridge, Fountain, Gate, Fruit-tree, Window,—
> at best: Pillar, Tower? . . . . but to *say*, remember,
> oh to *say* in such a way as the things themselves
> never intended to be.

> [Keins.
> Also die Schmerzen. Also vor allem das Schwersein,
> also der Liebe lange Erfahrung,—also
> lauter Unsägliches. Aber später,

unter den Sternen, was solls: die sind *besser* unsäglich.
Bringt doch der Wanderer auch vom Hange des Begrands
nicht eine Hand voll Erde ins Tal, die allen unsägliche, sondern
ein erworbenes Wort, reines, den gelben und blaun
Enzian. Sind wir vielleicht *hier*, um zu sagen: Haus,
Brücke, Brunnen, Tor, Krug, Ostbaum, Fenster,—
höchstens: Säule, Turm. . . . aber zu *sagen*, verstehs,
oh zu sagen *so*, wie selber die Dinge niemals
innig meinten zu sein.] (24–36)

We are here (perhaps) in order to say, although how we get from "Unsägliches" to "zu sagen" is not so clear. But to say what? A list of words, it seems, a list of names. Erich Heller, in "The Artist's Journey into the Interior," sees this naming (saying?) in the context of the Ninth Elegy's call for a transformation of the visible into the invisible within us:

True, the poet even today cannot be like Adam and name the things, saying "House, Bridge, Fountain, Gate, Jug, Olive Tree, Window," just as if no things had ever known before what it was. And yet in truth he is not quite like Adam anymore; he is now like Noah hammering together an invisible ark of inwardness in which he hopes to rescue the pure essentials of creation from the Flood that rages without and drowns the meaning of things. . . . Say: House, Bridge, Fountain, Gate, Jug, Olive Tree, Window—it is no longer enough to name these things in the same manner that Homer named the shield of Achilles, namely so that the shield appears to say: this is my idea of myself; no, "saying" now means a saying which takes by surprise and by storm the things "which never meant to be so intensely inward." For indeed: "earth, is it not this that you want: *invisibly* to arise within us?"[18]

Is it so easy, however, to pass from *nennen* to *sagen*, to transform the very things of the world that in their transforming being seemed to leave language behind? How will this saying rescue the meaning of things, the meaning that seemed to be lost in and by the act of naming? For on the page at least, this saying looks like naming, even like the problematic and inadequate naming of the "Klage" in the Tenth Elegy.[19] "Preise dem Engel die Welt, nicht die unsägliche. . . . Sag ihm die Dinge" ["Praise the world to the angel, not the unsayable. . . . Say to him things"] (53, 58) instructs the narrator in the Ninth Elegy. In the second Rodin essay, Rilke wants to talk about things rather than names; but in the passage quoted above, there are no things—not even descriptions of things. There is only a list of the names of things: "Haus, Brücke, Brunnen, Tur, Krug, Obstbaum, Fenster,—höchstens: Säule, Turm. . . ." (32–34). In seems unlikely that one of these could be the "erworbenes Wort, reines" of line thirty-one. Can this naming sayingly rescue meaning? In fact, three years later, discussing the Elegies for a translator, Rilke assembled some of these words in a list we have already seen: "*Noch* für unsere Großeltern war ein 'Haus,' ein 'Brunnen,' ein ihnen vertrautern Turm, ja eigenes Kleid, ihr Mantel unendlich mehr, unendlich vertraulicher," ["To our grandparents a 'house,' a 'well,' a tower familiar to them, even their own dress, their cloak, was still infinitely more, infinitely more intimate"]. Aren't these words already less by 1922, closer to *Schein-Dinge* than to *Dinge*; *sagen* seems to turn into *nennen* here, producing names that can't contain things or be the source of their flowing or raise them; names that cover things instead.

After the passage from the Elegy quoted above, Rilke writes of "the secret cunning of the reticent earth" ["die heimliche List dieser verschwiegenen Erde"] (36–37). Perhaps the cunning, the artfulness, the ruse of the earth is also its secret list ("die List*e*"): what the earth silently, speechlessly arranges but will not (need not) name. Our position is, however, inscribed within language: "*Wir* machen mit Worten und Fingerzeigen/uns allmählich die Welt zu eigen" [*We*, with words and finger-pointing, gradually make the world our own"].[20] Unlike the sculptor, we must work through words;[21] this is part of the danger of trying to say.

The Ninth Duino Elegy refuses to show how we could say "was ihr Apfel nennt" without losing it in a name. But perhaps there is still a way to say and not name, perhaps there is a possibility that words themselves might say something even if they didn't name that thing they claim to summon. Could the saying itself mean something? In his essay on Rilke, "Wozu Dichter?", Martin Heidegger identifies *sagen* with the risk, the venture, the *Wagnis*; for him to really engage in saying is to dare to venture into language, to dare language itself. "The more venturesome dare the saying" ["Die Wagenderen wagen das Sagen"].[22] Heidegger's text is obviously too complicated to explicate here, and it discusses saying in a context too large to address directly in this essay, but let me say simply that Heidegger proposes a daring of language that goes beyond *mere* saying:

When, in relation to beings in terms of representation and production, we relate ourselves at the same time by making propositional assertions, such a saying is not what is willed. Asserting remains a way and a means. By contrast, there is a saying that really engages in saying, yet without reflecting upon language, which would make even language into one more object. To be involved in saying is the mark of a saying that follows something to be said, solely in order to say it. What is to be said would then be what by nature belongs to the province of language. . . . The more venturesome are those who say in a greater degree, in the manner of the singer. Their singing is turned away from all purposeful self-assertion. It is not a willing in the sense of desire. Their song does not sollicit anything to be produced.[23]

The song which is more fully saying, the "sagendere Sagen," is the song of Orpheus: "Gesang ist Dasein"—"Song is existence."[24] Language cannot exhaust itself in signifying, stop at being a song or a cypher;

language, when risked and dared, when released from representation or assertion, becomes saying, becomes song.

Is Rilke venturesome enough to act out Heidegger's assertions, to abandon naming in order to speak in a song that says only itself? Other readers of Rilke have heard this in his poetry: Geoffrey Hartman, writing about Rilke and other poets, speaks of a path chosen to overcome the arbitrariness of symbols and language, a path

which is an exploration of the inner motion and incipient meaning of human speech as such: the discovery of the *voice* of the spoken word. Only in this way can poetry rival the example of painting. . . . Instead of giving conventional names to things, it would, like the painter, take them away and render instead the immediate "figure" of the senses, which in this case especially is that of speech as pure voice. "Wird euch langsam namenlos im Munde?" The poetry of Rilke and Valéry are living instances of anominization. . . .[25]

Paul de Man calls Rilke's poetry a poetry of figures rather than of metaphors, one which does not conceive of language "comme moyen de récupération d'une présence qui se situe en dehors de lui"; he finds in Rilke's poetry, especially in the late French poems, a "conversion de la fonction représentative et visuelle du langage en audition pure."[26]

How do we hear Sonnet XIII? Does Rilke achieve a purely vocative saying which is not evocative, which would renounce names entirely? Does he give up things, release from his touch that which is called an apple? There are indications of this in the poem: in the words disassociated in meaning, in the repeated "ig" suffixes at the end, in the almost entirely auditory motivation for "riesig" to utter the poem's last sound. However, as in the Ninth Elegy, the dare to say turns into the saying of a list: a sentence becomes an arrangement of separate words: "wach und transparent,/doppeldeutig, sonnig, erdig, hiesig-:/ O Erfahrung, Fühlung, Freude—, riesig!" (12–14). Does this indicate the same failure suggested by our reading of the Elegy and Rilke's letter? Yes and no; for I do not think this sonnet is meant to be the pure song that some readers have heard in Rilke's texts. I do not think that Rilke here gives up the language of names. The poem dares to say but it also risks naming. Its song may seek to go beyond words that inadequately point to things, but it sings within that language. "Wagt zu sagen, was ihr Apfel nennt." The poet dares to begin the poem with the name "Apfel," although its prefacing adjective "Voller" testifies to the incompleteness of the name. When Rilke says "Alles dieses spricht/Tod und Leben in den Mund. . . ." (2–3), the "dieses" refers not only to fruit but to the list of words we have just read: "Apfel, Birne und Banane,/ Stachelbeere. . . ." (1–2). Words speak death and life in the mouth, and in the poem, words speak of their own life and death. The poem speaks in a language of names while pointing to the failure of such language, hoping that in entering and disrupting these names it will find something said. Finally (and initially), the sonnet accepts a position inscribed within the problem of *nennen*.

However, this is the problem we are facing in trying to read the text. We are forced to consider it, not only to read about but to taste the problem of the poem. We try to read, to discover sense where words were, to touch something in the poem: to test it out, to move experimentally in search of its experience, accepting the peril contained in experience. We try to touch what can't be pointed to with pens and typing fingers, to ascertain what can't be fixed. This is why although we could never taste an experience behind the text, we can taste the experience of the text. The face we tried to read became a shadowed surface of lines and figures; but reading itself seemed to become the experience we were trying to read, what we could not know. The poem and the reader are face to face in and with the problem of the text. Rilke appears to be speaking from somewhere in between *nennen* and *sagen*: "Sprich und bekenn."[27] Speak and acknowledge.

The reader is called upon to do this, too. We are dared to risk saying, and to acknowledge what we have not said. Speak and confess. We find ourselves daring to name what is in the text, and we see the lines of the text looking back at us, leading back to us. The poem takes place in the mouth: the precinct of language and of tasting. We, as readers, are called upon to taste the words of the poem in our mouths, to taste the death and the life, the transformation. To decide whether the sonnet is a poem about language or a poem about tasting makes no sense at this point; both are the same thing, and if we try to point to one, it becomes the other.

But what are we left with? A list of names that can't really name what it says, that can't say what it names. The poem becomes a list which speaks of its failure and its proliferation of words and meaning. What do we hear in a list? In what we call a list we hear a command to listen, an expression of desire, that unsteadiness that interrupts a ship's course and prevents smooth sailing; we hear a catalogue of names that gets its name from the boundary, the edging, the strip that held them: a barrier enclosing space. A list, we see reading next to the dictionary (the most elaborate and self-generating of lists), contains words that name too much, just as they fall short of naming; released from syntax and grammar, they carry all their meaning, become "doppeldeutig." (Recall that "namenlos" gets its name from its excess of meaning; and recall that as we tried to translate Rilke's language into our understanding, a word gave way to words, a name could not be identified by a single name, a single word produced a list.) The list stands between *nennen* and *sagen*. It underlines *nennen* and appears at the boundary of *sagen*. The list is what encloses the space of saying, poses its limits, threatens to hold it in—while hoping to carry saying out, to gesture in its directions, to speak in the infinite space beyond its margin.

Are we left with a taste as the names disappear in our mouths? Wallace Stevens, at the end of one of his poems, noted that

> in this bitterness, delight,
> Since the imperfect is so hot in us,
> Lies in flawed words and stubborn sounds.[28]

Reading Rilke's poem we taste what is there and we taste what is not there; we become drunk with the changing taste, drunk with what has been said, drunk with absence.

> La vie est vaste, étant ivre d'absence,
> Et l'amertume est douce, et l'esprit clair.[29]

NOTES

1. Rainer Maria Rilke, *Sonnets to Orpheus*, a bilingual edition, trans. M. D. Herter Norton (New York: W. W. Norton, 1962), p. 40. All further citations to the sonnet refer to this text. The translation provided is based on Norton's, with revisions of my own and a phrase or two borrowed from C. F. MacIntyre's translation in his edition of the *Sonnets* (Berkeley and Los Angeles: University of California Press, 1960).

2. Rilke, quoted in the notes to the Norton edition of the *Sonnets*, p. 134. The German text is quoted by Martin Heidegger in *Holzwege* (Frankfort: Vittorio Klostermann, 1950), p. 268.

3. Paul Valéry, "Le Cimetière marin" in *Oeuvres* (Paris: La Pléiade, 1957), I, 149, line 268. Among others, C. F. MacIntyre has pointed out this connection in his tasteless notes to his edition of the *Sonnets*, p. 122.

4. Rainer Maria Rilke, *The Rodin Book* in *Selected Works*, trans. C. Craig Houston (London: Hogarth Press, 1954), I, 102, 108. Throughout my essay, I have provided English translations of prose passages from this text, although with some revisions. The German text of *Auguste Rodin* can be found in *Gesammelte Werke*, Band IV, *Schriften in Prosa* (Leipzig: Insel-Verlag, 1927), I.

5. *Rodin*, p. 132.

6. Ibid.

7. Ibid., p. 140.

8. Ibid.

9. *Die Bibel* (Nach der deutschen Übersetzung Martin Luthers), (Stuttgart: Württenbergische Bibelanstalt, 1969). Where the King James version differed significantly from the German, I have chosen to translate from the German.

10. *Rodin*, p. 95.

11. Ibid.

12. Ibid., p. 136.

13. Ibid., p. 140.

David Marshall

14. Ibid., p. 141–42.

15. Ibid., p. 112.

16. Rilke, *Sonnets*, II, 29.

17. Rainer Maria Rilke, *Duino Elegies*, a bilingual edition, trans. J. B. Leishman and Stephen Spender (New York: W. W. Norton, 1967), p. 72–76. Further citations from the Ninth Elegy refer to this edition, whose translation I have slightly revised.

18. Erich Heller, *The Artist's Journey into the Interior and Other Essays* (New York: Vintage, 1965), pp. 151–52.

19. Carol Jacobs discusses the problematic status of naming in the Tenth Duino Elegy in "The Tenth Duino Elegy or the Parable of the Beheaded Reader," *MLN*, 89:6 (1966).

20. Rilke, *Sonnets*, I, 16.

21. The epigraph to the Rodin essays is "Writers operate through words,/Sculptors through deeds" ["Die Schriftsteller wirken durch Worte,/Die Bildhauer aber durch Taten"]. Pomponius Gauricus, "De Sculptura," p. 94.

22. Martin Heidegger, "What Are Poets For?" in *Poetry, Language, Thought*, trans. Albert Hofstadter (New York: Harper and Row, 1971), p. 133. The German text, "Wozu Dichter," appears in *Holzwege*.

23. Heidegger, p. 137–38.

24. Rilke, *Sonnets*, I, 3.

25. Geoffrey H. Hartman, *The Unmediated Vision* (New York: Harcourt, Brace, and World, 1966), p. 163.

26. Paul de Man, Introduction to *Poésie, Rilke Oeuvres* (Paris: Seuil, 1972), 2, 32, 42.

27. "Ninth Elegy," l. 44.

28. Wallace Stevens, "The Poems of Our Climate" in *The Collected Poems* (New York: Alfred Knopf, 1972), p. 194.

29. Valéry, p. 149.

SEVEN

METAPHOR AND METONYMY: THE LOGIC OF STRUCTURALIST RHETORIC
Maria Ruegg

I

ONE OF THE CURIOUS by-products of French structuralism has been a revival of interest in classical rhetoric: curious, because whatever success the structuralist movement enjoyed was due, in large part, to the fact that it represented a "theoretical revolution" devoted, in particular, to overthrowing the very assumptions about language upon which classical rhetoric, no less than classical metaphysics, was based. Despite their repeated insistence that the new theoretical age—inaugurated by Saussurian linguistics, Freudian analysis, Nietzschean "symptomology" and Mallarmean poetics—constituted a "radical epistemological rupture" with the "pre-scientific" past,[1] a large number of structuralists were, at the same time, strangely attracted to the antiquated, elaborately constructed systems of tropes and figures offered by classical manuals of rhetoric, from Quintillian to Fontanier.

And what is even more surprising, they not only admired such works, but freely adopted, within their own "revolutionary" discourse, a good many terms directly, and uncritically, derived from the most traditional of rhetorical texts.[2] Of the many tropes and figures thus resurrected in the name of the "science of language," none proved so popular as the pair, "metaphor" and "metonymy." Introduced by Jakobson, in his article, "Two Aspects of Language and Two Types of

Maria Ruegg

Aphasic Disturbances" (which appeared in French translation, along with "Linguistics and Poetics" and other essays, in an extremely influential volume entitled *Essais Linguistiques*, published in 1963),[3] "metaphor" and "metonymy"—terms which Jakobson used to denote the "two fundamental poles of language"—quickly became key terms in the structuralist lexicon. Of the numerous articles which soon followed, based on Jakobson's distinction, the most significant was no doubt Lacan's "L'instance de la lettre dans l'inconscient" (published in *Ecrits*, 1966; translated "The Agency of the Letter in the Unconscious" in *Ecrits: A Selection*, 1977), which applied the Jakobsonian distinction to the context of psychoanalysis: metaphor and metonymy became the master figures of a "rhetoric of the unconscious," which it was the goal of the "Freudian science" to decipher.

The use of the terms "metaphor" and "metonymy" by both Jakobson and Lacan is of particular interest: first of all, because it illustrates a number of characteristic structuralist tendencies—the tendency to reduce complex givens to the terms of a simple binary opposition; the tendency to make universal generalizations on the basis of purely hypothetical and unverifiable "structures"; the tendency to ignore logical inconsistencies within the binary oppositions themselves. And secondly, the use of "metaphor" and "metonymy" is of interest because it reveals the extent to which structuralism, despite its pretense of radical novelty, remained firmly entrenched in the most traditional of metaphysical idealisms; for it was the use of such terms—terms which have always depended on classical theories of language, the very theories structuralists so categorically rejected—that permitted structuralism to dismiss the Western metaphysical tradition, while at the same time reaffirming it.

Jakobson's text is relatively simple, but it is in the very simplicity of the schema he proposes—the bipolarization of language in general terms of a binary opposition between "metaphor" and "metonymy"—that one can best trace the complexity of the logical problems that arise in structuralist methods of analysis. And while Lacan's treatment of metaphor and metonymy is more subtle, more difficult, and more complex, it is there that the very simple—and very conservative— metaphysical monism underlying structuralism's radical rhetoric reveals itself most clearly.

Jakobson derives his distinction between metaphor and metonymy from a fundamental differentiation of two linguistic faculties (a difference which he in turn derives from his empirical observation of certain speech disorders): the faculty of selecting and substituting one word *for* another, characterized as a "metaphoric" process; the faculty of combining words *with* one another, of putting words "in context," characterized as a "metonymic" process. The distinction between metaphoric "similarity" and metonymic "contiguity" appears, according to Jakobson, at all levels of language (morphological, lexical, syntactic, phraseological) in either of the two aspects common to both: positional (predicative) or semantic (substitutive).

This doubling of metaphor and metonymy (or, contiguity and similarity) along a positional/semantic axis is illustrated in Jakobson's text by a "well known psychological test," in which children were asked to respond to the stimulus of a signifier, "hut."[4] The responses were qualified as either "substitutive" or "predicative," according to whether the child "substituted" another signifier for the given signifier, or whether he "complemented" the given signifier with a chain of signifiers. To this horizontal, syntactic, positional axis, Jakobson superimposes a vertical semantic axis. The results can perhaps be best visualized with the help of the accompanying table.

	POSITIONAL (SYNTACTIC) AXIS	
SEMANTIC AXIS	(Predicative) Contiguity	(Substitutive) Similarity
Contiguity (Metonymy)	I . . . "burned down" . . . "shelters the old man"	III "straw" "poverty"
Similarity (Metaphor)	II . . . "is made out of straw" . . . "is a sign of poverty" . . . "is a little house" . . . "is a hut" . . . "is the opposite of palace" . . . "is like a lair" . . . "is a den of wickedness"	IV "hut" "cabin" "palace" "lair"

According to Jakobson, it is by manipulating these two types of connection (similarity and contiguity) in their two aspects (positional and semantic), that an individual "reveals his personal style, his tastes and his verbal preferences" (77). And since, for Jakobson, the "two types of connections" and their "two aspects" are in fact *doubles* of the *same* distinction—the distinction between the "two cardinal poles" of metaphor and metonymy—the key to understanding all human discourse, and all human behavior (literature, painting, film, dreams, "every symbolic process, whether it be intrasubjective or social" [80]) lies in the simple, but "primordial" dichotomy between metaphor and metonymy.

It is only on the most superficial level, however, that such a distinction can function, and even then, the grossly oversimplified caricatures to which it gives rise are so general as to be virtually mean-

Maria Ruegg

ingless (thus, to use Jakobson's own examples, lyric poetry is "meta-phoric," while epic is "metonymic"; romantics, symbolists and surrealists have a penchant for metaphor, realists have a penchant for metonymy [78]). But let us turn, for a moment, to the children's phrases cited by Jakobson: if we look at our little table, we can see that metaphoric "substitution" (Box IV) can become "contiguous" in the context of a predicative equivalence (or opposition or comparison or analogy) (Box II), and that metonymic "contiguity" (Box I) can become "substitutive" with the elimination of its syntactic context (III). If a simple phrase such as, "the den of poverty burned down" defies simple analysis in terms of the semantic/positional, contiguity/similarity axes (it doesn't fit in any one—or even two—of the boxes), then poetic discourse becomes a virtual nightmare for the modern rhetorician. Indeed, to reduce poetic language to two major "poles," the metaphoric (romantic, symbolist, surrealist) and the metonymic (realist), and to link this bipolarization onto the distinction between poetry and prose, can only generate a series of contradictory, "undecidable" interpretations.

Even in terms of the above schematization, the distinction between "metaphoric" and "metonymic" uses of language becomes clouded. A signifier becomes a metaphor only in certain syntactic contexts; thus "lair" or "palace" becomes a metaphor or an antinomy only *with reference to*, or in connection with another signifier—"hut." In Box II, the contiguous (syntactic) link between signifier and substitute is made explicit, and in the resulting paraphrase, tautology, antinomy, similitude, or metaphor, the predicate functions as a *substitute* for the subject, *within* and *as part of* a contiguous syntactic structure. Box IV is merely a truncated version of Box II, in that its terms have metaphoric meaning only in so far as they are contiguously linked (implicitly or explicitly) to the signifier "hut." In Box III, likewise, the terms (which are, syntactically, substitutes for the original signifier) are semantically metonymic only with reference to "hut"; when that contiguous link is made explicit (as in I), we once again have a predicate which functions as a *kind* of substitute for its subject (here indicating an "attribute" rather than postulating an equivalence or opposition) within, and as part of, a contiguous syntactic structure. The only opposition which remains is that between the narrative phrase, "burned down" or "shelters the old man" (which cannot be construed as metonymic) and the metaphoric/metonymic group of syntactically contiguous, but semantically substitutive phrases.

It is only by artificially abstracting both metaphor and metonymy from their syntactic contexts (and considering them only along the "semantic axis") that a comparison between metaphoric and metonymic poles of language can be made; if, however, semantic "value" can only be derived from the syntactic position occupied by the signifier in relation to the whole chain of signifiers, in the complex interplay between all possible combinatory positions of a given linguistic code (as in Wittgenstein's "meaning is use"), then the separation between "syntax" and "paradigm," between "contiguity" and "similarity" and between metaphor and metonymy is at best unfruitful, and at worst, a misleading oversimplification of what language does.

Even on a purely abstract, semantic level, the distinction between metaphor and metonymy is difficult to maintain with any certainty. If the metonymically minded realist calls his car his "wheels" while the metaphorically inclined romantic prefers to call it his "prancing steed," the fact remains that both involve a *kind* of substitution (of one signifier for another) and both involve some degree of semantic contiguity which provides the necessary link between the two signifiers—the road without which the transfer cannot be made. That the link of contiguity is based, in the first case, on a relationship of part to whole, and in the second, on a comparative relationship of functions or of "common quality" (that of providing transportation), is certainly insufficient grounds for constructing a bipolarization of all language.

In an article entitled "Théorie de la Figure"[5] Jean Cohen demonstrates the inseparability of paradigmatic (substitutive) and syntagmatic (contiguous) axes in the constitution of all rhetorical figures, and the consequent illegitimacy of all attempts to base a rhetoric on such a distinction (such as trope/non-trope, metaphor/metonymy). The basis of all figurative language is what he calls "syntagmatic combinatory incompatibility," in which a "gap" is perceived between the given phrase and what we would normally expect in that syntagmatic context (given our linguistic "contract" or "code"). Whether the "gap" exists "in absentia" (as in the metaphor) or "in praesentia" (as in simile), we reduce the syntactic anomaly by making a paradigmatic substitution. The reading of any figure depends first of all on the perception of an anomaly (syntagmatic incompatibility) and then on its "correction," through recourse to paradigmatic substitution.

But to be able to substitute word *for* word, one must have some notion of how words relate *to* words—that is, one must have an idea of the possible combinatory positions a word is able to occupy in the syntactic structures of a given linguistic code: or, more simply, the word's possible functions. Paradigms of substitution are based on abstractions of a word's function within the syntactic structures of the code; the place and function of a given signifier is always determined by its *context*, which is comprised *only* of other signifiers, whether "in praesentia" (in the actual syntactic phrase in question) or "in absentia" (in the variety of possible syntactic positions it *can* occupy according

Maria Ruegg

to the linguistic rules of the code). "Similarity" is derived from a *series* of contiguities or signifying chains and the play of all rhetorical figures (including metaphor and metonymy) is an extension of the ambiguous game of language itself—in which the rules for semantic replacement are nothing but abstractions (metaphors) for the rules of syntactic displacement.

Cohen's argument effectively underlines the inadequacies of the metaphor/metonymy paradigm in attempting to account for traditional rhetorical phenomena; but if his own theory of rhetoric is more consistent, it nonetheless reveals the classical logical/philosophical bias, in so far as it depends on the possibility of *deciding* whether a given message presents a "syntagmatic combinatory incompatibility" (and is hence "rhetorical") or not. In other words, it presupposes the possibility (and the necessity) of distinguishing between messages which are recognizably "rhetorical" and those which are "grammatical"—*and* the possibility of reducing rhetorical anomalies to grammatically "correct" syntagmas in so far as the meaning of the figure is concerned. What such a rhetoric fails to account for is what Jakobson himself later described as the "polysemic" nature of poetic discourse.

Referring to his earlier distinction between metaphor and metonymy, Jakobson—in "Linguistics and Poetics"[6]—attempts to modify his former position in an effort to make it include the play of multiple reference—the complexity, the "polysemic" nature—which characterizes poetic discourse. Thus, in *poetry*, "every metonymy is slightly metaphoric, and every metaphor has a metonymic tinge" (370). And this paradoxical admission of the failure of the metaphor/metonymy distinction to account for multiple reference is justified by the equally paradoxical explanation that the "essence" of poetry (its symbolic, polysemic nature) emerges from a *projection* of similarity *onto* contiguity (358).

First, as both communication theory and psychoanalysis have emphasized (and this, perhaps, is one of the most significant contributions of Freudian/Lacanian linguistic analysis), it is by no means the distinguishing characteristic of poetic discourse to be "polysemic"— even if poetic discourse *is*, in de Man's words, the "most advanced and refined mode of deconstruction."[7] All forms of discourse consciously or unconsciously exploit the polysemic potential of language to transmit ambiguous, undecidable messages. And secondly, that "polysemic essence" does not arise from a "metaphorization" of metonymy or a "metonymization" of metaphor; it comes, rather, from the impossibility of separating the two imaginary axes of "similarity" and "contiguity"— or rather, from the constant and inevitable mimetic *play* between a multiplicity of codes, texts, contexts: play which implicates *all* discourse in a complex, ambiguous, undecidable web. If poetry is the most "refined" mode of deconstructive discourse, it is because it systematically exploits that polysemic potential, while "ordinary language" attempts—consciously, at least (or, at least, it pretends to attempt)—to reduce that polysemic potential to an unambiguous single meaning.

If Jakobson's attempt to analyze language in terms of a simple binary rhetoric leads to logical inconsistencies, it is, first of all, because he treats what are in fact the very subtle, and often undecidable *differences* between metaphor and metonymy in terms of an absolute *opposition* which imposes an either/or choice at all levels of the analysis. And secondly, it is because he attempts to maintain a strict dualism between the two poles, even though he is forced to admit that the language of analysis (the "metalanguage") is itself essentially a "metaphoric" process, which naturally tends to *privilege* metaphor over metonymy.[8]

Lacan resolves these difficulties, as we shall see, first by transforming Jakobson's bipolarization of metaphor and metonymy along a single axis, into an opposition between two superimposed axes—one horizontal (metonymic), the other vertical (metaphoric)—in such a way that the two forms of discourse are no longer mutually exclusive, but on the contrary, always coexistent. And secondly, he makes no pretense of maintaining a symmetrically balanced, dualistic relationship between metaphor and metonymy: the Lacanian system is militantly monistic, and rigidly hierarchical.

II

Lacan's rhetoric, like Jakobson's, would include, in its analytic grasp, not merely what traditionally passes for "figurative" discourse, but *all* forms of discourse. In many ways, however, Lacan's treatment of rhetoric is more interesting than Jakobson's and more coherent as well—despite the relative obscurity of the Lacanian text. Not only does Lacan manage to avoid most of the logical problems that arise from the Jakobsonian dichotomization of language, but he offers a paradigm for the *interpretation* of rhetorical figures. While the question of *meaning* (or its "lack") is virtually ignored (or simply taken for granted) in Jakobson's text, Lacan provides a model which permits the analyst to account for the "true meaning" of all rhetorical discourse in terms of a limited number of key psychoanalytical concepts (castration, phallus, Other, Father, Law, etc.).

But the possibility of interpretation, in the Lacanian text, is made to rest on the *subordination* of rhetoric to a metaphysical order—The Symbolic—which is at once the "source" and the "truth" of rhetorical figures. And despite all the scientific clap-trap Lacan employs to prove its legitimacy—the algorithms, the knots, the Moebius strips, the Markov chains—"The Symbolic" remains as "scientific" and as "verifiable" as the Platonic realm of Ideas. The nature of rhetoric, in the Lacanian text, cannot be understood without reference to this "symbolic order"; but in order to understand the relationship between the two— and in particular, in order to understand the differentiation of the metaphoric and metonymic functions—some general remarks are first necessary.

Despite the elusive, enigmatic "style" of the *Ecrits*, one can hardly imagine a less "poetic" text—in de Man's sense of the word; for in fabricating its elaborate labyrinthian structure, filled with secret passages and hidden chambers accessible only to the initiated, it represents one of the most "refined modes" of what Derrida has aptly termed "phallogocentric" construction. The "play" of signification in which the text continually indulges itself—like the child's "game" of making objects appear and disappear—is no laughing matter; indeed, it is meant to reveal the impossibility of any play which is not determined by and which cannot be reduced to the Symbolic Order: illusory play, then, which is incessantly, with unrelieved monotony, referred, brought back, to the "inevitable" Truth which the text would have us stoically accept: the eternal, necessary *lack* of the object of desire.

If language plays such a central role in the Lacanian text, it is because language determines the "place" of the "subject." And if, in terms of the Saussurian distinction, the signifier is given absolute priority over the signified ("there is no master but the signifier"),[9] it is because the "signified" represents the concepts of a Cartesian rational consciousness which is based on an imaginary autonomy of the subject. Since, in a classical sign theory, the "signifier" corresponds to a "signified" (a conscious thought) which in turn corresponds to a reality, the signifier "je," for example (and the example is by no means randomly chosen), will correspond to the conscious concept "je" which will in turn correspond to the actual "being" of "je" (which exists, then, prior to both thought and language). Lacan sums up this hierarchical order of derivation, from real entity to thought to word, in the quasi-Cartesian formula "ubi cogito, ibi sum"; he then *reverses* that order with his own formula, "I think where I am not, therefore, I am where I do not think" (or, in its expanded form, "I am not wherever I am the plaything of my thought; I think of what I am where I do not think to think").[10]

The signifier, then, determines not only the imaginary concept (the signified) in terms of which our own, imaginary reality is constituted, but it also determines the *true* place of the subject (où il est), in revealing the *true* subject and the *true* object of all discourse. For the *subject* of "that which speaks" (the subject of the "énonciation") is not

the Cartesian "je" of "that which is spoken" (subject of the "énoncé"),
but rather the "id": "Ça parle" (and not "je")—the unconscious id, and
not the conscious ego. And it is because of this "splitting" of the subject
that the signifier is defined as "that which represents the subject for
another signifier," for the signifier "je" (of the énoncé) has the function
of *re-presenting* the subject *for* (in place of, as a substitution for)
another signifier: the subject of the enunciation, the "ça" of the unconscious, the "true" subject of discourse. In the corollary to this
formula, the subject is defined as "that which the signifier represents
for another signifier": subject caught ("split") between the "je" of
imaginary desire and the "ça" which truly speaks.[11]

The *object* of "its" discourse—that about which, from which,
according to which ("de qua") the subject speaks—is l'Autre, the
Other: the objects of desire which, since they exist only in the symbolic
order (phallus, father, etc.) can never be replaced or possessed. "La
vraie parole," true discourse, is then the discourse of the unconscious
subject derived from, determined by and concerning the non-existent
Object of its desire: "the unconscious of the subject is the discourse of
the other."[12]

Freud's "Copernican Revolution," according to Lacan, consists
precisely in this displacement of the subject, away from the center of
the linguistic universe in which the Cartesian "cogito" had imagined its
"sum" to be. But, if the "sum" of the now ex-centric subject is never
where its "cogito" thinks it is, its "place" can nonetheless be determined
by observing its trajectory as it revolves about the (center)—the Other
—which constitutes the object of its necessarily heliotropic desire. The
Lacanian revelation that the "sun" does not, in fact, exist (that it has
no real, material existence) by no means implies that the system is
not "solar": for even if the center is not "really" a center, but rather
a hole, an absence, a lack; and even if the Other exists "only"
Symbolically—that in no way changes the fact that the subject revolves
about and is determined by the "absence" which *functions* "as if" it were
a "presence," lodged in a "center."

The Lacanian text offers the subject only the necessity of recon-
ciliation (*Versöhnung*) with his own excentricity, and the necessity of
accepting the Revelation of Absence, of Eternal Lack. Whence his
insistence on the Freudian dictum, "Wo Es war, soll Ich werden"—
which, in Lacan's reading (which is indeed consistent with Freud), does
not mean that the "ich" should *replace* the "es" (the ego should "overcome" the id), but rather that the "je" should "come to be" there where
the "ça" already (is):[13] that the conscious subject should *accept* its
determination by the Symbolic Other.

The revelation of the Truth—of that Symbolic Order which "constitutes the subject"—is brought about by means of a rhetorico-linguistic analysis aimed at uncovering the laws of reference (or representation) which govern the seemingly chaotic displacements of signifiers. As we have just seen, the "I"—the conscious subject of the Cartesian cogito—is but an illusory figment of a narcissistic imagination, incapable of grasping the true meaning of the signifying chains "it" utters; for the meaning is never what the "I"—the conscious ego—*thinks* it is. For the "I" imagines that it is speaking a non-figurative, straight-forward language (in which signifier refers to a consciously "signified" concept), when *in fact,*—from the *true* perspective of the ex-centric, unconscious subject—its discourse is purely rhetorical, and has meaning only in so far as its rhetoric can be reduced to the "true" language underlying it.

The rhetoric which ultimately permits the Revelation of the Truth is divided, in "The Agency of the Letter in the Unconscious," into two branches, corresponding to the double function of the signifier: on the one hand, its function of combining with other signifiers in a horizontal, linear, syntactic chain (relationship of "mot à mot"); on the other, its function of replacing, of substituting itself for, of "re-presenting" *another* signifier, according to a vertical "semantic" axis (relationship of "mot *pour* mot"). Following Jakobson's model, the signifier, in its first "role"—horizontal, syntagmatic, contiguous, syntactic, associational—functions as "metonymy"; and in its second role—paradigmatic, substitutive, semantic, symptomal—it functions as a "metaphor."

But the Lacanian articulation of these "metaphoric" and "metonymic" signifying functions differs radically from that of Jakobson—and not simply in their correspondence to the "Verschiebung" (displacement) and "Verdichtung" (condensation) of the Freudian dreamwork (for Jakobson, elsewhere, makes the same association; association which—in the *Traumdeutung* itself—carries little of the hierarchical implications that it does in Lacan's text). It is, rather, in the association of "metonymy" with the Hegelian notion of desire for recognition by the Other (the dialectic of master and slave in the *Phenomenology*) and in the association of "metaphor" with the Heideggerean notions of Being and Truth (*alétheia*), that Lacan traces the fundamental qualitative difference between the two. For the metonymy is the "signifier of desire"; desire for the Other, which in Hegelian terms is at once a desire to *possess*—to own, to appropriate, to "subject"—the other, a desire to be recognized *by* the other, and a desire to replace, to substitute oneself *for* the other. But the Other can never be "replaced" or "possessed" by the desiring subject, for it symbolizes precisely that which is always beyond, that which exceeds the accomplishment of any particular desire. If one desire always leads to another, in an infinite self-perpetuating "metonymic" chain, it is because there can be no "real" satisfaction of desire, for there is no Object that can put an end to desire itself.

The discourse of the conscious "je" of the Cartesian cogito is thus nostalgically "caught in the rails—eternally stretching forth towards *the desire for something else*—of metonymy";[14] it can never "cross the bar" which separates signifier from signified, word from meaning, appearance from truth, for the "signified" to which it literally refers reveals only "le peu de sens," the *lack* of meaning it transmits. And to invest this fairly simple notion with the aura of scientific legitimacy, Lacan gives it the following "algorithmic" representation: $f(S \ldots S')S = S(-)s$.[15] (Formula which, thanks to Nancy and Lacoue-Labarthe's excellent work on Lacan, *Le Titre de la lettre*, [Paris: Galilée, 1973] can be simply translated: the signifying function, $f(\ldots)S$, of the syntactic combination of signifiers, $(S \ldots S')$, is equivalent to, $\cong$; the *maintenance* of the bar, $(-)$, which prevents the signifier, S, from grasping its signified, s. In this formula, it should be noted, the "signified" is used to symbolize the "true meaning," not the conscious concept.)

The metaphor, in contrast, is the "symptom" which provides access to "l'autre scène," the stage of the Unconscious, where lies the True Scenario hidden beneath the veil of the subject's metonymic displacements. And that is why its formula, based on the *substitution* of "mot pour mot," permits the "franchissement de la barre" permitting access to the realm of signification which had been denied the metonymy: $f\left(\dfrac{S}{S}\right)S = S(+)s$. (In other words, the signifying function of the substitution of one signifier for another $\left(\dfrac{S}{S}\right)$ is equivalent to a "crossing" of the bar which permits the revelation of meaning, the "grasping" of the "signified"—$S(+)s$.)

The real meaning of the signifier cannot be gleaned from its "literal," "mot à mot" syntactic displacements; it is only in substituting the "surface" signifier *for* another, in discovering *what* the conscious signifier is a substitute *for* (what repressed signifier it replaces—and, in replacing, attempts to hide) that the truth can be grasped. The strategy of the Lacanian metaphoric analysis is designed to break through the barrier separating language from meaning, the "I" from the "id," the rhetoric from the Logos; and the signifier provides access to the riches of this meaningful realm by showing us not only what is said (which is meaningless, the "peu de sens"), but more importantly by indicating what "it" does *not* say—the *lack* to which "it" points: "metaphor occurs (*se place*) at the precise point at which sense emerges from (*se produit dans*) non-sense."[16] For the real meaning of the

Maria Ruegg

signifier lies precisely in what it does *not* say, and in the absence "it" reveals: absence which points to a "being" and a "truth" which is present there, below the surface of conscious discourse, beyond the bar of resistance, in the Other Scene.

The function of the metaphor is then to reveal the "true discourse" of the unconscious: that is, the network of *symbols* which are, in fact, the origin of those metonymic displacements and those metaphoric veils —the rhetorical figures designed precisely to "cover up" (to repress, to resist the revelation of) their own (and the subject's) signification. The symbol—like the Platonic Idea and the Hegelian Concept (to which the Lacanian text refers us) is absolutely prior, autonomous, and determinant in relation to the "real" (physical reality) and the "imaginary" (conscious, rational thought). The symbolic order as Lacan repeatedly insists, "constitutes" man: ". . . (The) truth which emerges from (this) moment of Freudian thought is that it is the symbolic order which is, for the subject, constitutive"; "the order of the symbol can no longer be conceived as constituted by man, but as constituting him."[17]

What then is "the symbolic"? On the one hand, the symbolic functions, in the Lacanian text, as a purely abstract, structuring principle: reduced to its essence, it would be merely the structural alternative of "presence" and "absence," the scientifically objective, value-free mathematical sequence of "0" and "1." And as such, it would "constitute" man in so far as all desire, and hence all action, is desire for some thing, some object, some "presence," which must by definition be "absent" if it serves as an object of desire. An "absence" or a "lack" is, in that sense, always *prior* to and *constitutive of* man's desire for "presence"; but that desire is, of course, always illusory, since the moment we "possess" what we took to be the object of our desire—the moment the object becomes "present" to us—it is no longer, by definition, the object of our desire.

And it is in that sense, for Lacan, that man's life is symbolically structured by the "modulated couple" of presence and absence: "man literally devotes his time to deploying the structural alternative in which presence and absence each call the other forth" (où la présence et l'absence prennent l'une de l'autre leur appel).[18] And it is in that sense that the game described by Freud—in which a child makes an object appear and disappear—can serve, for Lacan, as the *model metaphor* of man's determination by the symbolic: "This game wherein the child plays at making an object disappear from view, only to bring it back, and then to obliterate it once again, an object whose nature is moreover indifferent, while at the same time he modulates this alternance of distinctive syllables ("Fort! Da!") this game, we say, manifests in its radical traits the determination that the human animal receives from the symbolic order."[19] Man 's life is nothing but a prolongation of that same game—game which, here, is regulated only by the abstract symbolic paradigm of a desire for presence *in general*, and the "truth" of an absence which is equally general.

But if Lacan's rhetoric consisted merely in reducing all language and all behavior to the simple, purely abstract structure of "presence" and "absence," it would be of as little use, of as little interest, and of as little effect as Jakobson's reduction of all linguistic phenomena to the abstract poles of "contiguity" and "similarity." What gives the Lacanian analysis its particular force is the fact that it *specifies the nature* of those symbolic "absences" that determine our desire; and in doing so, provides us with a *code*, a translation key, in terms of which all discourse can at last be truly understood.

The master symbol of that code—master symbol at once of absence and of desire—is the phallus. For Lacan, the phallus is the signifier of signifiers, "intended (destiné) to designate as a whole the effects of the signified."[20] Neither "real," nor "imaginary," the phallus represents *the* absence which makes it the ultimate object of desire: for the phallus in question is the phallus that Mother Never Had. And as such, it is the symbol that permits Lacan to articulate *female* desire in terms of penis-envy, and *male* desire in terms of the fear of castration:

Clinical experience has shown us that this test of the desire of the Other is decisive not in the sense that the subject learns by it whether or not he has a real phallus, but *in the sense that he learns that the mother does not have it.* This is the moment of the experience without which no symptomatic consequence (phobia) or structural consequence (Penisneid) relating to the castration complex can take effect. Here is signed the conjunction of desire, in that the phallic signifier is its mark, *with the threat or nostalgia of lacking it.*

Of course, its future depends on the law introduced by the father into this sequence.[21] (My emphasis)

If the object of desire—the symbolic phallus—is the *same* for both sexes, the social and cultural effects of that symbolic desire on the two sexes are radically *different*: for the actions of the one are determined by a "nostalgia" for what it "lacks," while the actions of the other are determined by the "menace" of *losing* what it "has": and in either case, it is the "law of the *father*" (who, in this case, is quite real) that will determine the future of both.

It is not by chance that Lacan compares the function of the phallus to the function of the Nous and the Logos in ancient philosophy.[22] For what the Lacanian text offers, far more than a "return to Freud," is a return to the comforting security of classical metaphysical idealism, and a return to the comforting security of the classical rhetorics which permitted readers to reduce all discourse to the terms of such a metaphysics. Despite the intentionally elusive games it constantly plays with the reader, there is no free play in the Lacanian text. And no way for the subject(s) to change the rules of the symbolically determined language game which determines his/her discourse and his/her desire.

The "revolutionary" theory of language upon which Lacan's "rhetoric of the unconscious" is based is, likewise, a reinscription of the most traditional, mimetic theories of language. If it is "the world of words" that engenders "the world of things" ("It is the world of words that creates the world of things"[23]), it is not by deriving the meaning of those words from any arbitrary metonymic displacements; for if things are constituted by words, words are in turn constituted and determined by *symbols* ("Man speaks, then, but it is because the symbol has made him man"[24]). For Lacan, "the word is already a presence made of absence";[25] that is, the word is a material "presence" (letter, body, appearance, veil) which represents an "absence"—a symbol which itself has no "material" reality, but which *determines* that reality . . . as its soul, essence, being, truth.

The Lacanian text offers at once the illusion of an openended poetic play, and the comforting reassurance that that "play" is, in fact rigidly controlled. The rhetoric of the text itself, like the crossword puzzles which Lacan would make part of the young analyst's training,[26] offers the vicarious thrill of solving problems to which the answers—however difficult to find—have always been carefully pre-arranged. But the seductive power of the Lacanian text does not lie in the self-gratifying pleasure of deciphering its all too obviously calculated hermetic style. It lies rather, on the one hand, in the metaphysical security which the text provides in the guise of an objective, "clinically proven" scientific truth: in its appeal, beyond the pleasure principle, to that desire for ontological certainty which manifests itself in the faith that man's fate, however grim, is once and for all decided. The "design of man's destiny," in Lacan's words, is always already traced "before he comes into the world" ("Symbols in fact envelop the life of man in a network so total that they conjoin, before he comes into the world, those who are going to engender him . . . so that they bring to his birth . . . the design (dessin) of his destiny."[27]), and for Lacan it is traced, like the handwriting on the wall ("les lettres de muraille") in such an indelible way that man has no alternative (barring madness, or worse yet, stupidity) but to accept it with stoic passivity. But on the other hand, and no doubt even more, the seductive power of the Lacanian text lies in the intoxicating promise of epistemological mastery implicit in the assumption that *all* discourse, including the most poetic, is constructed like a crossword puzzle, and that if anyone, it is the analyst who possesses the key.

Yet if the rhetorical force of the Lacanian text lies in its power to persuade the reader that rhetoric is subject to the force of analytic mastery, Lacan, like Socrates, is far too clever a rhetorician to claim mastery of that knowledge himself. And it is for that reason that he insists that the analyst is not the "subject who knows," but merely the "subject who is supposed to know" (le sujet supposé savoir); and the analyst, if he knows anything at all, knows, like Socrates, that it is only others who suppose that he knows. But the irony—which can quite properly be called Socratic, and which serves so effectively to transmit the same metaphysical idealism—is that the "subject who is supposed to know" has done everything in his rhetorical power to persuade others to attribute to him the very knowledge he so modestly disavows.

The irony of rhetoric, in the classical sense of the term (and Lacan's use of rhetoric is, as I have attempted to argue, highly classical), is that the subordination of rhetoric ultimately depends on a rhetorical gesture; and the effectiveness of that gesture has little to do with its epistemological qualifications, but much more with its power to *persuade* the reader that such a mastery of rhetoric is legitimate. The mastery of rhetoric ultimately rests on a rhetoric of mastery. And Lacan, like Socrates, is one of the few to have understood that irony—despite a whole tradition which accuses it of negativity and destructiveness—is in fact the trope of mastery par excellence. For it is the trope which legitimizes, in disarming its opposition, the "tour de force" by means of which rhetoric has already been subordinated to the master's Truth.

The rhetorical force of a figure like "les non-dupes errent" ("the non-dupes err": that is, those who think they are not dupes, those who think they "know," are mistaken; but at the same time, "les noms du père" and "les nons du père," referring to the simultaneous assumption of the Name of the Father and of His symbolic interdictions[28]) does not lie in the somewhat heavy-handed and strictly circumscribed polysemics of the pun. Like Lacan's metalinguistic disavowal of metalanguage ("There is no metalanguage. This affirmation is possible in as much as I have added one to the list of those that abound in the fields of science"[29]), it lies in the ironic manipulation of self-referential ambiguity: ambiguity which, in this case (as in the case so frequently made for Socrates), has the function of defusing the metaphysical charges which can only be avoided, but not denied.

Following the advice he gives the Minister at the end of the "Seminar on 'The Purloined Letter,'" Lacan consults his cards one last time before putting them on the table, and reading his own game, "he rises from the table in time to avoid the shame."[30] Lacan may err—as indeed he does, in the narrowness of his phallocentric determinism—but he is certainly no dupe: which is no doubt why he remains, in the eyes of his (non-) duped followers, a Master.

NOTES

1. The term "epistemological rupture"—which frequently appeared in structuralist texts of the 60's (in particular, the texts of Althusser, Foucault, and the *Tel Quel* group)—derives from Bachelard, who (in *La Formation de l'esprit scientifique*) used the term to apply to the "radical breaks" between scientific periods (the "pre-scientific" period thus refers to science before the nineteenth century; the "scientific" period is the nineteenth century; the "new scientific" period is the post-Einsteinean twentieth century: the notion of "radical rupture" obviously bears a close resemblance to Kuhn's concept of "scientific revolution"). The obsessive desire of structuralists to constitute a *science*—of man, of language, of literature—has yet to be analyzed.

2. Thus, Barthes published a résumé of classical rhetoric ("L'Ancienne Rhétorique: Aide-mémoire," *Communications*, No. 16, 1970) and at the same time used concepts derived from that rhetoric in his "structural" analyses (see, for example, "L'Analyse rhétorique" in *Littérature et Société*, Brussels, 1967; and "La Rhétorique de l'image" in *Communications*, No. 4, 1964). Groupe MU's *Rhétorique Générale* (Larousse, 1970) is an effort to construct a modern rhetoric. Genette (who edited Fontanier's classical *Figures du discours* [Flammarion, 1968]) has also made abundant use of classical rhetoric: see his "Métonymie chez Proust ou la naissance du récit," *Poétique* No. 2 (1970), and "La Rhétorique restreinte" in *Communications*, No. 16 (1970).

3. The original essay appeared in *Fundamentals of Language* (written in collaboration with Morris Halle) (The Hague: Mouton, 1956).

4. Ibid., pp. 76–77.

5. In *Communications*, no. 16 (1970).

6. In *Style and Language*, ed. Sebeok (Cambridge, Mass.: MIT Press, 1960).

7. Paul de Man, "Semiology and Rhetoric," *Diacritics* 3:3 (1973).

8. "Similarity in meaning connects the symbols of a metalanguage with the symbols of the language referred to. Similarity connects a metaphorical term with the term for which it is substituted. Consequently, when constructing a metalanguage to interpret tropes, the researcher possesses more homogeneous means to handle metaphor, whereas metonymy, based on a different principle, easily defies interpretation." Jakobson, "Two Aspects of Language and Two Types of Aphasic Disorders," p. 81.

9. Introduction to the Points edition of *Ecrits*, 1 (1966), 7.

10. "The Agency of the Letter in the Unconscious, or Reason Since Freud" ("L'Instance de la lettre dans l'inconscient, ou la raison depuis Freud") in *Ecrits: A Selection*, trans., Sheridan (New York: Norton, 1977), p. 166.

11. See "The Function and Field of Speech and Language in Psychoanalysis" ("Fonction et champ de la parole et du langage en psychanalyse") in *Ecrits*, ibid., pp. 90–91.

12. Ibid., p. 55.

13. "The Agency of the Letter in the Unconscious," ibid., p. 171.

14. Ibid., p. 167.

15. Ibid., p. 164.

16. Ibid., p. 158.

17. "Le Séminaire sur 'La Lettre volée'," in *Ecrits* (Paris: Seuil, 1966), pp. 12, 46.

18. Ibid., p. 46.

19. Ibid.

20. "The Signification of the Phallus" ("La Signification du phallus"), in *Ecrits: A Selection*, p. 285.

21. Ibid., p. 289.

22. Ibid., p. 291.

23. "The Function and Field of Speech . . . ," in *Ecrits*, p. 65.

24. Ibid.

25. Ibid.

26. Ibid., p. 56.

27. Ibid., p. 68.

28. The title of Lacan's seminar in 1973–74 (to appear as Livre XXI in the Seuil publications of the seminars).

29. Introduction to the Points edition of *Ecrits*, 1, p. 12.

30. "Le Séminaire sur 'La Lettre volée'," in *Ecrits*, p. 41.

EIGHT
CRITICISM AND ITS OBJECTS
Richard Eldridge

Our age is, in especial degree, the age of criticism,
and to criticism everything must submit.
Immanuel Kant, *Critique of Pure Reason*, Axii, n.a.

I

CRITICISM AND THE CONCEPT OF A MEDIUM

WHAT IS the relation of critical writing to the work it reads? The terms
"critic," "criticize," "criterion," etc., are derived from the Greek *krinein*,
meaning to separate, decide, or judge. *Krinein* in turn is derived from
the Proto-Indo-European *skeri-*, to cut, a root which also issues in the
Greek *krei-men* (crime, recriminate) and the Latin *scribere* (to scratch,
incise, or write; cf. scribble, script, etc.). The root is first noticed in
English writing in 1544 as a medical term, the adjective "critical"
meaning "relating to or involving the crisis of a disease, etc." (e.g., "a
day judiciall or creticke of the ague"). We see in this etymology death
and writing linked together in a concept of diagnosis and appropriation
(crime) at a moment of crisis.

Despite the etymological sedimentation of its name, criticism is
often considered to be a mode of discourse in which a truth independently constituted and borne by a literary work is simply revealed
and transmitted, a medium. What could be clearer? After all, we some-

times say such things as "I never (really) understood Wordsworth until I read M. H. Abrams," or "Michael Fried made me see for the first time what Morris Louis's veil series means." There are close parallels here with epistemology. Both criticism and epistemology tend to be characterized by such adjectives as "revealing," "penetrating," and "insightful," each of which suggests the transmission of some object through critical or epistemological writing.

But is this formula—"Criticism (or epistemology) is a mode of discourse in which . . ."—an adequate conceptualization of how criticism or epistemology works (on us)? Both critical writing and epistemological writing require the assent of their audiences to their analyses in order to become what they aspire to be, vehicles of truth. The claims they put forth are never established as insight-bearing until an audience confirms both their truth and their newness. Insofar as the satisfaction of the function of critical and epistemological writing, the mediate presentation of new truths about an old object, is always deferred beyond the moment of its production, the ability of these kinds of writing to control the satisfaction of that function, to control their media, is called into question.

If the attempt to do so is nonetheless made, it can only proceed by treating the object as already the bearer of the phenomena whose apprehension and description awaited only the forging of the terms of criticism controlling the analysis. But if the object of analysis is *necessarily* so treated, the confrontation between object and analysis which alone can directly confirm the analysis never takes place. If the analysis cannot fail, then the nature of its success is problematic. The ideal saturation of the object of analysis with the phenomena the analysis can treat, a saturation which takes place prior to the production of the analysis, means that the attempt of critical and epistemological writing to situate itself as a medium proceeds indirectly through an act of idealization. Critical and epistemological analysis cannot speak the truth of the object in itself. Hence the truth of any analysis will reside not in its ability to capture any such truth, but rather in its ability to insist to an audience on its characterization of an object. Describing the transcendental logic of analysis, a logic of insistence, will enable us to see that necessary evanescence of analytical understanding which continually calls forth new writing. To see what strategies of insistence writing has evolved, to see how it has (only) attempted to control its medium, is to test our possible modes of criticism and epistemology.

Hegel fastened on the paradox involved in construing theoretically a certain activity aiming at knowing—in his case, cognition—as a medium through which truth is transmitted and grasped. If the medium is taken to reshape its object actively in the course of the transmission, the object itself escapes the ability of the medium to capture it. But if the medium is taken to be wholly passive or the law of its refraction is independently known, then the concept of a medium becomes useless as a key concept in a theory of cognition: "Either way we employ a means [*ein Mittel*: that is, the concept of a medium in a theory of cognition] which immediately brings about the opposite of its own end [an understanding of cognition]; or rather, what is really absurd [*das Widersinnige*] is that we should make use of a means at all."[1]

Despite this seemingly unavoidable absurdity in considering the apprehension of truth to take place through a medium, even Hegelian Science found itself obliged to preface itself with a phenomenology designed precisely to serve as a medium for its apprehension. While apparently rejecting the concept of a medium, it cannot help making use of it. "Science, just because it comes on the scene [*eintreten*], is itself an appearance: in coming on the scene it is not yet Science in its developed and unfolded truth." Hence it must contest its title as a mode of knowledge with the other appearances which surround it on the scene.[2] The *Phenomenology of Spirit* is the place of this contest. Hegelian Science establishes itself as a known body of truths only by being revealed by the *Phenomenology*, its medium. Although it thus exists as Absolute Knowing only as apprehended through the *Phenomenology*, Science wishes to deny the contingency of that mediated apprehension, to control its medium. Hence Science attempts to pronounce truths which are fully rational and universal, truths which would make the contingency with which the *Phenomenology* begins impossible. Despite the fact that, as initially an appearance, it can arise only through a contest with other appearances in world history, Science denies that this contest ever took place in any real sense. It denies its medium by forgetting its origin in it. Science thus centers or fixes itself in its self-contemplation in virtue of its forgetting of its initial reasons for testing itself, a forgetting which is at the same time the memory that it was always already there, at all moments in history, behind all appearances.

This kind of turning against its origins as appearance is crucial to any system—including the systems of criticism—which attempts to pronounce necessary truths underlying and motivating the medium in which the system initially situates itself. A system of analytical understanding's denial of essential reality to its origin as an appearance is that system's denial that it has idealized its objects. By denying its performance of an act of idealization, it claims to apprehend the real essences of its objects. Only such a claim can inspire that conviction in the analysis's audience which is necessary for it to satisfy its function, to be an analysis. By turning against its origin as an appearance, an analysis attempts to reconcile the contingency of its appearance on the scene with the necessity it claims on behalf of its knowing.

In Hegel's writing, the ultimate transcendence of the medium of appearance in an Absolute Knowing which envelops all mediations is guaranteed by the logic of the transitions along the path followed by natural unreflective consciousness and its associated modes of expression and understanding. The presuppositions supporting various more or less unreflective philosophical systems are uncovered dialectically and collected into truth through each succeeding system's negation of the presuppositions of its predecessors. The moment of negation is a moment of skepticism on the part of consciousness about the possibility of understanding. The only function which binds these series of negations into a collective and progressive one is consciousness's ability, in skeptical despair, to retain even in its new stage the ideas and opinions now rejected as inadequate to secure understanding. By retaining these ideas and opinions, consciousness is able to establish their true significance as finite stages of its path to Absolute Knowing, to make them its media. It is this ability to remember the character of its earlier stages which makes consciousness's moments of negation determinate and significant and which ultimately validates consciousness as the vehicle of Spirit. In general then,

The skepticism that is directed against the whole range of phenomenal consciousness . . . renders the Spirit for the first time competent to examine what truth is. For it brings about a stage of despair about all the so-called natural ideas, thoughts, and opinions, regardless of whether they are called one's own or someone else's, ideas with which the consciousness that sets about the examination of truth *straight away* is still filled and hampered, so that it is, in fact, incapable of carrying out what it wants to undertake.

The necessary progression and interconnection of the forms of the unreal consciousness will by itself bring to pass the *completion* of the series.[3]

The ability of Spirit to master its medium, consciousness and its stages, thus turns on a specific property of consciousness in the grip of skepticism—its ability to preserve the ideas characteristic of its earlier stages so as subsequently to assign their proper meaning to them.

But what if skeptical doubt is not self-reflective in just this way? What if one always finds oneself forced, in moods of suspicion or incomprehension, to treat one's own ideas as those of another, to put those ideas in new words which *really express* (even if only momentarily) the essence hidden under the old ideas? Will this process of finding new words result in a recovery of what one once thought or meant? Or will it simply issue in a new, essentially *discrete* understanding? Just how do we explain the meaning to ourselves of something we find ourselves unable to understand when that something is one of our

Richard Eldridge

own ideas? Certainly simply repeating a set of words or running over ideas in a stupor will not do. Consider how we actually explain the meanings of some expressions to one another in conversation:

> If I say, "Sufficient unto the day is the evil thereof," which I take to be the literal truth, then . . . I shall perhaps not be surprised that you do not get my meaning. [Here I will not,] unless my disappointment pricks me into offense, offer to teach you the meaning of an English expression. What I might do is try to *put my thought another way*, and perhaps refer you, depending upon who you are, to a range of similar or identical thoughts expressed by others.[4]

Here someone who does not understand may not be unaware of the meanings of the words or the significance of the ideas proper. Rather, one lacks the voice in which they were uttered, and what one needs is a way back to the voice, a hint as to what those words could (be used to) mean. And when teaching the meaning of an expression is not in order, more words are—words that will aim at the voice that uttered a certain expression, appropriate it, and make it our own.

If the need for new understanding which arises in moments of skepticism about our past understandings and the present possibilities they allow is like the need for understanding which requires a direction to new expressions, then the logic of critical understanding will be broken and nonprogressive. Once we have begun to *put our thoughts another way*, we have begun to remove ourselves from an understanding of our first words and ideas as much as we promote it. The necessary attempt at interpretation will never attain its object in a way which is fully satisfying, for the new words we produce are in turn soon subject to their own attendant doubts and misunderstandings. In attempting to find our way about in language, we follow a path of themes and connections which, while allowing the discovery of ever-greater linguistic treasures, constantly both removes us further from our point of departure and suggests further steps to be taken. In the hope of attaching to one another with essential security our ways of putting our thoughts, we attempt to recover what Mallarmé called a root or origin (*racine*) lying underneath the surface of a language now problematized by doubt:

> Qu' est-ce qu'une *racine*? Un assemblage de lettres, de consonnes souvent, montrant plusieurs mots d'une langue comme disséqués, réduits à leurs os et à leurs tendons, soustraits à leur vie ordinaire, afin qu'on reconnaisse entre eux une parenté secrète: plus succinct et plus évanoui encore, on a un *thème*.[5]

But, as Mallarmé argues by observing his own progress in tracing actual linguistic connections, this project of recovery both spirals into the infinite distance of human prehistory and circles back on itself:

[D'] où l'on pourrait conclure à bon droit que les milliers de mots d'une langue sont apparentés entre eux. Tout est de savoir commencer et finir ou de préciser à quel degré se rompra, plus ou moins prolongé, le lien familial: discernment très subtil, car il ne dépend d'aucune règle absolue. De racines et de thèmes, à proprement parler, il n'y en a plus, puisqu'on a été obligé de remonter à des époques immémoriales pour trouver ceux-ci . . . .[6]

If the need that is felt in skeptical moods is indeed a need for this kind of always evaporating explanation of the source of a given expression, then Hegel's progressive logic of negation will be a myth. If we doubt the real significance of our expressions in this way, then no attempt to connect expressions whose significance we have lost with new ones will result in an essentially guaranteed way back to the consciousness which once voiced them, to a consciousness no longer present, a consciousness lost behind a veil of doubt and misunderstanding. The explanatory power of the new words will evaporate in the ideality, the nonessentiality, of their connection with the old. New words will not master the medium of language.

Nonetheless, Hegel's attempt to secure understanding is not altogether misplaced. Any words able to do the work which needs doing must be at least momentarily fixed. It is possible to carry out in a way which will hold for a moment a rational reconstruction of the meaning of an expression. Similarly, just because analytical writing consists of expressions putatively attached under the authority of a common theme to an experience or work to be recovered, it can sometimes rationally reconstruct its object—an experience or a literary work—in a way which satisfies present intents and purposes. Such reconstructions must relate in a stable fashion the words or ideas to be recovered to the present moment and its words or ideas. It must repeat in its own terms what has been lost. Hence any words which can carry out this task of reconstruction must, in the interests of the stability and the power of relation that are required, repress or forget their own status as identically unsecured linguistic entities and deny, at least for the moment, that they will no more be able to ground themselves essentially than was the stage of consciousness which is their object.

What is left is a dialectical movement from particular moment to particular moment, controlled, with only relative success, by our current interests and situations. Descriptions, answering to current interests, of objects and experiences which we wish understood are produced. Then, as the power of such descriptions is analyzed, as the ability of such descriptions to constitute thematically a medium of understanding is considered, the nonessential character of the connection between the descriptions and the object described is uncovered. The principles of the medium of understanding constituted by the initial descriptions are formulated. These principles claim to represent, as a partial mode of necessity relative to the wider new thematic descriptions they provide, the necessity connecting description and object described. But just because these principles come on the scene, they can lay claim to necessity only by repressing the contingency of their own appearance and apprehension as necessary for understanding. Hence, in attempting to describe the necessary relation between description and object described, these principles repeat the very act of repression which they uncovered as the source of the stability of the initial description.

The recovery of the repression stabilizing the principles of a given set of descriptions, a recovery which leads to a recasting of those principles as appearances (relative now to the medium constituted thematically by the new principles which made the diagnosis and recovery possible) defines criticism. And if criticism begins by treating its object as an appearance whose necessity it will explicate, it thereby also displays its own submission to the logic of appearance. It is perhaps for such reasons that Hegel, hoping vainly to avoid the use of principles in Absolute Knowing, observed that

a so-called basic proposition of philosophy, if true, is also false, just because it is *only* a principle. It is, therefore, easy to refute it. The refutation consists in pointing out its defect; and it is defective because it is only the universal or principle, is only the beginning. If the refutation is thorough, it is derived and developed from the principle itself, not accomplished by counterassertions and random thoughts from outside. The refutation would, therefore, properly consist in the further development of the principle.[7]

Criticism develops the principles of its objects. It repeats them aloud, bringing to consciousness their repressions. But this repetition takes place and completes itself only insofar as critical writing represses its own origins in the vain hope of eternally mastering its medium, thereby repeating the initial gesture of its object. Analytical writing is the repetition of this situation. The convincingness with which any such writing can manage to repeat the principles of its object is our measure of its truth.

II

READING POULET

Poulet's writing begins by redescribing thematically the fundamental project of a given writer. The terms, those of subjective time and subjective space, which provide Poulet with his themes—terms whose claim to metaphysical privilege as the proper terms for the description of human experience is argued abstractly through a blend of Bergson and Sartre—are not as important in themselves as they are in establishing the parameters of Poulet's critical investigation. Poulet does not investigate subjective space and time in themselves. Rather he assumes a certain necessary and fully conscious understanding of subjective space and time as places of experience and proceeds to sketch the paths of various individual writers through these places. Poulet's writing is important precisely because, taking for granted the theme provided by the concept of a path through subjective space and time, it takes up the project of the description of its objects and because Poulet pushes this writing to its limits of intelligibility, to the point where the space in which it locates itself begins to evaporate. Here Poulet can only insist on the ability of his chosen themes nonetheless to promote understanding. That Poulet's writing may be seen to issue at its limits in insistences about the necessary thematic character of its objects will lead to a description of the understandings it makes possible in general as depending upon the repetition of the attempt to master a medium. The terms of this *act of repetition* constitute the identity of Poulet's writing.

The space of Poulet's writing, the medium within which Poulet attempts to repeat other writers' repetitions of a journey through an experiential field, is opened by a claim about the location of thoughts in general. The claim to direct knowledge of this location or medium of the experience of thinking furnishes Poulet with the analytical terms which will enable him to describe the experiences of the objects of his investigations as repetitions within this medium:

Ma pensée est un espace où ont lieu, où ont leur lieu mes pensées. Les voici qui arrivent, passent, s'écartent ou s'enfoncent, et je les distingue à des distances spatiales ou temporelles qui ne cessent de varier. Ma pensée n'est pas faite seulement de mes pensées; elle est faite encore, et bien plus peut-être, de toute la *distance intérieure* qui me sépare ou me rapproche de ce qui je puis penser.[8]

This gesture, the naming of the container outside the contained, repeats exactly Kant's gesture in naming space and time as the media of experience. It has been remarked that Kant bore no animus towards metaphysics, he simply thought that no one before him had ever done any because of a universal failure to appreciate the proper media of metaphysical investigation. The same thing could be said of Poulet and criticism.

Like Hegel, Poulet denies that his command of the principles of the medium proper to critical investigation is essentially a contingent achievement. Whatever contingency inhabits his criticism as an achievement Poulet will ascribe to the failure of others to appreciate what they have always already been doing while reading. Thus Poulet remarks that

"[When I read] I am aware of a rational being, of a consciousness; the consciousness of another, no different from the one I *automatically assume* in every human being I encounter, except that in this case the consciousness is open to me, welcomes me, lets me look deep inside itself, and even allows me, with unheard-of license, to think what it thinks and feel what it feels."[9] Poulet here takes "the intervention of language," the author's writing, to provide him with access to the author's mode of existence in the medium of consciousness, interior distance. The ability of his criticism to reveal or elucidate the consciousness of the author is due to his *a priori* grasp (he mentions both an act of "apperception" and a "fundamental *cogito*") of the possibilities for consciousness given by its medium. Hence his reading "might rather be called a *phenomenon* by which mental objects rise up from the depths of consciousness into the light of recognition."[10]

The appropriation of other writers' writings takes place then through the formulation of a description of those writings which locates them in the medium of interior distance. This description brings out both the identity of all writings and the differences among them by focusing on shared structures of self-representation, determined by the possibilities permitted by the medium, which are filled in with various particular awarenesses. After describing the circle as "a structural principle for all types of consciousness" (one identical structure, different consciousnesses), Poulet goes on to describe the metamorphoses of the circle as "the changes of meaning to which it has never ceased to adapt itself in the human mind. These changes of meaning coincide with corresponding changes in the manner by which human beings represent to themselves that which is deepest in themselves, that is to say, the awareness of their relationship with the inner and the outer worlds; their consciousness of space and duration."[11] Poulet's criticism is the perception of the continual adaptations of this identical structure, carried out by other writers in the interest of self-representation, within the given space of experience. Poulet's writing repeats these adaptations.

This repetition of adaptations produces in Poulet's writing a union of being (the eternal identity of this structure) and becoming (the new content), a union that is characteristic of critical understanding's analytical appropriation of earlier writing. "Poulet conceives of literature as the eternally repeated sequence of new beginnings."[12] It is this conception which allows Poulet himself to aim at transcending that repetition by naming it.

Mallarmé's writings, despite their difficulty, allow the perfect operation of Poulet's method, for, in reading Mallarmé according to that method, all the work is done at the very beginning. Though Mallarmé may seem to resist appropriation to a consciousness-bounded structure

of space and time, once the appropriation has been initially carried out,
Mallarmé's writings immediately cast themselves as representations of
a series of practical confrontations between desire and the bounded field
of consciousness. Each of these confrontations issues in a particular
movement within this field, subsequently represented in a poem or a
set of poems.

Poulet begins this appropriation by characterizing Mallarmé's
poetic desire as a wish to express an ideal which exists in virtue of the
poet's dream alone. This desire is clearly impossible, for a dream only
exists as a dream in virtue of its specific opposition to wakefulness. If
our dreams generate our ideals, we must nonetheless acknowledge that
our dreams require for their specific existence an alternation with wakefulness. Thus, given this impossible situation, the chief question in
writing poetry becomes for Mallarmé, "How can I even begin to express
an impossible ideal?" or, in Poulet's terms, "Comment trouver un point
de départ?" In so styling the question opening Mallarmé's writings,
Poulet himself is actually asking "What can my criticism, which depends
upon the existence of such a point within a specific field, say about
Mallarmé?" And here the answer is found, the work is done, in making
"Comment trouver un point de départ?" Mallarmé's question, for the
point of departure is already a key concept in Poulet's writing, the moment at which a consciousness begins to exist in the medium of interior
distance. Poetic desire wells up, the question is uttered as a sigh, and
Mallarmé situates himself within the field of Poulet's criticism. For
Poulet, the sigh represents Mallarmé's first practical response to a
theoretically impossible situation, and *as a practical action* it determines
itself as an originating motion in the field of subjective experience. In
reality, a sigh is no more adequate as an expression of an absolutely
impossible desire (why should one *sigh* at absolutely nothing? how can
an ideal which cannot have been even vestigially present be lost and
sighed for?) than any other action. But as an action which Mallarmé
happened to perform, this sigh gives Poulet's criticism a foothold. The
notion of the practical projection of a desire governs the subsequent
course of Poulet's writing on Mallarmé. This projection is taken to be
the mode of Mallarmé's repetition of consciousness's characteristic
action, a motion, in the field of subjective space and time in which it
is situated.

In their very practicality, Mallarmé's impossible projections come
to represent for Poulet the purest form of writing as a positive operation
carried out by a specific consciousness in an eternally recurring situation. It is thus no accident that Poulet honors Mallarmé with his highest
praise: Mallarmé's voluntary combinations of words reflect the very
structure of time which is presupposed in Poulet's own criticism. Poulet

might be describing his own writing when, after characterizing the structure of projection in Mallarmé's poetry, he writes: "Ainsi l'opération volontaire de la parole a le même office que le mouvement involontaire du temps. Reléquant en l'oubli tout contour réel, elle décompose le monde en ses éléments spirituels, pour qu'il n'en émane plus que les 'notions pures.' "[13]

Poulet finds that in virtue of Mallarmé's voluntary combinations of words, an exchange with the reader takes place: the pure notions shine through the writing. Poulet banks everything on the power of his own writing to effect such exchanges. In an exchange between author and reader carried out in the light of the pure notion, thought finds and founds itself—achievements which are the objects of Poulet's criticism: "Ainsi poème et lecteur, spectacle et spectateur se fondent en une même pensée, qui est tout simplement la pensée réflexive. Je me fonde et me trouve dans le moment parfait et dans le lieu absolu où je crée ma pensée, et la reconnais pour mienne. L'espace, la durée, l'univers de mon poème, c'est moi.

Moi projété absolu."[14]

Moi protégé absolu! Poulet here writes in the full assurance of his method. Mallarmé is the perfect example of a writer situated in Poulet's medium. But has the appropriation really taken place? And if so, where? Granted that Poulet may have found (as have others) the only way to read Mallarmé by reading his poems as the result of an action practically motivated by a desire. But has he invested anything in his reading of Mallarmé? Does Mallarmé test his categories of reading? No. Poulet repeats Mallarmé's project, but he does not repeat its action of fixing its own categories of experience and terms of understanding as it utters them. The appropriation of Mallarmé takes place outside the act of reading. The terms of this reading are fixed before it begins and are never tested.

Some such fixing is no doubt necessary for reading to begin, to take place, and to end. But the use of fixed terms of understanding seems to block the sort of confrontation between author and reader where the outcome is in danger. Not only that, but in fixing his terms of understanding, Poulet makes those terms necessary and directly obvious, thereby engendering a paradox concerning the obviousness and necessity of these terms and the status as appearance of the contingent mode of knowledge—Poulet's own critical writing—they were to constitute. This paradox makes critical understanding, the insightful application of these terms to specific writings, *essentially problematic.*

How does this problem of application arise? The categories of subjective space and time are designed to apply to all writing, indeed to all experience. All acts of writing are taken to repeat, whether by identity, inversion, condensation, etc., a certain pattern of movement in the field of subjective space and time. Since these categories and this pattern of movement are universal, they must apply to Poulet's own writing. But this blocks the ability of these terms to perform new epistemological functions, critical functions, in Poulet's writing. If Poulet's writing is only one writing among many, as his principles of reading tell us it must be, what power do those principles have to master and organize the very medium in which they are situated as a phenomenon? Similarly, if Poulet's categories fail to apply to his own writing, then they likewise lose their universality and organizing power. Poulet's writing would transcend all writing, and yet at the same time remain writing. It is impossible.

Poulet's genius is that in the face of this paradox his writing comes to display the kind of insistence which can momentarily force understanding. Just when the categories Poulet uses to describe various authors' situations in the field of subjective space and time are beginning to rigidify—simple location and movement within that field are placed under the authority of the organizing figure of the circle—he reconfronts writers who stretch the figure out of shape. Yet Poulet continues to write, and the result is a criticism which repeats the aims of its objects in advancing our understanding from particular point to particular point through the thematic production of an organizing figure which holds for a moment.

The circle as an organizing figure begins to break down—Poulet's writing begins to test itself as a mode of knowledge—when Poulet confronts Romantic writing where the conditions of understanding have become problematic (a problem Poulet's writing shares). Where once God had been an omni*present* organizing force, "the circle whose center is everywhere and circumference nowhere," man becomes in Romantic writing situated within a circle similar in outline but no longer held in place as a figure for God's presence. "The infinite sphere is nothing now but the field encompassed by human consciousness."[15] And once God is no longer present to this field, the outlines of the circle begin to evaporate. The self finds itself within a field without clear horizons. And without clear horizons, there is no longer a limited field to be traversed and understood through a simple journey.

God's initial absence meant that for the first time consciousness appeared as a consciousness of loss. In the Romanticism exemplified by Tieck's writings, Poulet finds that "For the first time there clearly appears the consciousness of the non-identity which distinguishes the self-center from the circumferential nonself."[16] But without God's presence determining the horizons of experience and understanding, the non-self soon lost its circumferential status. And with this loss, the self lost its reciprocally determined status as center. Writing after the Romantic turn becomes an attempt to recenter experience by establishing a central self and a circumference which will limit in the interest of understanding the field it is required to traverse: "All philosophy therefore becomes a study of the similarities existing between center and circle, and even more, of their dependence one upon the other. 'Just as,' writes Friedrich Schlegel, 'the center is center in relation to the periphery, and the periphery is periphery by reference to the center, thus the Self and the Non-Self exist only by this reciprocity.'"[17] In light of this reciprocity, once the circumference is lost, the center is lost as well. The self remains without location in an unlimited and unorganized field.

Poulet's writing participates equally with the writings of the authors he examines in the attempt to establish a center. The situation necessarily determining Poulet's participation in this attempt is clear. In discussing the subjective situation in which Coleridge's writing originates, Poulet observes that, "Everything takes place as if human thought when it finds itself given over to a centrifugality without control, begins to break up in small fragments, or to turn in circles and become crazed. At the end of this movement, thought slips away, or it vanishes in its own fragmentation, or else it becomes the prey of a kind of demented vertigo."[18] Poulet's own fear is speaking here. It is as a response to this fear that Poulet's writing participates in the attempt to establish a center, thereby repeating the gestures of its objects and genuinely appropriating them in the act of reading them. Poulet appreciates the centered self-presentness of Goethe's remark, "To be in a circle is to be happy."[19] How can a circle in which the self might center itself be drawn when there is no horizon of experience?

What is required is a term which will relate thematically two or more moments of experience: the present experience of the writer and the experiences which form the topic of his writing. Poulet here appeals to an identity between moments which is constituted by vibration, by the echo of all past moments in the present. This vibration makes possible the determinate relation of discrete time bound moments: for Poulet, crucially, the moment of his writer-object's point of departure and the moment of his own departure. Vibration makes possible the critic's repetition of the point of departure. The vibration engendered in the critic by his writer-object's writing is the mark of an identity and the condition of the intelligibility for the critic of his writer-object's experience, and hence the condition of the possibility of his own criticism.

Poulet gives the poetic theory of this kind of criticism where the critic's own identity is at stake in the act of reading in his writing on

Baudelaire. Substitute "Poulet" for "Baudelaire" in the following passage and the critical project of self-recovery through the repetition of an organizing moment within a medium becomes clearer:

> Baudelaire [Poulet] does not in the least wish to establish, outside of time, an identity of essences between the separated moments, but, on the contrary, to suggest that in the interval between the moments time has never ceased to reign, an always identical time. Repetition proves the identity of a duration; a duration constituted by the continuity of a resonance, sometimes so feeble that it is imperceptible, and sometimes given its original strength by the action of a sensorial event of the same nature. All the sensations of the past continue to last and to quiver in our depths, sometimes so faintly that we no longer perceive them.[20]

Here Poulet sees in Baudelaire's writing an act which opens the bare possibility of criticism. Baudelaire's writing is held to be the essentially contingent connection of temporally discrete moments in virtue of their resonance. It is this act of contingent connection which constitutes the medium of subjective time by establishing a scheme of identity and difference among its moments. Poulet's writing attempts to voice the *a priori* possibilities of just this medium, possibilities whose law Baudelaire is held to be obeying. Poulet aims at connecting with the proper *a priori* terms of understanding Baudelaire's contingent act of connection with his own necessary one. Hence Poulet finds the possibility of his own writing in his perception of an identity between Baudelaire's subjective situation and his own—the identity of both writing within and constituting at a particular moment a medium—but an identity which is brought to consciousness only by the critic's possession of the proper names (resonance, vibration) for the modes of identity. Baudelaire's act, the act of connection, is thematized in the writings of Poulet. Thus, in a method precisely opposed to that exercised in his reading of Mallarmé, the terms of understanding which make his own writing possible are here crystallized in the very reading of Baudelaire.

As a result, the critical theory and the perception of Baudelaire stand or fall together. The author's text as a guaranteed mode of access to the author's consciousness has been replaced by the text as an object of anxiety. If resonance and vibration are not, whether or not Baudelaire is taken to be conscious of them, agreed to be Baudelaire's fundamental themes, then both the perception of Baudelaire and the theory which necessarily finds these themes in its objects will be flawed. Poulet's critical theory and critical consciousness in general are at stake in his reading of Baudelaire. If the act Poulet discerns in Baudelaire's writing, connection through vibration and resonance, turns out to be frustrated or inadequate to fix an understanding which is later fixed in other terms

Richard Eldridge

in Baudelaire's writing, then Poulet's writing will likewise turn out to be frustrated or inadequate. Thus Baudelaire remains essentially problematic for Poulet precisely because the vibration which constituted an identity among moments and made Baudelaire's (Poulet's) perception possible fails to hold in Baudelaire's writing. The vibration dissipates and vaporizes: "Vaporization is therefore the decomposition and the disappearance of the mental world, at the extreme limit of its excentric development. In the final analysis, everything is dissolved in space. Everything, too, is dissolved in forgetfulness."[21]

Poulet cannot bear this turn in Baudelaire's writing, for it undermines the critical poetics of echo and repetition. He thus forces Baudelaire continually to repeat his attempts at self-discovery and self-representation so that he, Poulet, can analyze the structure of this repeated action. This forcing takes place despite the fact that the last poem in *Les Fleurs du Mal* is "Le Gouffre" which records the withdrawal from all such attempts at self-representation in such lines as:

> —Hélas! tout est abîme, —action, désir, rêve,
> *Parole!*

and

> Je ne vois qu'infini par toutes les fenêtres.

Poulet forces Baudelaire's work into a structure of repeated and repeatedly frustrated positive attempts at the connection of moments of consciousness despite such lines. He can do nothing but insist on his characterization, an insistence which is essential to the possibility of his criticism.

This insistence of Poulet's contests with Baudelaire's own lines for the characterization of Baudelaire's consciousness. Instead of immediately assimilating Baudelaire's consciousness to a pre-existing paradigm, Poulet enters into a struggle to characterize Baudelaire's consciousness by making use of terms latently structuring Baudelaire's writing—vibration and dissipation—in an attempt to find a convincing description. Poulet's effort will succeed or fail depending on whether we, his audience, endorse his attempt at appropriation.

Baudelaire himself, in the lines cited, is content to conclude his writing with the announcement that he is *en abîme* (there is a certain tone of smugness in this announcement), thereby suggesting that he is the first to appreciate the situation of all consciousness. This conclusion is no longer open to Poulet, who, in order to read and understand Baudelaire's problematic writings, must appropriate them by casting them in new terms, by describing those writings as one of the less than fully conscious stages of self-representation in a movement which is brought to full consciousness only in his critical writings. Here in giving his reading Poulet genuinely repeats Baudelaire's gesture in writing. He attempts to appropriate the consciousnesses of his predecessors by voicing the general condition of consciousness.

Far then, despite his characterizations of his enterprise, from treating the consciousness of Baudelaire *automatically* as he treats the consciousnesses of others in general, Poulet enters into a struggle with Baudelaire to describe thematically the condition of Baudelaire's consciousness. The outcome of this struggle is not guaranteed by a fundamental *cogito* or fundamental act of apperception on either Poulet's or Baudelaire's part. It issues instead only from their audience's test of the depths of self-perception of both Baudelaire and Poulet. The self-consciousnesses of Baudelaire's and Poulet's consciousnesses are invested in the moment when the convincingness of the criticism is tested.

If Poulet's insistence on the thematic character of the consciousness he and Baudelaire must share can win through in this struggle, it will be because the complex of description and object described in Poulet will have been adjudged by us, in light of the situation of our consciousness which we feel needs description (its confrontation with Baudelaire and the moments of his writing), to be more insightful than the similar complex in Baudelaire. If Poulet is held genuinely to have understood Baudelaire, it will be because he has come closer than Baudelaire to voicing the condition of consciousness generating Baudelaire's writing, his own, and our needs.

It is then perhaps no accident that Poulet, upon being forced (1) by German Romanticism and its effects in the writing of Baudelaire to abandon the figure of the circle as a concept which organizes *a priori* the medium of experience, and (2) by the logic of critical understanding to insist nonetheless on his ability to characterize the experience of Baudelaire better than Baudelaire himself, produces the figure of the thyrsus to describe Baudelaire's writing. Just as both line and spiral in the thyrsus aim, without quite touching, in a common direction, so Poulet describes the experience represented in Baudelaire's writing and the experience represented in his own as identically directed without quite being able to make them touch. Our experience of Poulet will here turn on our response to the ability of his criticism (the spiral)—claiming a wider experience of the possibilities of the medium of experience—to insist that it has Baudelaire's experience (the line) accurately located at its center. This insistence will always be essentially contested by the abysmal insistences of Baudelaire's writing which will likewise claim to spiral about Poulet's.

If this contest must always take place insofar as no terms of understanding can be essentially grounded, then we shall have to count Poulet's criticism as a failure when assessed against the universal

Richard Eldridge

ambition it necessarily sets itself. Perhaps Poulet was thinking of his own inability to escape from the necessity of insistence into the pure description of consciousness when he confessed: "I am above all attracted by those for whom literature is—by definition—a spiritual activity which must be gone beyond in its own depths or which, in being unable to succeed in this, in being condemned to the consciousness of a failure to go beyond itself, affirms itself as the experience and verification of a fundamental defeat."[22] Yet if Poulet's criticism is the record of a failure, it is nonetheless, in its ability to occupy a position in a struggle with Baudelaire, a register of the humanly possible modes of critical success. Poulet, repeatedly, insists to us on the necessity of his themes.

III

DESCRIPTION AND CONVICTION

The reality for us of the contest between Baudelaire and Poulet means that criticism with Poulet now shares the condition of literature, drawing its worth from its occasional ability to locate particular experiences within an organized medium and, at the very moment of its insistent act of location, opening itself to the possibility of appropriation to another, momentarily more general, medium of experience. The logical structure of the act of critical understanding—its repeated insistences aimed at reconciling the contingency of its appearance and reception with the necessity it claims on its own behalf—entails the omnipresence of the possibility of appropriation.

If we continue, given our uncertainties, to need the kind of understanding criticism and art aim at, the thematization of the straits of consciousness, we can only proceed by producing what Wittgenstein called a perspicuous representation: "A main source of our failure to understand is that we do not *command a clear view* of the use of our words.—Our grammar is lacking in this sort of perspicuity. A perspicuous representation produces just that understanding which consists in 'seeing connexions.' Hence the importance of finding and inventing *intermediate cases*."[23]

Perspicuous representations will characteristically consist of descriptions which unite thematically, through their insistence, moments of consciousness in a way which convinces an audience. But insofar as this conviction is itself a moment of consciousness, an appearance, it will not provide an essentially secure understanding of the situation of consciousness. The moment of conviction will, in order to continue to secure understanding and to allow the seeing of connections, itself have to be located within the always expanding, non-horizoned medium

Criticism and Its Objects

of consciousness in general. Just because moments of conviction are located in the medium of consciousness, the appearance of further moments of consciousness will inevitably convict our convictions of the insistences on which they depend. We will always be becoming strangers to ourselves, we men of knowledge, and we shall repeatedly have to be brought back from this estrangement.

Donald Barthelme, commenting on the constructions of Wittgenstein, has figured the fate of all writing which aims at securing critical understanding:

. . . but of course it is not that query that this infected sentence has set out to answer (and hello! to our girl friend, Rosetta Stone, who has stuck by us through thin and thin) but some other query that we shall some day discover the nature of, and here comes Ludwig, the expert on sentence construction we have borrowed from the Bauhaus, who will—"Guten Tag, Ludwig!"— probably find a way to cure the sentence's sprawl, by using the improved ways of thinking developed in Weimar—"I am sorry to inform you that the Bauhaus no longer exists, that all of the great masters who formerly thought there are either dead or retired, and that I myself have been reduced to constructing books on how to pass the examination for police sergeant"—and Ludwig falls through the Tugendhat House into the history of man-made objects; a disappointment, to be sure, but it reminds us that the sentence itself is a man-made object, not the one we wanted of course, but still a construction of man, a structure to be treasured for its weakness, as opposed to the strength of stones.[24]

It will thus not have escaped notice that the act of describing the transcendental logic of analysis in terms of a repeated insistence on the necessity of certain descriptions is itself submitted to that very logic. In insisting on a set of analytic descriptions of analysis, we have ourselves risked, in the hope of critical penetration, voicing the necessary condition of consciousness. How far or how fruitfully this voicing will be heard is not ours to say, for there is no description of the general condition of consciousness which will not be tested by what comes on the scene.

NOTES

1. Georg W. F. Hegel, *Phenomenology of Spirit*, trans. A. V. Miller (Oxford: Clarendon Press, 1977), p. 46. *Phänomenologie des Geistes*, ed. Johannes Hoffmeister, 6th ed. (Hamburg: Felix Meiner, 1952), p. 64.

2. Ibid., p. 48.

3. Ibid., p. 50.

4. Stanley Cavell, "Aesthetic Problems of Modern Philosophy," in *Must We Mean What We Say?* (Cambridge: At the University Press, 1976), p. 78. I have modified the passage to fit this context.

5. Stephane Mallarmé, "Les Mots anglais," *Oeuvres complètes* (Paris: Editions Gallimard, Bibliothèque de la Pléiade, 1945), p. 962. "What is a root (source, origin)? A collection of letters, often of consonants, showing a

number of the words of a language as, though they were dissected, reduced to their bones and tendons, plucked out of their ordinary [unreflective] life, so that one can recognize a secret consanguinity among them. If this collection is taken at the same time more succinctly and more faintly, one has a *theme* (subject, topic)" (my translation).

6. Ibid., p. 963. "From which one could with good reason conclude that the thousands of words of a language are wedded among themselves. Everything is in knowing how to begin and finish, or in how to determine the place where the familial bonds, more or less drawn out, will break: a very subtle discernment, for it depends on no absolute rule. Properly speaking, there are then no such things as roots and themes, since one is obliged to return to immemorial ages in order to find them" (my translation).

7. Hegel, p. 13.

8. Georges Poulet, *Etudes sur le temps humain*, vol. 2., *La Distance intérieure* (Paris: Plon, 1952), p. i (hereafter cited as *La Distance intérieure*). "My thought is a space in which my thoughts take place, in which they take their place. I watch them arrive, pass on, wander aside or sink out of sight, and I distinguish them at spatial and temporal distances which never cease to vary. My thought is not made up solely of my thoughts; it is made up also, even more perhaps, of all the *interior distance* which separates me from, or draws me closer to, that which I am able to think" (George Poulet, *The Interior Distance*, trans. Elliott Coleman [Baltimore: Johns Hopkins Press, 1959], p. vii).

9. Georges Poulet, "Criticism and the Experience of Interiority," in *The Structuralist Controversy*, ed. Richard Macksey and Eugenio Donato (Baltimore: Johns Hopkins Press, 1970), p. 57 (emphasis added).

10. Ibid., p. 60 (emphasis added).

11. Georges Poulet, *The Metamorphoses of the Circle*, trans. Carley Dawson and Elliott Coleman in collaboration with the author (Baltimore: Johns Hopkins Press, 1961), p. i.

12. Paul de Man, *Blindness and Insight* (New York: Oxford University Press, 1971), p. 90n.

13. Poulet, *La Distance intérieure*, p. 342.

14. Ibid., p. 354.

15. Poulet, *Metamorphoses*, p. xxvii.

16. Ibid., pp. 92–93.

17. Ibid., p. 101.

18. Ibid., p. 109.

19. Johann W. v. Goethe, cited in Poulet, *Metamorphoses*, p. 113.

20. Ibid., p. 271.

21. Ibid., p. 278.

22. Georges Poulet, cited in J. Hillis Miller, "Geneva or Paris? The Recent Work of Georges Poulet," *University of Toronto Quarterly* 39 (1970), 220.

23. Ludwig Wittgenstein, *Philosophical Investigations*, trans. G. E. M. Anscombe, 3d ed. (New York: Macmillan, 1968), 122, p. 49e.

24. Donald Barthelme, "Sentence," in *City Life* (New York: Bantam Books, 1971), p. 121.

I would like to thank Françoise Meltzer and Andrew Parker for comments on earlier drafts of this paper and for cooperation in the study of Poulet and French Symbolism. Paul Gudel and Stephen Melville promoted my study of Hegel.

NINE

DECONSTRUCTION AS CRITICISM
Rodolphe Gasché

IN SCIENCE, conceptual progress as well as "the wandering off into different fields," without which there is no such progress, leads to the impossibility of asking questions and explaining problems which were essential to the previous theoretical configuration. Indeed, such a loss is not considered a serious one for "there is no need to possess such knowledge," as the only *one* thing legitimately to be demanded of a theory "is that it should give us a correct account of the world, i.e., of the totality of facts *as constituted by its own basic concepts*."[1] What is true of science is in principle also true of literary criticism. If "the context of discovery" comes into conflict with "the context of justification,"[2] if the reading devices produce discoveries that the previous theories can no longer account for, and if in the eyes of the traditional critic it becomes undecidable "whether a new view *explains* what it is supposed to explain, or whether it does not wander off into different fields,"[3] then one may speak of what Paul Feyerabend calls the *incommensurability* of approaches. Yet, is this incommensurability as securely established as some of the Newer Critics—the so-called deconstructive critics—and most of their opponents would like to believe? Implicitly, a distinction such as Wayne C. Booth's between monism and limited pluralism (i.e., liberalism) acknowledges already that the seemingly mutually exclusive approaches to literature are about the same. What Booth's conceptual system vouches for—an intimate affinity of

Rodolphe Gasché

traditional academic criticism in all its forms and deconstructive criticism, a commensurability without the knowledge of the critics (Booth included)—is one of the presuppositions of this article. However, rather than representing a conciliatory gesture in the direction of a "critical commonwealth" whose access depends on the critics' statements seen as "a passport into the country of debate"[4] and far from being a belief into the continuity of tradition, the stand taken here is critical of deconstructive literary criticism, and maintains that it is incapable of living up to its pretensions. For the problem of either thematic criticism and/or New Criticism (only disguised by a new and sometimes fashionable vocabulary) still dominates the post-structuralist approaches,[5] in spite of their rhetoric. Apart from this rhetoric there is no trace of what Bachelard called an epistemological break.[6] In no way does such a judgement disqualify or impair the contributions of modern deconstructive criticism. On the contrary: in the wake of New Criticism deconstructive criticism has developed now indispensable insights into the very object of literary criticism, the text. But just as science textbooks represent a sort of obstruction within the ongoing activity of scientific research,[7] much of what appears as deconstructive criticism contributes more to prolonging the impasses of traditional academic criticism than to opening up new areas of research. Hence the generalized discomfort about, in particular, deconstructive criticism. But the critical malaise of modern critics that makes them long for a "beyond-deconstruction" and simultaneously allows the attacks of the rear-guard, stems in the first place from a mutual misunderstanding of the notion of deconstruction. It is precisely this misinterpretation that makes its accommodation by American criticism possible, and, by the same token, transforms it into a mechanical exercise similar to academic thematism or formalism.

Before trying to clarify the misinterpretation of the notion of deconstruction, some of the *evidence* guiding so-called deconstructive criticism has to be pointed out.[8] In the wake of New Criticism, which rightly showed that literary criticism was not derivative and was not simply a parasitic response to literature, but an autonomous discipline, it has become fashionable to conceive of literary criticism as *theory*. Yet, what does theory mean in this context except the all too often naive and sometimes even, for its uncontrolled and unwanted side-effects, ridiculous *application* of the *results* of philosophical debates to the literary field? It is on this unproblematized and rarely justified application, as well as the lack of any questioning of the applicability of such philosophemes to the specific levels of texts, that the theory rests. It rests especially on a generally intuitive understanding of conceptual systems situated as it is in the (institutionally motivated) absence of all rigorous formation in pilot sciences such as anthropology, linguistics, psychoanalysis, and especially philosophy.[9] With this, *theory* is no different from the impressionistic approaches and loose conceptual instruments of traditional academic criticism which seldom reflects its own presuppositions. In fact, the unproblematized application of borrowed tools to the analysis of literary texts already proves the affinity of deconstructive and traditional criticism. Indeed, the newly fashionable *a-theoretical* stand which in the present configuration pretends to come to the rescue of literary, aesthetic, and ethical values is by its very definition not only *violently* theoretical, but this hypocritical innocence in matters of theory stems from its blindness and an ignorance of its own presuppositions that are in the end all dependent on various extra-literary disciplines such as psychology, history, and philosophical aesthetics. The origins of these disciplines in nineteenth-century philosophy are never admitted or made explicit.

If deconstructive criticism does not simply coincide with such an ill-founded application of conceptual tools borrowed from certain pilot sciences to the analysis of literary texts, its theoretical pretensions end with the elaboration of the cognitive aspects of these texts. Such an approach, however masterful it may be, by taking the information and knowledge explicitly or implicitly displayed by a text for granted or by taking the reflections a text confers about itself literally, not only fosters a theoretical eclecticism that raises the critic to the status of characters like Bouvard and Pecuchet, but also makes him subject to the same kind of criticism that Levi-Strauss directed against Mauss: to have tried to explain the melanesian notion of *mana* with the help of a native theory.[10]

A second evidence predominant in deconstructive criticism is the conviction that everything is literature, text or writing. This evidence of Newer Criticism only radicalizes the purely aesthetic and a-historical vista of its academic antecedents. It also continues the conservative function of traditional criticism by neutralizing and blurring the capital differences and critical functions between different kinds of discourses. In the case of the so called deconstructive criticism, this evidence originates in an illicit application of the Derridean notion of *écriture* to all forms of discourses. This precipitated application in question is made possible—as always—through a confusion of levels in a specifically philosophical debate with Husserl's phenomenology. These levels are in fact distinguished carefully by Derrida himself. The notion of *writing* (of text, and of literature, as well) as used by modern deconstructive criticism refers in general only to the *phenomenological experience of writing* as something present in all discourses and texts. Yet, in *Of Grammatology* Derrida clearly warned of mistaking writing (as arche-writing) for the colloquial meaning of writing. Indeed, writing as arche-

Rodolphe Gasché

writing "cannot occur *as such* within the phenomenological experience of a *presence*." The notion of the trace, he adds, "will never be merged with a phenomenology of writing."[11] Derrida's notion of writing and of the trace presupposes a phenomenological reduction of all the mundane regions of sensibility (but also of the intelligible). Being anterior (yet not as an essence) to the distinctions between the regions of sensibility, and consequently to any experience of presence, the trace or writing is not something which can be said to be *present* in all discourses. The regions of sensibility and of presence are "only" the regions where writing as arche-writing appears *as such*, becomes present by occulting itself. Thus, the evidence in question, since it confuses and is unaware of distinctions as important as those between appearance and appearing, between appearance and signification, consists of a fall back into a phenomenological apprehension of writing as something readable, visible, and significant in an empirical medium open to experience. However, criticizing this evidence does not entail (as will be shown) that there is a tangible outside to literature, to the text, and to writing, nor does the rejection of such an exteriority necessarily imply one's entanglement in the pure immanence of the text.

The major evidence of deconstructive criticism, also shared by its opponents, is its understanding of the operation of deconstruction. The evidences already mentioned, the priority of theory and the universalization of literature, are linked to modern criticism's understanding of deconstruction. According to these presuppositions, Derrida's philosophical work can be turned into a theory to be applied to the regional science of literary criticism as well as to the literature it deals with, without the categories of literature and criticism (and the institutions supporting them) being put into question. This naive and intuitive reception of Derrida's debate with philosophy, its reduction to a few sturdy devices for the critic's use, represents nothing less than an extraordinary blurring and toning-down of the critical implications of this philosopher's work.

Since it requires only a little more than skimming Derrida's major works to know what deconstruction *is not*, let us briefly enumerate what it certainly cannot be identified with. Deconstruction is *not* to be mistaken for a nihilism, nor for a metaphysics of absence, nor for a negative theology. It is *not* a demolition and a dismantling to be opposed by or calling for a rebuilding and a reconstruction.[12] It is *not* to be taken for what Heidegger calls *destruction*. At the same time, deconstruction is not what is asserted by positive definitions in Newer Criticism. Here deconstruction is said to represent the moment where in a text the argument begins to undermine itself; or, in accordance with Jakobson's notion of the poetic and aesthetic function, the relation of a message of communication to itself that, thus, becomes its own object; or, finally the self-revelation and indication by the text of its own principles of organization and operation. Consequently, deconstructive criticism seldom appears to be more than a very sophisticated form of structural analysis. The only difference with structural analysis is that the diacritical principal of meaning, that is to say its dependence on differentially determined opposites, on the correspondence and reciprocity of coupled terms, is applied in a negative fashion. Meaning, as well as the aesthetic qualities of a text, then spring forth from the self-cancelling of the text's constituting oppositions.[13] But not only is this interplay of binary terms that parody and debunk one another called deconstructive, to increase the confusion it is often also said to be dialectical.[14] Yet, in terms of logic, the diacritical relations do not even represent the threshold to (negative or not) dialectics, not to speak of deconstruction.

As a negative diacritical approach to literature and the text, deconstructive criticism consequently asserts and simultaneously depends on the idea of the self-reflexivity and the autonomy of the text. It is this rationale of almost all of modern criticism that, as the third evidence, totally distorts the notion of deconstruction.

Here again, in order to avoid some all too hasty conclusions, a few remarks are indispensable. The self-reflexivity with its idea of a more or less infinite *mise en abyme* of the text, as well as the idea of its autonomy assumed by modern criticism is not to be criticized from an, if you will, extrinsic approach. Besides, such an approach, historical, sociological, psychological, psychoanalytical, and so forth, goes perfectly with the assumption of the text's self-reflexivity and self-referentiality as constitutive of its autonomy. Nonetheless, the contributions based on such a notion of the text cannot be minimized. Compared to the traditional approach which, in spite of its erudition is scarcely more than an unflagging effort to avoid the object of literary studies, modern deconstructive criticism has shown itself to be able to investigate the manifold linguistic density of the *work of literature itself*. Moreover, the self-reflexivity of the text is in no way to be denied. Undoubtedly, its self-reflexive stratas *almost* constitute its entirety. But what is at stake here is this *almost*, the point of nonclosure of the reflexive space of the text.

In general, modern deconstructive criticism attributes this self-reflexivity of the text to certain specific totalizing emblems such as tropes, images, similes, and so on. Never questioning the nature and the status of *representation in* the text, deconstructive criticism conceives of these emblems of the whole as hyperbolically reinscribing the act of writing.[15] Through such images, the text *itself* (or the writer) is said to perceive "the act of constituting—that is, of writing—(its, or) his nascent *logos*."[16] This is certainly true, but this is precisely the problem as well. Indeed, as an especially modern aesthetic device this self-reflexivity of texts depends on the totalizing consciousness of an author, or on an equally questionable assertion of a consciousness or unconsciousness of the text. Thus a textual reading would precisely have to account for these cognitive functions of the text, for the images or scenes where its production is staged and for its self-reflexive stratas, by inscribing them into the *global* functioning of the text. As the self-perceiving function of the text is subject to the same aporias which haunt perception and consciousness in general, as the act of production of the text will never coincide with its reflection through totalizing emblems (or concepts), such a move toward a global apprehension of the functions of the text becomes imperative. Yet since the (neither *de facto* nor *de iure*) overlapping of the two languages—writing on the one hand and its reflection on the other—never takes place, that overlapping or that identity, which is supposed to engender the text, would also call, in a global apprehension of the functions of the text, for another notion or concept of the text. The current notion of the text's autonomy and self-reflexivity only continues the claim of American formalism to a totalizing principle, to what is called the integrity of the literary form. The idea of self-reflexivity indeed reconfirms, but also —and this is its historical importance—represents the development of what makes the idea of contextual unity possible. Modern deconstructive criticism, a faithful offspring of New Criticism, significantly enough was able to think the mode of totalization of texts in terms of what makes such a unity possible by borrowing from European thematic criticism.[17]

A compromise between formal and thematic criticism on the one hand and on the other hand a radical development of the metaphysical implications of the formalist's idea of contextual unity, deconstructive criticism cannot hope to escape the, it is true, usually dull critique of its opponents. A more radical critique, however, is to be directed against deconstructive criticism (a critique that affects traditional criticism so much the more), which by erroneously mistaking the reflexive stratas and the cognitive functions of the text that it describes for the text as a whole, seriously reduces and restricts the play of the text, a play it was one of the first to take into account.

Reassessing deconstruction thus faces several tasks. Besides the necessity of restoring its rigorous meaning against its defenders as well as against those who argue against it, deconstructive criticism will have to break away from its formalist past and to resituate its loans from thematic criticism, in order to open the notion of the text to its outside. That will not, however, mean that the text is to be precipitously connected to the real and empirical outside.[18] It is true, that far from being an operation *in the limits* of the text, deconstruction proceeds *from and at the limit* of the text. But the outside of the text, that which limits its reflexive stratas and cognitive functions, is not its empirical and sensible outside. The outside of the text is precisely that which *in* the text makes self-reflexion possible and at the same time limits it. While, on the one hand, the position which consists of criticizing the self-reflexivity of a text from one of its possible sensible and empirical outsides is still privy to what it criticizes, deconstructive criticism, on the other hand, is incommensurate with one of these corresponding alternatives. Proceeding from that limit that traverses the text in its entirety, deconstructive criticism reasserts literariness and the text as *play*: as the unity of chance and rule. In this perspective, the reflexive strata which constitute *almost* all of the text, appear as *almost* parasitical in relation to the text and its play. In short, such a deconstructive criticism reaffirms all of the text. More complex than a totality solely based on a self-reflexive autonomy, the global situation of the text encompasses both the text's reflexive inside and that outside from which it proceeds, an outside that it harbors in its core. This approach to the play of the text (still called literature in the absence of a better term[19]), which unlike conventional criticism inevitably limits this very play by its mere investigation, accounts for its own desire to limit and induce changes in this play.[20]

Thus, in the pages that follow, one aspect of deconstruction only will be analyzed. Indeed, if Derrida's work can already provide a superficial reader with enough material to invalidate most of the critic's contentions, this one aspect in particular has misled philosophically untrained readers. This one aspect, more than obvious to the philosopher, is that deconstruction in the first place represents a critique of reflexivity and specularity. It is the unawareness of this essential feature of deconstruction that has caused the easy accommodation of deconstruction by contemporary American criticism.

I

Although Jacques Derrida was the first to introduce the notion of deconstruction (in the context of a debate on Husserl's phenomenology), for reasons soon to become clear, it may be convenient to start with an analysis of Jean-François Lyotard's use of this notion in *Discours, Figure*.

However different Lyotard's work may be from that of Derrida, *Discours, Figure* is a monument of deconstruction similar to *Of Grammatology*. Indeed, the notion of the *figural* which Lyotard develops in this book, a notion whose meaning shifts as the book unravels from an at first sensible connotation to a libidinal definition in order to finally be determined by the concept of difference, is the result of a decon-

Rodolphe Gasché

structive operation. The production of the notion of the figural takes place in two distinctive steps.[21] Setting out from one particular conceptual dyad structuring the discourse of Judaic and Christian metaphysics—the opposition of writing and the figure[22]—Lyotard first reprivileges the hitherto secondary and necessarily inferior term of the dyad, that is to say, the figure. This first step is achieved by *reversing* the hierarchy of the given dyad. The second step consists of *reinscribing* the newly privileged term. This reinterpretation of the notion of the figure takes place in *Discours, Figure* by moving away from phenomenology and turning to psychoanalysis. This second step of deconstruction— the reinscription of the newly privileged term—is indispensable in order to prevent the naive solution of wanting "to pass to the other side of discourse," which is nothing but a simple inversion of metaphysical values. The reinterpretation of the phenomenological notion of the figure is achieved through an *extension* of its range and scope. No longer simply opposed to writing and discourse, the figure, or more precisely, the figural now broaches them from the inside:

The figure is both outside and inside . . . . Language is not an homogenous medium, it is [. . .] divided because it interiorizes the figural in the articulated. The eye is inside speech because there is no articulated language without the exteriorisation of something "visible," but also because there is an at least gesticulatory, "visible," exteriority at the heart of discourse, that is its expression.[23]

Hence, the figural which represents a sort of margin to discourse while already broaching it from the inside (and which, consequently, no longer corresponds to the notion of the figure which remains caught in the dissymmetrical and hierarchical space of the initial dyad) becomes the very space of the inscription of discourse. Discourse, in this way, appears surrounded and undercut by the figural. This (double) inscription—a term whose meaning is strictly limited to the derivation of the central from the marginal—gives the final touch to the operation of deconstruction. Now, what is of interest here and explains the detour through Lyotard's use of deconstruction is that he dates the necessity of an operation such as deconstruction back to what the late Maurice Merleau-Ponty called *hyper-reflection (sur-reflexion)*.

Before discussing the term of *hyper-reflection* and its relation to deconstruction, let us, in a very succinct manner, recall the problematics of Husserlian phenomenology. The answer to the traditional question of the origin of the world, reformulated by Kant as a question concerning the conditions of possibility of a world for a subject, is rejected by Husserl. Indeed, for Husserl the transcendental categories are still mundane categories and will not explain the absolute origin of the world. Husserl, on the contrary, by bracketing the world discovers its absolute origin in the subject of the *epoche*. This is a subject which after having suspended the world becomes evident to itself, evident in an apodictic manner. A mundane object no longer and distinct from both the psychological and the transcendental subject, it derives this apodictic self-evidence from the gaze of consciousness at itself. It is a gaze which becomes possible only through an eidetic reduction. Although this apodicticity does not entail equality in content, adequation, or the certitude of self-knowledge, it represents the condition of possibility of a subject fully conscious of itself, which, no longer a thing, is an absolute freedom in regard to the world which, consequently, is contingent.[24]

Merleau-Ponty, however, in interrogating the primary openness upon the world in *The Visible and the Invisible* puts the very possibility of such an apodicticity of a subject into question. This interrogation of the gaze of consciousness at itself, a gaze which is different from every possible object-relation and which gives access to the new mode of transcendental existence as an absolute present existence, takes in *The Visible and the Invisible* the form of a critique of reflexivity in general and of all philosophy of reflection. This critique interrogates the very possibility of reflection. Such a critique becomes inevitable, indeed, as soon as one proceeds to question the problem of perception. Thus, while analyzing the perceptual and pre-reflexive faith (in *one* same world shared by all subjects) to which all sciences and (intuitive, reflexive, and dialectical) philosophies remain tributary, Merleau-Ponty ascertains that the opacity of the body of the subject of perception, that is to say, the distance or depth between me and the thing suspended at the end of my gaze, represents the condition of possibility of all perception of the thing itself. However, if it is true that my body as an opacity opens up the space of my glance, then this condition of possibility of all perception also entails the impossibility of self-perception. Merleau-Ponty gives here the famous example of the experience of touching and being touched: "If my left hand is touching my right hand, and if I should suddenly wish to apprehend with my right hand the work of my left hand as it touches, this reflection of the body upon itself always miscarries at the last moment: the moment I feel my left hand with my right hand, I correspondingly cease touching my right hand with my left hand."[25] Hence, the body while opening the indispensable depth of perception is equally the space where self-affection and reflexive conversion miscarry.[26] This impossibility will negatively affect all reflexive movements in general.

In order to prevent an all too hasty misunderstanding of Merleau-Ponty's critique of reflexivity, it will certainly not be misplaced to underline the fact that this exhibition of the impossibility of reflection to engender a self-identity, does not imply a sacrifice of the intelligible universe of philosophical *cogitata* at the profit of the irrational and the sensuous. It is absolutely necessary to realize that for Merleau-Ponty:

> The remarks we made concerning reflection were nowise intended to disqualify it for the profit of the unreflected or the immediate (which we know only through reflection). It is a question not of putting the perceptual faith in place of reflection, but on the contrary of taking into account the total situation, which involves reference from the one to the other.[27]

No doubt, the movement of reflection remains inevitable: "in a sense it is imperative, it is truth itself, and one does not see how philosophy could dispense with it." Thus, if reflection is not only an unavoidable temptation, but also "a route that must be followed," the question becomes a different one. In light of the paradoxes constitutive of reflection, "the quesion is whether the universe of thought to which it leads is really an order that suffices itself and puts an end to every question." The question, consequently, aims at its presuppositions, "which in the end reveal themselves to be contrary to what inspires the reflection,"[28] in order to account for the total situation of reflection.

After having demonstrated how science and the philosophy of reflection remain tributary to perceptual faith, to the pre-reflexive openness upon the world which presupposes our participation in one and the same world, a world which in the case of philosophy coincides with the world of the spirit, Merleau-Ponty defines philosophy of reflection as an attempt to *undo* the world in order to *remake* it.[29] This rebuilding of the world from "a center of things from which we proceed, but from which we were decentered," from a center that as "a *source of meaning*" is identical to the spirit, makes that reflection a "coming back over the traces of a constitution." Yet, between this original constitution and the *après-coup* moment of reflection, between the movements of re-travelling to the origin on a "route already traced out from that center to us," on a route that can only be used after one has already come back from the center, Merleau-Ponty discovers divergences so unsurmountable as to impede all internal adequation. These divergences are, for Merleau-Ponty, of a temporal nature: "The movement of recovery, of recuperation, of return to self, the progression toward internal adequation, the very effort to coincide with a *naturans* which is already ourselves and which is supposed to unfold the things and the world before itself—precisely inasmuch as they are a return or a reconquest, these operations of reconstitution or of re-establishment which come second cannot by principle be the mirror image of its internal constitution and its establishment, as the route from the Etoile to the Notre-Dame is the inverse of the route from the Notre-Dame to the Etoile: the reflection recuperates everything except itself as an effort of recuperation, it clarifies everything except its own role." This left over (*reste*) or blind spot of "the mind's eye"[30] which characterizes perceptual faith and consequently reflection, the massive "assurance that the things under my eyes remain the *same* while I approach them to better inspect them," and "according to which it is always *the same* thing I think when the gaze of attention is displaced and looks back from itself to what conditions it,"[31] coincides with the act of reflection itself. However, the temporal differences between the always belated movement of recovery and return on the one hand, and on the other hand the originary constitution, their dissymmetry, forbid all contemporaneity of reflection with itself:

The search for the conditions of possibility is in principle posterior to an actual experience, and from this it follows that even if subsequently one determines rigorously the *sine qua non* of that experience, it can never be washed of the original stain of having been discovered *post festum* nor ever become what positively founds that experience. This is why we must say not that it proceeds the experience (even in the transcendental sense) but that it must be able to accompany it, that is, that it translates or expresses its essential character but does not indicate a prior possibility whence it would have issued. Never therefore will the philosophy of reflection be able to install itself in the mind it discloses, whence to see the world as its correlative. Precisely because it is reflection, re-turn, re-conquest, or recovery, it cannot flatter itself that it would simply coincide with a constitutive principle already at work in the spectacle of the world, that, starting with this spectacle, it would travel the very route that the constitutive principle had followed in the opposite direction. But this is what it would have to do if it is really a *return*, that is, if its point of arrival were also the starting point.[32]

The aporia between the constitutive principle and reflection as a retrospective construction is non-existent for the philosophy of reflection. As it has nothing to say about this gap "since it is literally *nothing*,"[33] philosophy exempts itself from accounting for it, albeit, or precisely because its foreclosure is constitutive of philosophy itself. Now, with Merleau-Ponty this *nothing*, this non-space of philosophy literally becomes the space of *hyper-reflection*. *Hyper-reflection* then is that other "operation besides the conversion of reflection, more fundamental than it"[34] that takes "the twofold problem of the genesis of the existent world and of the genesis of the idealization performed by reflection" seriously in order to account for the global situation. Therefore *hyper-reflection* by taking the paradoxes and contradictions of the reflexive conversion into account becomes "not a superior degree at the ultimate level of philosophy, but philosophy itself."[35] As "another point of departure," *hyper-reflection* as "a philosophy of total reflection" assumes the task of not losing sight of the unsublatable antinomies of reflection as well as of the specific nature of the sides involved in this operation (these sides

Rodolphe Gasché

being brute perception and the transcendence of the world on the one hand, and, on the other, the world of idealization) so as to be able to account for the total situation and for "the changes it introduces (itself) into the spectacle."[36]

In *The Visible and the Invisible* Merleau-Ponty distinguishes *hyper-reflection* from Hegelian dialectics. This happens in some remarkable pages where Merleau-Ponty shows why *hyper-reflection* is a "hyper-dialectics," that is to say a "dialectics without synthesis."[37] Yet this *hyper-reflection* which is fundamentally self-critical, which does not model itself after any historically given form of dialectics, which resists the temptation of its being "stated in these, in univocal significations," and, thus, its becoming "what we call *a philosophy*,"[38] still longs for the rediscovery of "the being that lies before the cleavage operated by reflection."[39] The desire for such a pre-reflexive *being* keeps hyper-dialectics in the bonds of philosophy. It is not *a* philosophy, but, as Merleau-Ponty admitted, philosophy itself. Nonetheless, *hyper-reflection* came close to anticipating the *strictly speaking* no longer philosophical operation of deconstruction.

Merleau-Ponty's *hyper-reflection*, which phenomenology, weary of ruminating over intentionality, felt urged to develop, led already through its critique of the always retrospective and belated construction of reflection to a reverie about the language of philosophy. In *Discours, Figure*, Lyotard while continuing this investigation of the language of philosophy, however, transforms Merleau-Ponty's reverie on language into a questioning of the language of dreams. Such a move becomes necessary if the linguistic conditions of reflexivity are to be explored. Remember that Merleau-Ponty had made reflexivity dependent on the opacity of the body and the transcendence or depth of the object suspended at the end of my gaze. Now, since all reflexivity takes place in a language game, Lyotard can question discursive reflexivity in terms of what makes that play possible, that is to say in terms of the Saussurian notion of language (*langue*) as opposed to speech (*parole*). But, it is precisely when trying to combine the negativity specific to speech and discourse (the spacing of referential transcendence which, like the visual depth out of which the pictorial redoubling originates, makes reflection possible) with the negativity characteristic of language (*langue*) (its closed system of distinctive and differential features which not only prohibits the transgression of the differences and the free play of the subject, but also forbids all reflection on that level), that Lyotard sees himself compelled to go beyond that distinction and, consequently, beyond linguistics altogether. Thus, taking up again Merleau-Ponty's idea of *hyper-reflection*, but reformulating it "in the shape of deconstruction,"[40] Lyotard posits a "third" negativity which, however, is not the dialectical identity of the first two. This "third" negativity is the *figural* which not unlike the death-drive silently constitutes both the reflexive discourse of speech as well as the non-reflexive system of language (*langue*) presupposed by all speech-acts as their condition of possibility. With this "third" negativity, deconstruction then seeks to account for the irruption of the extra-linguistic into both the reflexive discourse and into its invariable system of differential traits. It is an operation that takes aim at elucidating the linguistic and non-linguistic conditions of the possibility of reflection.

It is important here to remark that the negativity of the *figural* on which reflexivity appears to rest, a negativity that represents the limits of reflexivity, takes its most radical shape for Lyotard as poetry, as a poetry, however, that assumes what Mallarmé called a critical function. This radical poetry, which is not identical with literature in general, *is* deconstructed language *par excellence*. It is deconstructed language, because it is a language that by delaying communication through the intervention of extra-linguistic procedures and by exhibiting (*faire voir*) the laboratory of the images causing the seductive power of poetry, accommodates what impedes its reflection by means of a "regressive flexion."[41]

The space of inscription of reflexivity that Lyotard calls the *figural* corresponds to what for Derrida is the *text*.

II

After having established how deconstruction with Merleau-Ponty and Lyotard takes the operation of reflection as its target, not to destroy it, but to account for its antinomies, let's now consider the writings of Derrida. After Merleau-Ponty and Lyotard demonstrated how the mundane exteriority of the body on the one hand, and the non-mundane exteriority of the figural on the other prevent all reflection from coinciding with itself, one could still dream the dream at the bottom of *all* of Western Philosophy of a pure reflection that would not have to rely on a non-proper mediator. This dream takes—in Husserl's phenomenology in particular and in philosophy in general—the shape of the idea of self-affection, of an auto-affection of the voice in the "medium of universal signification" that is the voice itself.[42] This idea of self-affection is the matrix of all forms of self-reflexivity. Now, what Derrida's deconstruction has in view is precisely the undoing of the idea of self-affection, and, consequently, of all forms of self-reflexivity.

Speech and Phenomena is a critical essay about Husserl's doctrine of signification as developed in particular in the *Logical Investigations*. At first, Derrida's critique of this theory comes close to resembling what

one calls *immanent criticism.*[43] For instance, Derrida reproaches Husserl
for insisting on the necessary absence of presuppositions while, in fact,
constructing his theory of signification on the metaphysical presupposition par excellence: "i.e. the original self-giving evidence, the *present*
or *presence* of sense to a full and primordial intuition."[44] In addition to
this *implicit* contradiction Derrida points out *explicit* contradictions.
This kind of contradiction is either overtly admitted by Husserl himself
or becomes visible through contradictory stratas of description in
Husserl's work. To give an example: one such stratum recognizes the
idea of an originary presence while other strata cannot avoid linking
presence to "an irreducible nonpresence as having a constitutive value."[45]
Let's add to this inner turmoil and contestation of Husserl's philosophy
from within the following critical move: by showing that Husserl
privileges a certain region of language only, a region he raises to "the
dignity of a telos, the purity of a norm, and the essence of a determination" by means of a simple *de facto* delineation "of the logical *a priori*
within the general *a priori* of language,"[46] Derrida not only pins down
a contradiction between the philosophical necessity of foundation and
a philosophy's discursive practice, but he also specifies certain very
precise *ethico-theoretical decisions* that are responsible for an actual
discursive state of a particular philosophy, as well as of philosophy in
general. It would not be very difficult to continue analyzing Derrida's
critique of Husserl in terms of immanent criticism though, already,
such a notion becomes questionable as the survey of contradictions in
Husserl's theory of signification is not undertaken in view of greater
logical coherence of the discourse of philosophy, but in order to demonstrate that they are a function of the ethico-theoretical decisions constitutive of philosophy. But if this is so, then the contradictions Derrida
has been pointing out are not simple contradictions, but, on the contrary
contradictions constitutive of philosophical discourse in general, and of
Husserl's philosophy in particular. They represent inevitable contradictions, contradictions which cannot be overcome, as long as the ethico-
theoretical decisions they spring from privilege the idea of presence, the
logicability of language, and so forth.

It is only after having emphasized the contradictions inherent in
philosophical discourse, from a position which as could easily be shown
is not skepticism,[47] that the operation of deconstruction becomes possible, not to say imperative. In *Speech and Phenomena* it takes place in
Chapter 4, entitled "Meaning and Representation."

Let's summarize as briefly as possible the argument of this chapter.
Using several descriptions by Husserl concerning the nature of the sign
and representation in general, descriptions which stem from different
strata of Husserl's text, Derrida recalls that a sign as a necessarily ideal

identity (ideal, because a sign must remain the *same* if it is to be repeated) always implies a threefold relation to representation: "As *Vorstellung*, the locus of ideality in general, as *Vergegenwärtigung*, the possibility of reproductive repetition in general, and as *Repräsentation*, insofar as each signifying event is a substitute (for the signified as well as for the ideal form of the signifier)."[48] Indeed each effective discourse, that is every discourse that uses signs and has, consequently, an indicative function, must, in order to take place at all, set to work all these representative modalities. However, Husserl, in his theory of signification, wants to reserve the modality of *Vorstellung* (the locus of ideality in general) for the inner discourse alone, for the soliloquy of the soul as a silent speech independent of (even imagined) words, which is, according to Husserl, a discourse of expression radically different from all effective and indicative discourse. Husserl needs the quality of *Vorstellung* conferring ideality in general to be able to establish the purely representational and imaginary nature of the expressive inner voice. Yet, since Husserl has already (in other strata of his text) implicitly attributed this particular modality of representation to the sign in general, Derrida can rightly infer the equally imaginary and expressive nature of the so-called effective or indicative discourse. And, conversely, the discourse of represented communication which Husserl wants to be radically different from the discourse of real communication appears then to be as effective as the latter. Consequently, a total blurring of the distinctions between expressive and indicative signs, between representation and reality takes place. Yet these distinctions are capital to Husserl's whole enterprise which consists of trying to exclude all indication from expression so that the soliloquy of the silent inner voice can achieve an unmediated and apodictically self-evident presence to itself.

It has to be noted that the conflicts between the distinct stratas of Husserl's philosophical discourse do not represent a weakness of his philosophy. They cannot be ruled out through an attempt at greater logical coherence.[49] They are functions of the ethico-theoretical decisions of philosophy itself. Thus the question why Husserl would sacrifice the coherence of his discourse in order to be able to maintain his distinctions —an incoherence that coincides with the very coherence of philosophical discourse—and why "from the same premises . . . (he) refuse(s) to draw these conclusions,"[50] is to be answered by the "ethico-theoretical act that revives the decision that founded philosophy in its Platonic form."[51] This decision is the theme of full presence. It is indeed "the obstinate desire to save presence and repetition," to juggle away death and "to reduce or derive the sign,"[52] which in the name of this *evidence* of philosophy[53] makes Husserl maintain the differences between expression and indication, between two kinds of signs, between representation and reality. Now, to suspect that this very evidence of philosophy (the evidence being the privilege of the present-now and everything it governs: sense and truth) gains its life from an attempt at excluding the other and death, becomes possible only "from a region that lies elsewhere than philosophy." Such an enterprise would represent "a procedure that would remove every possible *security* and *ground* from discourse," for such a security can only be grounded in *the* evidence of the idea of presence constitutive of philosophy as a whole.

Husserl, as remarked, tries to evacuate the sign from the living presence of the self-affecting voice. It is, indeed, an obstacle, a non-proper mediator to a pure act of self-affection. What Husserl tries, is to reduce the sign's originality and originarity. This, then, becomes the precise moment when deconstruction occurs. It reads as follows:

But there are two ways of eliminating the primordiality of the sign . . . . Signs can be eliminated in the classical manner in a philosophy of intuition and presence. Such a philosophy eliminates signs by making them derivative; it annuls reproduction and representation by making signs a modification of a simple presence. But because it is just such a philosophy—which is, in fact, *the* philosophy and history of the West—which has so constituted and established the very concept of signs, the sign is from its very origin and to the core of its sense marked by this will to derivation or effacement. Thus to restore the original and nonderivative character of signs, in opposition to classical metaphysics, is, by an apparent paradox, at the same time to eliminate a concept of signs whose whole history and meaning belong to the adventure of the metaphysics of presence.[54]

A few lines later, Derrida notes that with such a restoration of a nonderivative notion of the sign which simultaneously coincides with the elimination of its traditional concept, "a whole system of differences involved in language is implied in the same deconstruction."[55] What does such a deconstruction then consist of, what does it accomplish, and to what effect is it being carried out? Using the complex representative structure of the sign developed (by referring against Husserl's express intentions to various descriptions of this philosopher) to subvert the notion of an inner expressive discourse that Husserl wanted to be free of all indicative relation, Derrida reprivileges the hitherto derivative notion of the sign. This reprivileging, however, does not go without a total redefining of the notion of the sign itself. Two movements are thus characteristic of deconstruction: a *reversal* of the traditional hierarchy between conceptual oppositions (expression/indication, presence/sign) and a *reinscription* of the newly privileged term. What makes such an operation possible is the fact that all conceptual dyads constitutive of the discourse of philosophy are "dissymmetrical and hierarchial spaces that are transversed by forces and in whose closure the repressed outside is at work."[56] But, the inferior and derivative term of these non-homogenous oppositional spaces reprivileged through a reversal of the given hierarchy is not yet the deconstructed term. The newly reprivileged inferior term in the process of deconstruction is as Derrida says only "the negative and atheistic face (an insufficient, but indispensable phase of the reversal),"[57] "the negative image" of the "radical Otherness."[58] To pause at this negative face of the radical Otherness, at an interminable negative theology, and at a metaphysics of absence, is to remain in the immanence of the dyad or system to be deconstructed. The deconstructed term, however, as a result of a reinscription of the negative image of absolute exteriority and otherness, of what Derrida also names *displacement* or *intervention*, is no longer identical with the inferior term of the initial dyad. The deconstructed term indeed escapes "the specular reflection of philosophy which is only able to inscribe (understand) its outside by assimilating its negative image."[59] Although it uses the same name as its negative image, the deconstructed term will never have been given in the conceptual opposition it deconstructs.

Hence, what does deconstruction accomplish? If the sign and its threefold structure of representation is privileged over presence and over the ideal expressive discourse of the silent inner voice, then the medium of presence, representation as *Vorstellung*, becomes dependent on the very possibility of the sign. In other words, ideality is not without the repetitive nature of the sign. Derrida writes: "We thus come— against Husserl's express intention—to make the *Vorstellung* itself, and as such, depend on the possibility of re-presentation (*Vergegen-wärtigung*). The presence-of-the-present is derived from repetition and not the reverse."[60] The deconstructed term, the reinscription by elimination of the traditional notion of the sign (as derivative of presence) thus coincides with "the primordial structure of repetition" governing the structure of representation and, therefore, "all acts of signification,"[61] plus those of indicative and expressive communication as well. Thus, "the primordial structure of repetition," "the possibility of re-petition in its most general form," serves to *account for*[62] the *terms* of the initial conceptual dyad and for the *contradictions* and tensions that make the dyad a hierarchy. This primordial structure functions indeed like a sort of *deep structure* underlying the system of differences and oppositions for which it is not to be mistaken.

Such a structure of originary repetition is "more 'primordial' than what is phenomenologically primordial."[63] As, however, the notion of the primordial is necessarily linked to presence, this structure cannot be called primordial in the traditional sense. Moreover, it manifests a strange kind of temporality. Indeed, as the primordial structure of repetition derives the ideal from repetition, from that which until this point was thought to be derived from presence, it obeys what Derrida terms "the strange structure of the supplement . . . : by delayed reaction, a possibility produces that to which it is said to be added on."[64] Thus *accounting* for both presence and absence, the structure of originary repetition as a product of deconstruction represents "a meditation on non-presence—which is not perforce its contrary, or necessarily a meditation on a negative absence, or a theory of non-presence *qua* unconsciousness."[65]

Let's recapitulate: by analyzing the ethico-theoretical decision constitutive of philosophy—a decision in favor of the *presence* of the *present* to be achieved in the medium of a silent voice free of all signs and of all indication (and even of imagined words) that purely affects itself—Derrida shows that such an idea of presence has to rest on "the primordial structure of repetition," on a structure which both makes something like presence possible and impossible. Indeed, "without this nonself-identity of the presence called primordial," "how can it be explained that the possibility of reflection and re-presentation belongs by essence to every experience?" Without an originary trace, i.e., "a bending-back of a return," and without "the movement of repetition"[66] constitutive of the possibility and impossibility of self-affection, how could there even be (and not be) something like self-reflection?

Thus, deconstruction, in this precise case—the deconstructed term of "the primordial structure of repetition," or the trace,—"is inconceivable if one begins on the basis of consciousness, that is, presence, or on the basis of its simple contrary, absence or nonconsciousness."[67] Or, put another way, deconstruction is an operation which accounts for and simultaneously undoes self-reflection.[68]

III

Already in *Speech and Phenomena* Derrida remarks that the difference constitutive of the self-presence of the living present reintroduces as a *trace* the impurity of spatial depth, that is to say a nonidentity into self-presence. This trace "is the intimate relation of the living present with its outside, the openness upon exteriority in general, upon the sphere of what is not 'one's own.'" Moreover, as the *spacing* of self-presence, this trace coincides with the origin of time. And, finally, because sense, as Husserl recognized, is always already engaged in the order of "signification," that is to say in the "movement" of the trace, it is also as "proto-writing (*archi-écriture*) . . . at work at the origin of sense."[69]

The *primordial structure of the arche-trace* with its three functions is that which determines the scope and significance of deconstruction. This threefold structure simultaneously accounts for the possibility (and impossibility) of the self-presence of the present, of time, and of sense. Deconstruction aims at nothing less than producing such a primordial threefold structure that can account for the exteriority constitutive of three fundamental and interrelated *topoi* of Western Metaphysics: presence, time, and sense. Since Western Metaphysics conceives of these three concepts or ideas as generating themselves in a movement of unmediated auto-affection, the primordial structure of the arche-trace assumes the role of reinscribing them back into the non-reflexive and non-present exteriority of the absolute other of the arche-trace. Indeed, philosophy, already against its will and unknown to it, could never avoid linking presence and self-reflexivity to an irreducible non-presence which has a constitutive value. In order to show how the arche-trace with its threefold structure assumes this function of both engendering and reinscribing presence, time, and sense, let us now turn to analyzing the "theoretical matrix" outlined in the first part of *Of Grammatology*.

Of Grammatology examines the possibility of a "science" of writing in a historical epoch that a) determines as language the totality of its problematic horizon, while already pointing at the limits of that horizon, that is to say, at its other, at writing. It is thus an epoch in which b) science as *episteme*, while still determined by the idea of *logos* as *phone* and presence, paradoxically, opens itself more and more to non-phonetic forms of writing. This epoch, moreover, is characterized by c) a challenge to the traditional idea of the book as something that refers to a natural totality by what is profoundly alien to it: writing and the text. These are for Derrida the signs through which the *other* of science as *episteme*, of language and of the book as a natural totality, *empirically* comes into manifestation; empirically, that is to say, through an effect of specular reflection still inscribed in philosophy. As the negative image only of a radical otherness, writing and the text are what *can appear* and become visible of this invisible radical otherness. And *as such*, that is as text and writing, this otherness will remain the object of a phenomenology, of a phenomenology of writing, for instance. A grammatology, however, would reach out for that radical otherness beyond writing and the text which are nothing but the negative faces under which it can appear, that is to say, become present *as such*. Indeed, in *Of Grammatology*, Derrida clearly stresses that what grammatology (a "science," that while reinscribing all the concepts on which sciences rest, can no longer be called a science) designates as trace or arche-trace "will never be merged with a phenomenology of writing."[70]

Thus, after the deconstruction of the conceptual dyad of presence

Rodolphe Gasché

and the sign in *Speech and Phenomena, Of Grammatology* deconstructs the opposition between speech and writing. But before dealing with this deconstruction itself, it is imperative to consider its preliminaries.

Deconstruction does not operate from an empirically present outside of philosophy since that outside is only the outside *of* philosophy. Deconstruction does not proceed from a phenomenologically existing exteriority (like literature, for instance) that would claim to represent the truth of philosophy, because that truth is only the truth *of* philosophy itself. In order to shake the heritage to which concepts belong, *all* the inherited concepts have, on the contrary, to be mobilized. They are all indispensable. Here is what Derrida says:

> The movements of deconstruction do not destroy structures from the outside. They are not possible and effective, nor can they take accurate aim, except by inhabiting those structures. Inhabiting them *in a certain way*, because one always inhabits, and all the more when one does not suspect it. Operating necessarily from the inside, borrowing them structurally, that is to say without being able to isolate their elements and atoms.[71]

Consequently to prevent the danger of a regression, before deconstructing one has "at first . . . [to demonstrate] the systematic and historical solidarity of the concepts and gestures of thought that one often believes can be innocently separated."[72] It is, of course, impossible here to exhaustively describe as does *Of Grammatology* the field of forces constituting the conceptual dyad of speech and writing. Let us then only recall that the privilege of speech over writing in Western Metaphysics is founded on the idea that speech as logos is the logos of Being. What makes speech in the Western tradition the medium *par excellence* of Being (as logos) is the "fact" that in a language of words "the voice *is heard* . . . closest to the self as the absolute effacement of the signifier: pure auto-affection that necessarily has the form of time and which does not borrow from outside itself, in the world or in 'reality,' any accessory signifier, any substance of expression foreign to its own spontaneity. It is the unique experience of the signified producing itself spontaneously, from within the self, and nevertheless, as signified concept, in the element of ideality or universality. The unworldly character of this substance of expression is constitutive of this ideality."[73] Compared to speech as *phone*, to this self-effacing signifier that raises the voice to the universal medium of signification, all other signifiers necessarily appear as being exterior, non-proper, sensible, and derivative. Writing, moreover, for being understood as the graphic signifier of the verbal signifier that signifies the signified (that, in the last instance, is always, what Derrida calls the transcendental signified) is doubly exterior to the sense. It has solely a technical and representative function. Compared to the self-affecting logos in self-effacing speech, to a signification, consequently, that take place without any obstructing and obscuring signifier, all sensible signs, and writing in particular, are necessarily inferior and secondary. This is the relation between speech and writing in the discourse of philosophy from Plato[74] to Husserl. There are only a few exceptions where the hierarchy is reversed, as in the case of the Leibnitzian characteristic violently criticized by Hegel.

The deconstruction of this opposition takes place in the second chapter (entitled "Linguistics and Grammatology") of Part One of *Of Grammatology*. It is preceded by a critique of linguistics as deriving its claim to scientificity from its *phonological* foundations, thus as reiterating the classical opposition between speech and writing at the benefit of the articulated unities "of sound and sense within the phonie."[75] Therefore, it is only by overthrowing linguistics that it becomes possible to develop a "science" such as grammatology. Yet, as Derrida points out, this overthrow is already being carried out by linguistics itself. After a meticulous analysis of Saussure's attempt to exorcise writing at the moment he promotes linguistics—"the modern science of the logos"[76]— to scientific heights, Derrida writes: "It is when he is not expressly dealing with writing, when he feels he has closed the parentheses on that subject, that Saussure opens the field of a general grammatology which would not only no longer be excluded from general linguistics, but would dominate it and contain it. . . . Then something which was never spoken and which is nothing other than writing itself as the origin of language writes itself within Saussure's discourse."[77] With this the traditional opposition of speech and writing ceases to be clearcut. It becomes blurred in Saussure's writing. Thus, when asserting that the inner system of language is independent from the phonic character of the linguistic sign, it becomes apparent "why the violence of writing does not *befall* an innocent language."[78] Indeed, how could writing represent speech without an originary violence already at work in speech itself? But it is especially Saussure's famous thesis of the arbitrariness of the sign that completely blurs the traditional opposition of speech and writing. Saussure excluded writing from language and chased it to its outer fringes because he considered it only to be an exterior reflection of the reality of language, that is, nothing but an image, a representation or a figuration. The thesis of arbitrariness according to Derrida "successfully accounts for a conventional relationship between the phoneme and the grapheme . . . [and] by the same token it forbids that the latter be an 'image' of the former."[79] But without a natural relation between speech and writing (as it is true of the symbol which for that reason is excluded from linguistics), writing cannot be chased from speech.

This blurring of the distinctions of the conceptual dyad: speech

Rodolphe Gasché

and writing, a blurring brought about by a play on incompatible strata of Saussure's *Course* ("an entire stratum . . . [which is] not at all scientific"), leads then to the operation of deconstruction. It reads as follows:

> Now we must think that writing is at the same time more exterior to speech, not being its "image" or its "symbol," and more interior to speech, which is already in itself a writing. Even before it is linked to incision, engraving, drawing, or the letter, to a signifier referring in general to a signifier signified by it, the concept of the *graphie* [. . .] implies the framework [instance] of the *instituted trace*, as the possibility common to all systems of signification.

Implicitly, Derrida has *reversed* the hierarchy and *displaced* the newly privileged term: writing. This displacement and reinscription rests on the notion of the *instituted trace*. As writing coincides in this context with the concept of the trace, or, more precisely, the arche-trace, it will be necessary to distinguish what this concept implies in order to understand what this deconstruction is able to account for.

First, it has to be remarked that the deconstructed term: the *instituted trace*, entails a detachment of "these two concepts from the classical discourse" from which they obviously are borrowed.[80] Generally speaking, a trace represents a *present* mark of an *absent* (presence). But this is not what the *instituted* trace or the arche-trace is about. The notion of an institution, on the other hand, refers in general to a cultural and historical instauration. The trace, in its colloquial sense is instituted this way, but not the *instituted trace*. What then is the arche-trace or the *instituted trace* if it is neither a trace in the colloquial sense, nor simply instituted? The arche-trace, on the contrary, is the movement which produces the difference of absence and presence constitutive of the colloquial sense of trace as well as the difference of nature and culture constitutive of the idea of institution. To understand this, let us unravel the major functions of the *instituted trace*. Derrida writes: "The general structure of the unmotivated trace connects within the same possibility, and they cannot be separated except by abstraction, the structure of the relationship with the other, the moment of temporalization, and language as writing."[81] At the risk of oversimplifying, it is nevertheless necessary to separate these *three* possibilities characterizing the general structure of the *instituted trace* (or archetrace, or arche-writing):

1. *The arche-trace as the origin of all relation to an other.*

The arche-trace is "the irreducible absence" (i.e., an absence that is not the absence of a presence) or "the completely other" that announces itself *as such* within all structure of reference as the *present* (mark or trace) of an *absent* (presence). This manifestation of the absolute other *as such* (that is to say, its appearing within what is not it, its becoming present, tangible, visible), consequently, coincides with its occulation. "When the other announces itself as such, it presents itself in the dissimulation of itself." What becomes present of the absolute other, through "the dissumulation of its 'as such,'" is but a *present* mark that retains it as other in the same and refers to it as an *absence*. Thus, the arche-trace actively manifesting itself as such in the dissimulation of itself, engenders the *difference* of sign and referent, of presence and absence. It opens up the possibility of all relation to an other, of all relation to an exteriority, in short, the structure of reference in general. If this constitution, through announcing and dissimulation, can be viewed as an *active* synthesis, the fact that the *absence* of the irreducible other is constitutive of the *presence* in which it appears *as such* makes it equally a *passive* synthesis.

To conclude: the empirical trace or mark "where the relation with the other is marked,"[82] or the sign which always stands for an absent presence, depends on (and becomes possible only through) the arche-trace as "the completely other," that precedes all particular relations to an other.

2. *The arche-trace as the origin of temporality.*

As the origin of the experience of space and time, the fabric of the arche-trace "permits the difference between space and time to be articulated, to appear as such, in the unity of an experience."[83] The arche-trace as "an absolute past" (a past that is not a past presence or a present-past), as an irreducible "always-already-there," also opens up "the difference between the sensory appearing (*apparaissant*) and its lived appearing (*apparaître*)," of appearance and appearing.[84] In other terms: the absolute past announcing itself *as* such through its own occultation, appears as *time*. The "*dead time* within the presence of the living present, within the general form of all presence,"[85] within the sensory appearing of time without which no such appearing is possible, however, is *space* as the lived appearing of time. Indeed, without spacing, no such experience as time, as the presence of the present, is conceivable.[86]

Consequently, this spacing of time (passive synthesis) and this appearing *as such* of the absolute past as time (active synthesis) accounts for the origin of temporalization (of time *and* space). For Saussure this means, that the arche-trace represents the possibility of signification which is always dependent on articulation.

3. *The arche-trace as the origin of language and sense.*

While trying to define the order of language (*langue*) in its inde-
pendence from the phonic nature of language, Saussure compares this
inner system of language to writing. Speech "draws from this stock of
writing, noted or not, that language is."[87] But: "Before being or not being
'noted,' 'represented,' 'figured,' in a '*graphie*,' the linguistic sign implies
an originary writing."[88] Yet how is language on the one hand, and
notation on the other founded on the general possibility of the arche-
trace as arche-writing?

The originary writing or the arche-trace is not to be mistaken for
writing in the narrow sense as it appears in the given opposition of
speech and writing. It is neither to be identified with the stock of
writing from which speech draws its possibility. The arche-trace or
arche-writing is the condition of possibility of these differences. Arche-
writing, which unlike speech and writing in the colloquial sense has no
sensible existence,[89] by announcing itself *as such*, thus by simultaneously
dissimulating itself, engenders *speech* as haunted by what it is not:
the system of differences that Saussure compared to *writing*. This active
synthesis of speech and writing (in a truly phenomenological sense) by
the very movement of the arche-trace does not exclude a passive
synthesis as well.

Indeed, through what Derrida calls "the being-imprinted of the
imprint," which differs from the imprint as much as the being-heard
of speech is different from the sound-heard, the arche-trace is passively
constitutive of speech. Derrida develops this passive synthesis of speech
when reflecting Saussure's reduction—a reduction not unlike a phenomenological reduction—constituitive of the very object of structural
linguistics: the object of structural linguistics, actually, is not the real
material and physical sound, the sound-heard, but its acoustic image,
the being-heard of the sound.[90] Defending Saussure's notion of "psychic
image" against Jakobson's objection of mentalism, and preserving the
Husserlian distinction "between the appearing sound and the appearing
of the sound in order to escape the worst and the most prevalent
confusions," Derrida stresses that Saussure's linguistics, whose object
is the internal system of language, that is to say, a system independent
of the phonic nature of language, is not to be mistaken for "a mundane
science . . . , [for] a psycho-physic-phonetics." On the contrary, this
investigation into the non-mundane region of the "psychic image" (an
image that is not another natural reality) and into the being-heard of
the sound leads to a definition of the *form* of language as a system of
differences constitutive of each particular speech-act. Yet this specific
space of differential features passively constituting speech "*is already
a trace.*"[91] For this system of differences is only the negative face, the

face through which the arche-trace appears as one term of an opposition that it engenders as a whole.

With having shown how the arche-trace (or the instituted trace, arche-writing, or differance) as an "irreducible arche-synthesis [opens] in one and the same possibility, temporalization as well as relationship with the other and language,"[92] it becomes possible to present a necessarily provisional and reductive draft of the theoretical matrix of deconstruction (Table 1). On its horizontal axis, this matrix displays the arche-trace's active and passive synthesis of presence, time, and speech (while all three, traditionally, are thought to engender themselves through auto-affection and self-reflection) as well as of their canonical derivatives: absence, space, and writing. The vertical axis of this diagram inscribes the structural possibilities simultaneously realized by the arche-trace. The diagram is consequently a layout of the various levels simultaneously to be observed in a deconstruction. Yet, since for didactic reasons this originary synthesis had to be broken down in its successive moments so as to clarify the scope of deconstruction, its diagram is also an inadmissible simplification. The notion of the arche-trace (and all of its non-synonymical substitutions: arche-writing, differance, and so forth) refers to an order which resists (and *accounts for*) the founding conceptual oppositions of philosophy. Thus, most of the concepts used to describe the movement of the arche-trace are inappropriate. Originary constitution, active and passive synthesis, genetic and structural production are still terms that belong to meta-

TABLE 1. THE THEORETICAL MATRIX OF DECONSTRUCTION

ARCHE-TRACE : as condition of possibility of metaphysical dyads

:: as originary synthesis						
	the origin of all relation to the OTHER	act.	manifests itself *as such* as	PRESENCE	of an	ABSENCE
		pas.	is, as	ABSENCE	constitutive of	PRESENCE
	the origin of TEMPORALITY	act.	manifests itself as the experience of	TIME	through the dead time of	SPACE
		pas.	is, as	SPACE	constitutive of	TIME
	the origin of LANGUAGE	act.	manifests itself *as such* as	SPEECH	as *a priori*	WRITTEN
		pas.	is, as	WRITING	the form of	SPEECH

Rodolphe Gasché

physics in general and to transcendental phenomenology in particular. Consequently, using them to account for a constitution of presence, time, and language—a constitution that reveals the self-referential term present in the dyad not only to represent *as such* its absolute other, but also to necessarily depend on the negative image of that other—can only be strategic. Actually, this synthesis is neither passive nor active, it is a "middle voice, that expresses a certain intransitiveness,"[93] and that remains undecided. For the same reason, the notion of structure is to be rejected as well as its opposite (the genetic point of view).

Although deconstruction investigates the conditions of possibility of the *conceptual systems* of philosophy it is neither to be mistaken for a quest of the transcendental conditions of possibility of knowledge (Kant), nor for a new version of Husserl's transcendental philosophy.[94] As the transcendental question in Derrida represents at first a precaution against falling back into a naive objectivism, or an even worse empiricism, it is a strategic question. Regarding the notion of the arche-trace, Derrida writes:

The trace is not only the disappearance of origin—within the discourse that we sustain and according to the path that we follow it means that the origin did not even disappear, that it was never constituted except reciprocally by a nonorigin, the trace, which thus becomes the origin of the origin. From then on, to wrench the concept of the trace from the classical scheme, which would derive it from an originary nontrace and which would make of it an empirical mark, one must indeed speak of an originary trace or arche-trace. Yet we know that the concept destroys its name and that, if all begins with the trace, there is above all no originary trace. We must then *situate*, as a simple *moment of the discourse*, the phenomenological reduction and the Husserlian reference to a transcendental experience.[95]

These remarks having been made, a few of deconstruction's prerequisites and prior conditions can finally be underlined. If deconstruction and the production of a particular deconstructed term such as the arche-trace, a notion that comes to account for a series of interrelated metaphysical pairs of oppositions, cannot simply be reduced to the questions of transcendental phenomenology, it can just as little be said to simply have broken with these questions. Deconstruction, consequently, presupposes the scholarly knowledge of transcendental phenomenology, in order to distinguish and not "confuse very different levels, paths and styles."[96] It is imperative to be able to rigorously separate what in deconstruction corresponds to the regions of natural experience and what to the transcendental experience in order to understand how this operation leads to the production of an irreducible non-phenomenal that can no longer be explained in terms of a phenomenological reduction and a transcendental phenomenology. In the last instance, deconstruction is an operation that accounts for the conceptual difference between factual or regional experience and transcendental experience.[97] It is precisely for paying little or no attention to these distinctions that notions like trace, writing, supplement, and so on could as easily find their way into a regional science such as literary criticism where they either served to denote existing and apprehensible marks or, at its best, in Husserl's sense *reell* (as opposed to *real*) traits characterizing differential systems and the phenomenological notion of writing.

This leads then to another problem. The diagram of deconstruction shows how the arche-trace through an active and passive synthesis engenders presence, time, and speech on the one hand, and on the other, absence, space, and writing. Consequently, showing how time, speech, and presence (or, the word, the logos, God) are always already broached and contaminated by their other is not yet deconstruction. Such an operation does not lead a single step outside metaphysics. It is as Derrida says "nothing more than a new motif of 'return to finitude,' of 'God's death,'" etc. and consequently, nothing more but negative theology, negative dialectics and negative specularity.[98] Deconstruction begins only where the difference of a term such as presence, for instance, and its other, absence, is accounted for from an absolute other. Or, to put it differently, deconstruction begins when a concept that designates a real, empirically apprehensible experience and the concept of its "ideal" and phenomenal opposite that vouches for a transcendental experience are explained by means of an irreducible non-phenomenal structure that accounts for the difference under examination.

A further confusion also stems from an insensibility to philosophical distinctions. It concerns the "status" of the deconstructed term. The spacing as well as the order of the differential traits represent the origin of signification (of language and of sense, in general). Yet, in spite of their general invisibility and nonpresence they are still phenomenal and represent only the negative image of the absolute other. Thus pointing out blanks, pauses, punctuations, intervals, etc., that is to say negatives without which there is no signification, or in short, establishing the textuality of a discourse, is not yet deconstruction. Deconstruction aims at something that can never become present "as such," and that without concealing itself can only appear *as such*. The *text* as a deconstructed term will never be identical to the visual features of the black-on-blacks[99] or to the generally unperceived (but structurally present) intervals and differences that form signification.[100]

IV

This brings us back to Lyotard's use of the notion of deconstruction. As *Discours, Figure* demonstrates at least two different kinds of deconstruction, the question that appears in what we have developed up to this point, is this: how is this double deconstruction possible, and how are these two notions interrelated? The first notion of deconstruction is silently at work in Lyotard's book and coincides with the *stricto sensu* definition elaborated by us. This deconstruction leads to the development through its various substitutions and levels of the concept of the figural as difference. But at the same time, this notion serves as a framework for another use of deconstruction that designates the irruption of the extra- or non-linguistic: of the figural, into the differential and structural order of discourse. Since, however, the figural deconstructs the linguistic order according to three possible articulations of the figural, it becomes necessary to distinguish as many as three different kinds of *transgressive deconstructions*: (1) the *figure-image* which deconstructs "the contour of the silhouette," or the outline of the image; (2) the *figure-form* which transgresses the unified form and is "indifferent to the unity of the whole"; and (3) the *figure-matrix* that deconstructs the very space of the phantasmatic matrix and that is "a space that simultaneously belongs to the space of the text, to the space of the scenario and of the theatrical scene: writing, geometry, representation, all being deconstructed by their mutual mingling." Lyotard, consequently, calls the last form of the figural: "difference itself."[101] Now, none of these particular transgressive deconstructions relative to the particular level of intervention of the figural can claim priority over the others:

In each case the presence of the figural is negatively indicated by disorder. Yet there is no privileged disorder. One cannot ascertain that the deconstruction of a space of figurative representation is less provocative than that of "good" abstract forms. The critical force of a work of art derives much more from the nature of the deviation (*écart*) on which it rests than of the level (of figures, here) on which it brings the effects of this deviation to bear.[102]

If the fact that a particular deconstruction reaches "deeper strata of the generation of discourse,"[103] cannot hold as a pretext to privileging such a deconstruction, and if, moreover, the very presence of non-discursive instances in discourse is not yet sufficient to "make the other scene present," then this implies that deconstruction—as we understand it at this point, as a transgression of linguistic discourse, a transgression that as a regression affirms what language negates—is linked to the "logic" of desire.

Before continuing, it is important to remark that the denegation (*Verneinung*) founding language and its deconstruction by an affirmative recess are not symmetrical. One has to be attentive, says Lyotard, to "the impression of a return produced by the prefix re- which clearly indicates that going back and having gone for the first time are not the same since in the meantime one had to come back."[104] This asymmetry and non-specularity of the two movements that gives birth to critical poetry derives from the unfulfillment of desire in poetic language. Indeed, if the work of art is said to originate in the phantasmatic matrix that produces images and forms, it also has to represent the non-fulfillment (*inaccomplissement*) of that same matrix, for otherwise the work of art would remain a clinical symptom. Phantasms elaborate scenarios for the sole purpose of fulfilling the desire. For that reason a transgression of the linguistic space by phantasms will remain caught in the form this transgression takes. Yet this form, since it is the form of the phantasm, is also as a necessarily bad form "the at least potential *transgression of form*."[105] It is the death drive as a re-gressive compulsion that in the work of art comes to prevent the form of deconstructive regression from becoming an identity and a unity mirroring the good form of communicative language. The deconstructive recess by transgressing its own form, thus, prevents the desire from fixing and fulfilling itself in a particular scenerio. This way, desire is prompted into becoming a critical instance and thereby achieves the dissymmetry of the deconstructive recess and the order of language that it transgresses.

Poetical language then—a language where desire remains unfulfilled, alive, where the constitutive and destitutive moments do not mirror or reflect each other—is, so to speak, a "superficial" or "surface" *scene* of deseizure and dispropriation (*désaisissement*) of both phantasms and the order of language. But because poetical language, as Lyotard understands it, represents a language that under the impact of the death drive restores difference and dissymmetry by hampering desire's fulfillment, and that undermines the philosophical and pathological specularity and reflexivity in a work of art, it therefore shows the figural at work as difference. Hence, two remarks, at least:

1. With the idea of the non-fulfillment of deconstructive transgression, Lyotard makes all particular transgressions of the linguistic order work at the production of the figural as difference, and, thus, circles back to a *stricto sensu* definition of deconstruction. Only if a transgression is prevented from becoming the fulfillment of a desire, and consequently the negative specular image of what is transgressed, can one start speaking of deconstruction.

2. If poetic language as critical language represents a sort of "surface" scene (and not a *structure*, for Lyotard, from his premises, has to reject that term) where the reflexive opposition is transformed into heterogeneous difference, then it is to be understood as the scene whence all the particular and necessarily symptomatic transgressions of the differential order of language can be accounted for. It represents a scene which as soon as one turns one's back to it[106] gives birth to

critical theory and theoretical discourse in general with its understanding of literariness as self-reflexivity.

Undoubtedly a theory that identifies deconstruction with self-reflexivity was, and to some extent still is, in the present state of critical consciousness a better instrument for freeing the mind of traditional approaches than what necessarily would be understood as an out and out nihilism liable to paralyze the mental faculties of almost everyone. If, however, such an approach reveals its philosophical implications by straining the notion of self-reflexivity, the confusion between self-reflexivity and deconstruction can become fruitful. Indeed, a rigorous application of the idea of self-reflexivity leads to the elevation of thought (*Erhebung des Gedankens*) and the work of the concept (*Arbeit des Begriffs*) that deconstruction measures swords with. It is thus not surprising that Paul de Man, who in his early work equates deconstruction with the self-reflexivity of the text, not only keeps identifying deconstruction with the generally more American methodology of self-reflexivity, but also abstains—with some irony, no doubt—from calling his more recent readings deconstructive.

In this context, de Man's discussion of Derrida's interpretation of Rousseau in *Of Grammatology* is of particular interest. In "The Rhetoric of Blindness: Jacques Derrida's Reading of Rousseau," de Man recognizes that "Derrida's work is one of the places where the future possibility of literary criticism is being decided."[107] Yet, to become fruitful to literary criticism, Derrida's work has first to be submitted to a critique by literary criticism itself. This is why "The Rhetoric of Blindness" reproaches Derrida's reading of Rousseau—a reading that leads to the development of the notion of "a structure of supplementarity" that has to account for the numerous "contradictions" of Rousseau's discourse, and which de Man neglects to mention in his review—as nothing but "Derrida's story of Rousseau."[108] This story is a bad story opposed to the good story of Rousseau. But why is Derrida's story a bad one? In the process of determining Rousseau's place in the history of Western thought, Derrida is said to "substitute Rousseau's interpreters for the author himself," and thus while "the established tradition of Rousseau criticism . . . stands in dire need of deconstruction . . . , instead of having Rousseau deconstruct his critics, we have Derrida deconstructing a pseudo-Rousseau by means of insights that could have been gained from the 'real' Rousseau." But is this distinction between the good and the bad story not dependent on de Man's own story which reads as follows: "there is no need to deconstruct Rousseau" himself? De Man's story is indeed a function of his understanding of deconstruction as supplying the reflexive moment to the inevitable blindness of critical texts, as well as of his notion of literariness as the text's self-reflexivity.

For being a literary text, Rousseau's "text has no blind spots: it accounts at all moments for its own theoretical mode."[109] In an attempt to bypass the deceitful academic distinction between an author's consciousness and unconsciousness, de Man, indeed, attributes a self-awareness and a self-control to literary language itself. Of Rousseau's language, he writes: "The key to the status of Rousseau's language . . . can only be found in the knowledge that this language, as language, conveys about itself, thereby asserting the priority of the category of language over that of presence—which is precisely Derrida's thesis."[110] Deconstruction as self-reflection would consequently be grounded in the self-consciousness of the text. Self-consciousness, however, is only the modern mode of presence being understood as subjectivity. Indeed, de Man attributes a series of cognitive functions to the text:

The text . . . accounts for its own mode of writing, it states at the same time the necessity of making this statement itself in an indirect, figural way that knows it will be misunderstood by being taken literally. Accounting for the "rhetoricity" of its own mode, the text also postulates the necessity of its own misreading. It knows and asserts that it will be misunderstood.

If de Man calls " 'literary,' in the full sense of the term, any text that implicitly or explicitly signifies its own rhetorical mode and prefigures its own misunderstanding as the correlative of its rhetorical nature; that is, of its 'rhetoricity,' "[111] then literariness, writing, and the text are understood according to the model of a conscious subjectivity, that is, of a self-reflexive presence. Consequently, it comes as a surprise when de Man still claims that it is precisely this self-reflexivity of the literary text[112] that preserves it from metaphysics: "Rousseau escapes from the logocentric fallacy precisely to the extent that his language *is literary*."[113] Thus, deconstruction and self-reflexivity are for de Man the same. Such a conclusion becomes inevitable when literariness, textuality, and writing are being thought in terms of self-consciousness. But *writing*, a notion which has, as the result of a deconstruction, an irreducible non-phenomenal meaning, deconstructs and disrupts all reflexivity. Derrida writes:

Constituting and dislocating it at the same time, writing is other than the subject, in whatever sense the latter is understood. Writing can never be thought under the category of the subject; however it is modified, however it is endowed with consciousness or unconsciousness, it will refer, by the entire thread of its history, to the substantiality of a presence unperturbed by accidents, or to the identity of the selfsame (*propre*) in the presence of self-relationship.[114]

If deconstruction has been developed by Derrida (and Lyotard, as well) to account for the contradictions inherent in the conversion of reflection, it was precisely because deconstruction and self-reflection are not identical. Moreover, the ideas of self-reflection, specularity, self-referentiality, and so on, are essentially metaphysical and belong to logocentrism. Deconstruction, on the other hand, by showing how the two asymmetrical moments of self-reflection are engendered by either a "deep" *structure* or ι "surface" *scene*, opens a breach in the ideological closure of self-reflection.

In "Action and Identity in Nietzsche" de Man further develops his understanding of the self-reflexivity of the text, and, consequently, of literariness. As was already suggested in *Blindness and Insight*, the text's self-deconstructing movement is here said to rest essentially on its tropological level. In this manner, de Man distinguishes a variety of deconstructions based on the metaphor, the metonymy, the synecdoche, the metalepse, and so forth. At close sight all these particular deconstructions appear either to be operations of immanent criticism or to reveal the ways in which a text refers to itself. They relate propositions of the text to their implicit presuppositions, they indicate the necessity of all discourse to criticize itself in the language of what it criticizes, and so on. Yet, of these different operations which were shown above to precede deconstruction properly speaking, de Man ascertains that they represent "moments in the deconstructive process" by means of which the "rhetoric becomes the ground for the furthest-reaching dialectical speculations conceivable to the mind."[115] Is the presupposed autonomy and self-reflexivity of the text, its literariness as well, related to the life and self-becoming of the Hegelian concept (*Begriff*)? As the following passage proves, de Man's notion of literature derives only negatively from Hegel's dialectics and is conceived after the model of negative dialectics:[116] "a text . . . allows for two incompatible, mutually self-destructive points of view."[117] This negative specularity that undoubtedly corresponds to certain reflexive strata of the text does not account for the global situation of a text. Already in "Action and Identity in Nietzsche" de Man allows for a speculation about the whole of the text that is not identical to its (reflexive) totality, when he writes: "Moreover, the reversal from denial to assertion implicit in deconstructive discourse never reaches the symmetrical counterpart of what it denies . . . . The negative thrust of the deconstruction remains unimpaired; after Nietzsche (and indeed, after any 'text'), we can no longer hope ever 'to know' in peace."[118] Paradoxically, it is de Man's unflagging investigation into tropology and rhetorics that undermines the possibility of knowledge by putting into question the metaphysical integrity of the text as constituted by cognitive rhetorics. Consider, for instance, "The Purloined Ribbon," where de Man undertakes a "deconstruction of the figural dimension" of the text, that is, of its cognitive tropes, its reflexive metaphors that stand for the totality of the text and produce the illusion of "specular symmetry." This deconstruction which "is a process that takes place independently of any desire," which is "not unconscious but mechanical, systematic in its performance but arbitrary in its principle, like a grammar," opens up to what de Man terms "the absolute randomness of language, prior to any figuration or meaning."[119] This prefigurative dimension of the text—its limit as de Man shows in his forthcoming reading of Shelley's *The Triumph of Life*—"never allowed to exist as such," where language or fiction "stands free of any signification," this moment of its *positing* becomes tangible through a figure such as the anacoluthon or the parabasis.[120] Both reveal disruptions and sudden discontinuities between codes. As such, this dimension of the prefigural is akin to the performative rhetoric of a text which the cognitive rhetoric can never hope to dominate. Indeed, the process of the text's own production figures in the text only as a disruption of the cognitive rhetoric attempting to account for it through reflection. It is precisely this dissymmetry, "this disjunction of the performative from the cognitive,"[121] which, in "The Purloined Ribbon," vouches for a practice of deconstruction which no longer rests on the idea of the text's self-reflexivity. De Man, despite the weight of the philosophical tradition that stands behind this notion, calls this practice irony.

While in *The Purloined Ribbon* he accounts for the inability of cognitive rhetoric to exhaust and dominate the text's performative function (in which cognitive rhetorics, moreover, appear to be inscribed), in *The Epistomology of Metaphor* de Man undertakes a deconstruction of the metaphor of the subject as the totalizing instance of the text. De Man here shows that the impossibility of controlling tropes, an impossibility due to an "asymmetry of the binary model that opposes the figural to the proper meaning of the figure,"[122] implies an inextricable entanglement of the self-reflecting subject into a narrative. The subject, as well as his cognitive function in the text, is, consequently, neither outside the signifier's play, nor outside the *positing* of the text. This, of course, calls then for a concept of text that goes beyond its narrowly regional conception and its reduction to a self-reflexive and self-deconstructive totality.

Yet, such a notion of the text, as well as the *literally* deconstructive practice it presupposes, proceeds from the border of the text. This outside of the text, an outside that does not coincide with naive empirical or objective reality and whose exclusion does not necessarily imply the postulate of an ideal immanence of the text or the incessant reconstitution of a self-referentiality of writing,[123] is in fact *inside* the text and is what limits the text's abysmal specularity. This infinite, as well as the finitude of the text's signification, finds its limits in the non-reflexive margins of the text.

NOTES

1. Paul Feyerabend, *Against Method* (London: Verso, 1978), pp. 283–84.
2. Ibid., p. 167.
3. Ibid., p. 283.
4. Wayne C. Booth, "Preserving the Exemplar: or, How Not to Dig Our Own Graves," in *CI* (1977):420.
5. Post-structuralism is an exclusively American label that reveals more about the departmentalizing spirit in power or in search for power than about the phenomenon in question if we accept that there is such a thing as post-structuralism at all.
6. The notion of the epistemological break as a passage from sensible to scientific knowledge is not only a much more complex notion than is usually believed, but also cannot serve to conceptualize the incommensurability between theories. We will try to show this elsewhere.
7. See, Edward W. Said, *Beginnings* (New York: Basic Books, 1975; Baltimore: Johns Hopkins University Press, 1978), pp. 202–?.
8. It is with the evidence of modern criticism that I am concerned here and not with the at least as questionable evidences of literary criticism in general. Of these evidences one can assert that they belong "to the deepest, the oldest, and apparently the most natural, the least historical layer of our conceptuality, that which best eludes criticism, and especially because it supports that criticism, nourishes it, and informs it; our historical ground itself." Jacques Derrida, *Of Grammatology*, trans. Gayatri Chakravorty Spivak (Baltimore: Johns Hopkins University Press, 1976), pp. 81–82.
9. See for instance the "Polemical Introduction" by Northrop Frye to his *Anatomy of Criticism* (Princeton: Princeton University Press, 1973).
10. Claude Lévi-Strauss, "Introduction à l'oeuvre de Marcel Mauss," in Marcel Mauss, *Sociologie et Anthropologie* (Paris: Presses Universitaires de France, 1968).
11. Derrida, *Of Grammatology*, p. 68.
12. In this context Lionel Abel commits a philosophical blunder. Abel's contention that deconstruction is identical with Husserl's notion of *Abbau* is particularly revealing since it provides the philosophical base, so to speak, of all the misinterpretations of deconstruction. See Lionel Abel, "It Isn't True and It Doesn't Rhyme. Our New Criticism" in *Encounter* 51:1 (1978):40-42.
13. It is precisely this self-undermining and self-cancelling of the text's constituting oppositions that brings about what J. Hillis Miller in a first attempt to analyze the anti-deconstruction's rhetoric calls "strong language" ("The Critic as Host," in *CI* [1977]:442). Indeed, the modern critic's approach to the text as a self-reflexive totality fills the traditional critic with strong moral, political, and religious indignation. The apocalyptic titles such as Abrams' "The Deconstructive Angel" and Booth's "Preserving the Exemplar: or, How Not to Dig Our Graves" (in the same issue), speak for themselves. Booth, moreover, in analyzing criticism in terms of a pluralistic (yet limited) community of critics, accuses the deconstructionists of a sacrilegious claim to superiority—a superiority which would spring forth from their nihilistic destruction of moral and aesthetic values. Booth, consequently, demands the banishment (as foreign agents) of those who from the very beginning refuse the openess demanded of them from the "country of debate" (Booth, pp. 420–23).

Deconstruction as Criticism

14. Besides this naive confusion as to the nature of deconstruction, Derrida foresaw in *Of Grammatology* the philosopher's critique of deconstruction as dialectics: as "the enterprise of deconstruction always in a certain way falls prey to its own work . . . , the person who has begun the same work in another area of the same habitation does not fail to point [this] out with zeal. No exercise is more widespread today and one should be able to formalize its rules," (*Of Grammatology*, p. 24). We might at this point note the erroneousness of the nonphilosopher's common identification of deconstruction with dialectics. Since it is precisely an operation *on* dialectics, this mistake nevertheless confers an inkling of the rigors of deconstruction. Deconstruction indeed vies with dialectics in what Hegel called the seriousness and the work of the concept.

15. Though not using the notion of deconstruction Cary Nelson's approach in "Reading Criticism'" (*PMLA* 91:5 [1976]) to reading critical language as literary language rests also on the idea of the self-referentiality of language. Cary Nelson's analysis provides provocative insights into the nature of criticism as a discourse, no doubt. Yet, since this approach leads, in particular in Nelson's analysis of the critical works of Susan Sontag, to a definition of criticism as an endless process of self-appropriation and self-actualization through the object and the other at distance, consequently to dialectics in a genuinely Hegelian way (pp. 807–8), it is therefore an excellent example of the presuppositions and implications of the so-called deconstructive criticism.

16. Said, *Beginnings*, p. 237.

17. The major critics in question are Auerbach and Poulet. Poulet's notion of a harmony of vision that gives a sense of unity to the work of each individual writer, as well as Auerbach's germinal notion of a self-referring, self-interpreting, and self-criticizing text (see, in particular, *Mimesis* [Princeton: Princeton University Press, 1953] p. 486) allowed for the transformation of the totalizing mode of formalism into a contextual unity based on the self-reflexivity of the text.

18. "Chaque fois que, pour brancher précipitamment l'écriture sur un dehors rassurant ou pour rompre très vite avec tout idéalisme, on en viendrait à ignorer telles acquisitions théoriques récentes (. . .), on regresserait encore plus surement dans l'idéalisme avec tout ce qui . . . ne peut que s'y accoupler, singulièrement dans la figure de l'empirisme et du formalisme." Derrida, *La Dissémination* (Paris, Seuil, 1972), p. 5.

19. See also Derrida, *La Dissémination*, p. 62.

20. Derrida, *Of Grammatology*, p. 59.

21. For the distinctions of the two steps of deconstruction, see Derrida, *Positions* (Paris: Minuit, 1972).

22. See also *Of Grammatology* where Derrida argues that Christianity only privileged a highly metaphorical notion of writing, as for instance God's or Nature's writing, while all other forms of writing were seen as derivative (p. 15).

23. Jean-François Lyotard, *Discours, Figure* (Paris: Klincksieck, 1971), pp. 13–14.

24. Jean-François Lyotard, *La Phénomenologie* (Paris: Presses Universitaires de France, 1954), pp. 23–24.

25. Maurice Merleau-Ponty, *The Visible and the Invisible* (Evanston: Northwestern University Press, 1968), p. 9.

26. See also Derrida, *Speech and Phenomena* (Evanston: Northwestern

Rodolphe Gasché

University Press, 1973), p. 78–79: "Every . . . form of auto-affection must either pass through what is outside the sphere of 'ownness' or forego any claim to universality. When I see myself, either because I gaze upon a limited region of my body or because it is reflected in a mirror, what is outside the sphere of 'my own' has already entered the field of this auto-affection, with the result that it is no longer pure. In the experience of touching and being touched, the same thing happens."

27. Merleau-Ponty, *The Visible and the Invisible*, p. 35.

28. Ibid., pp. 31–32.

29. It should already become obvious here that speaking of deconstruction versus reconstruction turns deconstruction erroneously into a *moment* of the speculative process.

30. Merleau-Ponty, *The Visible and the Invisible*, p. 33.

31. Ibid., p. 37.

32. Ibid., pp. 44–45.

33. Ibid., p. 44.

34. Ibid., p. 38.

35. Ibid., p. 46

36. Ibid., p. 38.

37. Ibid., p. 94.

38. Ibid., p. 92.

39. Ibid., p. 95.

40. Lyotard, *Discours, Figure*, p. 56.

41. Ibid., p. 60.

42. Derrida, *Speech and Phenomena*, p. 79.

43. Immanent criticism, as defined by Theodor W. Adorno, consists of measuring culture or a discourse against their own ideal or concept (*Begriff*). "Immanent criticism of intellectual and artistic phenomena seeks to grasp, through the analysis of their form and meaning, the contradiction between their objective idea and that pretension. It names what the consistency or inconsistency of the work itself expresses of the structure of the existent" (p. 32). Yet, this notion of immanent criticism is not without "consciousness transcending the immanence of culture" (p. 29), and is "founded in the objectivity of the mind itself" (p. 28). This insures that the immanent procedure is essentially dialectical, or to be more precise, negatively dialectic. Adorno writes: "A successful work, according to immanent criticism, is not one which resolves objective contradictions in a spurious harmony, but one which expresses the idea of harmony negatively by embodying the contradictions, pure and uncompromised, in its innermost structure" (p. 32). Theodor W. Adorno, *Prisms* (London: Neville Stearman, 1967). It is thus not so much through its procedure, but through its perspective that what we call here immanent criticism in Derrida differs from Adorno's approach.

44. Derrida, *Speech and Phenomena*, p. 5.

45. Ibid., p. 6.

46. Ibid., p. 9.

47. For indeed, as Wayne C. Booth points out, every skeptic shows "at his climatic moment of total doubt: that valued enterprises need not end when conceptual doubt has done its worst, that . . . various enterprises including life itself are both more important than any one conceptual blind alley, and that they can be pursued and defended, once entered upon," as rational ("Preserving the Exemplar . . . , p. 417). But that is precisely the question in deconstruction as the self-evidence of those ethical and pragmatic

issues become problematic. Booth's assimilation of common-sense and self-evidence, his valorization of the pragmatic of life over conceptual enterprises, moreover, does not diminish the conceptual status of his values which, like the concept of life, are tributary to a metaphysics of presence.

48. Derrida, *Speech and Phenomena*, p. 50.

49. As these contradictions are an inevitable function of the ethico-theoretical decisions of philosophy, no renewal in terms of greater logical coherence can *master* them. For that same reason, deconstruction is no longer a simple attempt of mastery.

50. Derrida, *Speech and Phenomena*, p. 97.

51. Ibid., p. 53.

52. Ibid., p. 51.

53. Ibid., p. 62.

54. Ibid., p. 51.

55. Ibid., p. 52.

56. Derrida, *La Dissémination*, p. 11.

57. Ibid., p. 62.

58. Ibid., p. 39.

59. Ibid., p. 39.

60. Derrida, *Speech and Phenomena*, p. 52.

61. Ibid., p. 57.

62. Although deconstruction provides a justifying analysis of the global situation of reflection, it does not account for this situation without residues. If an account is a record of debit and credit to be balanced, deconstruction is precisely an operation which makes such a mastery impossible.

63. Derrida, *Speech and Phenomena*, p. 67.

64. Ibid., p. 89.

65. Ibid., p. 63.

66. Ibid., p. 67–68.

67. Ibid., p. 88.

68. Thus, if one still insists on using the notion of the self and of the *auto*—(which to a certain extent is unavoidable) one has to account for everything that makes that self a decentered self. For the notion of self-decentering see Hugh J. Silverman, "Self-Decentering: Derrida Incorporated," in *Research in Phenomenology*, Special Issue on "Reading(s) of Jacques Derrida," vol. 8, (Atlantic Highlands: Humanities Press, 1978), pp. 45–65.

69. Derrida, *Speech and Phenomena*, pp. 85–86.

70. Derrida, *Of Grammatology*, p. 68.

71. Ibid., p. 24.

72. Ibid., pp. 13–14.

73. Ibid., p. 20.

74. See "La pharmarcie de Platon," in Derrida, *La Dissémination*.

75. Derrida, *Of Grammatology*, p. 29.

76. Ibid., p. 34.

77. Ibid., pp. 43–44.

78. Ibid., p. 37.

79. Ibid., p. 45.

80. Ibid., p. 46.

81. Ibid., p. 47.

82. Ibid., p. 47.

83. Ibid., pp. 65–66.

84. Ibid., p. 66.

85. Ibid., p. 68.

86. *"Spacing* (notice that this word speaks the articulation of space and time, the becoming-space of time and the becoming-time of space) is always the unperceived, the non-present, and the non-conscious. *As such,* if one can still use that expression in a non-phenomenological way; for here we pass the very limits of phenomenology. Arche-writing as spacing cannot occur *as such* within the phenomenological experience of *a presence"* (ibid., p. 68).

87. Ibid., p. 53.

88. Ibid., p. 52.

89. The arche-trace as arche-writing "does not depend on any sensible plenitude, audible or visible, phonic or graphic. It is on the contrary, the condition of such a plenitude" (ibid., p. 62).

90. "The sound-image is the structure of the appearing of the sound which is anything but the sound appearing. . . ." And: "Being-heard is structurally phenomenal and belongs to an order radically dissimilar to that of the real sound in the world" (ibid., p. 63).

91. Ibid., p. 64–65.

92. Ibid., p. 60.

93. Derrida, *Speech and Phenomena*, p. 93.

94. Derrida responds to such a possible objection all throughout the first part of *Of Grammatology*. Yet in *Edmund Husserl's "Origin of Geometry": An Introduction* (New York: Nicolas Hays, 1977) Derrida most extensively deals already with that question.

95. Derrida, *Of Grammatology*, p. 61.

96. Ibid., p. 62.

97. Defining deconstruction in this manner leaves the problem of its relation to notions like the text, textuality, literariness, and so forth suspended. This relation is neither obvious nor self-evident. That is why we intend to deal with it separately on another occasion.

98. Derrida, *Of Grammatology*, p. 68.

99. Meyer H. Abrams, thus, mistakes the priority of writing over speech for a shift of elementary reference to the "black marks on white paper as the sole things that are actually present in reading," to "already existing marks" that, consequently, lead him to accuse Derrida of "graphocentrism," as if such a concept did not already destroy its very name ("The Deconstructive Angel," pp. 439–30). Abrams "impudently makes of visibility the tangible, simple and essential element of writing" (*Of Grammatology*, p. 42).

100. "It should be recognized that it is in the specific zone of this imprint and this trace, in the temporalization of a *lived experience* which is neither *in* the world nor in 'another world,' which is not more sonorous than luminous, not more *in* time than *in* space, that differences appear among the elements or rather produce them, make them emerge as such and constitute the *texts,* the chains, and the systems of traces" (*Of Grammatology*, p. 65).

101. Lyotard, *Discours, Figure*, pp. 278–79.

102. Ibid., p. 324.

103. Ibid., p. 326.

104. Ibid., p. 296.

105. Ibid., p. 350.

106. Ibid., p. 387.

107. Paul de Man, *Blindness and Insight* (New York: Oxford University Press, 1971), p. 111.

108. Ibid., p. 119.

109. Ibid., p. 139–40.

110. Ibid., p. 119.

111. Ibid., p. 136.

112. De Man also links this self-reflexivity and self-cognition of literary language to "the necessarily ambivalent nature of literary language" (p. 136). But *ambivalence* and *ambiguity* are not the presupposition of deconstruction. Ambiguity, says Derrida, "requires the logic of presence, even when it begins to disobey that logic" (*Of Grammatology*, p. 71). Merleau-Ponty already had criticized ambivalence as a characteristic of negativist thought (as Sartre's), as in fact something proper to the ventriloqual sophists, a thought that "always affirms or denies in the hypothesis what it denies or affirms in the thesis," oscillating between "absolute contradiction and the identity" (*The Visible and the Invisible*, p. 73). Moreover, as the idea of *simultaneity* always "coordinates two absolute presents, two points or instants of presence, and . . . [thus] remains a linear concept" (*Of Grammatology*, p. 85), it fosters a kind of negative specularity and dialectics.

113. *Blindness and Insight*, p. 138.

114. Derrida, *Of Grammatology*, pp. 68–69.

115. Paul de Man, "Action and Identity in Nietzsche," in *YFS* 52 (1975): 26–28.

116. Properly speaking this is no negative dialectics in the Adornian sense. For Adorno, in short, negative dialectics is a dialectics which for *historical* reasons cannot sublate its conflicting opposites. It is a dialectic without synthesis which tries to keep the conflict going. It refuses both *Aufhebung* and the annulment of the opposites. De Man's notion of negative dialectics is more precisely linked to the romantic interpretation of dialectics by Schelling as a neutralization, as a mutual annulment (and, actually, constitutive of the *Witz*).

117. De Man, "Action and Identity in Nietzsche," p. 29.

118. Ibid., p. 23.

119. Paul de Man, "The Purloined Ribbon," in *Glyph* 1 (1977):44.

120. Ibid., p. 40.

121. Ibid., p. 45.

122. Paul de Man, "The Epistemology of Metaphor," in *CI* 5:1 (1978):28.

123. Derrida, *La Dissémination*, p. 42.